THE STRENGTH
OF WATER

KARIN K. JENSEN

THE STRENGTH
OF WATER

An Asian American Coming of Age Memoir

BALESTIER PRESS
LONDON · SINGAPORE

Balestier Press
Centurion House, London TW18 4AX
www.balestier.com

The Strength of Water:
An Asian American Coming of Age Memoir
Copyright © Karin K. Jensen, 2023

First published by Balestier Press in 2023

A CIP catalogue record for this book is available from the British Library.

ISBN 978 1 913891 29 9

Cover design by Sarah and Schooling
Cover illustration by Andre D'Rozario

CONTENTS

PROLOGUE

In my heyday, I was a bit over five feet tall. Today, I am four feet eight inches. I am a little person, but I have lived a big life. China, the country of my heritage, traded silk for gold with Rome and Carthage, and millennia after the Roman Empire and Carthage fell, China still endures. I like to think of myself that way. I did not have much formal education or encouragement as I grew up. Some think my ways are a little backward, but I have persisted.

During my life, I have been criticized as sometimes too boisterous or sometimes too quiet or sometimes not smart enough, or sometimes not big enough. Still, as long as I try my best, I know that I have value and am deserving.

The most important thing I have looked for is an appreciation for who I am, which is hard to find in the world. Cultural and educational barriers are difficult to overcome. Those we love most are sometimes our greatest detractors.

However, where once I shared two rooms with eight family members, now I live in a hilltop home with a view of San Francisco. Where once I did not have the opportunity to finish high school, now both my daughters have college degrees. Where once I was alone and lonely, now I have family and friends.

This is my story.

1

WHAT'S IN A NAME?

I was born June 26, 1923, in St. Luke's Hospital, San Francisco, California. My father, an immigrant of the Guangdong province of southern China, was twenty-five. My mother was twenty-one. I was their first child to live past birth.

My father named me Yee King Ying, Yee being my family or clan name and King Ying being my given name. As a Chinese person, I am first a member of my clan and, secondly, an individual.

My father asked the doctor to suggest an American name. "Well," he said graciously, "she is a beautiful child. You might name her Helen."

Father did not get the allusion to Greek mythology. However, understanding that Helen meant beauty, he consented that among Westerners, I would be Helen Yee. For as an American, I am first an individual and, secondly, a member of my family.

We lived in a small apartment above some stores on Clay Street in Chinatown. Chinatown then, as now, was defined by Broadway, California, Kearny, and Powell Streets, with Grant Street bisecting it. The architecture was new, being done in the Edwardian style, for Chinatown had wholly burned down during the 1906 earthquake.

Thanks to a wealthy businessman named Look Tin Eli, the new Chinatown was designed to be more distinctly "Oriental" to draw tourists. Edwardian architecture decorated with theatrical chinoiserie replaced the old Italianate buildings. Chinatown rose from the ashes like the phoenix with a new façade dreamed up by an American-born Chinese man, built by white architects, looking like a cross between Chinese and Western ideals.

Far from being a wealthy businessman, my father did laundry work in this Chinatown or other odd jobs wherever he could find work. This fact had come as a great shock to my mother upon marriage. A pretty girl born into a wealthy family where servants did everything for her, she immigrated to America with my father, knowing nothing about housework, cooking, or raising children.

It was a difficult, long voyage in the ship's steerage, and my mother was pregnant. Steerage is the lower deck of a ship, then providing the lowest class of travel for Chinese immigrants to North America. Often crowded with poor food, little fresh air, inadequate sanitary conditions, and a good deal of pitching and rolling, steerage was often decried as inhumane. Under these conditions, my mother gave premature birth to my stillborn brother.

Grandmother had arranged the marriage through a matchmaker. Mother met Father shortly before their wedding in his village in the Kaiping District of Guangdong. Grandmother thought this a good match for Father since Mother came with an impressive dowry. On their wedding day, a splendid procession started from the village entrance, led by a lady deemed by the elders to have lived a blessed and prosperous life.

Following her was my mother, carried in a red sedan chair by servants. Before her path, the honored lady strewed puffed rice with a ladle to ward off evil spirits. Puffs caught in the breeze and floated a little before landing. Mother's dowry came next. There were two personal maids, one to care for Mother and one for my grandmother since it was always a bride's duty to care for her mother-in-law. Several pigs and furniture carried by servants followed. The furniture consisted of a sizable, red-painted bed with a hand-embroidered silk canopy and a carved teak wood dining table, chairs, and washbasin stand with porcelain washbasin. Following these were bed linens, household items for the kitchen, and then Mother's carved wooden trunk filled with silk clothing, embroidered scarves for furniture, and exquisite gold and jade jewelry.

Bringing up the rear was the food provided by the groom's family for the wedding feast that the village would share and for the couple to start their new life. There was a whole roasted pig, cooked fish and fowl, tea cakes, candy, dried lychee nuts, persimmons, and other fruits, and a thousand wedding cookies for good luck. Chinese wedding cookies are a kind of thin pastry shell, usually with a traditional pattern imprinted on the top and filled with sweet beans.

It was also considered a good match for Mother. She thought she would be going to the "Gold Mountain," the Chinese name for San Francisco, so her new husband could make his fortune. It would be a great adventure, and she could return someday the proud mother of sons and the wife of a wealthy man like her father. The name Gold Mountain stems from the gold rush days in California when there were stories of pioneering overseas Chinese from America returning home with bushels of gold sand.

By the 1920s, immigrants were no longer returning with gold sand. However, the Gold Mountain still represented a chance to attain comparative financial security. Over previous centuries, South China had become densely populated, making it difficult to earn a living. The wars, uprisings, and natural calamities of the 19th and early 20th centuries struck this region hardest.

By 1846, the Chinese population had swelled to 421 million from just 200 million in 1762, resulting in ever-increasing rents for tenant farmers and concentrations of wealth among landowners. In Guangdong, the soil yielded enough crops to feed only one-third of its people. Farmers reacted by taking matters into their own hands and chopping down entire forests on mountains near major rivers in the hope of growing more crops. The resulting soil erosion caused floods that led to famine, epidemics, and the death of tens of millions. Relief money sent by the central government ended up lining the pockets of local officials instead of people in need.

Moreover, beginning in the 18th century, Britain began

exporting opium from India to China, which solved the trade imbalance created by the West's desire for Chinese products. Opium spread addiction and corruption in its wake, ensnaring every level of society from the bored socialite desiring escape to the laborer seeking to ease the pain of heavy loads.

When the Chinese government tried to stop the trade in 1839 by confiscating and destroying 20,000 chests of opium, Britain responded by waging the First Opium War of 1839-1842 to ensure an open market. Following their victory, Britain forced China to make humiliating concessions to foreign powers. Unfair treaties with the West wreaked havoc in the countryside when the Qing government shifted the burden of their losses to the peasants by increasing taxes.

As feelings against foreigners and the corrupt Manchu rulers of the Qing dynasty grew, there was then the Taiping Rebellion of 1851–64. Over twenty million Chinese died attempting to oust the Manchus, and scores of millions more were wounded or made homeless. Later, there was the so-called Boxer Rebellion of 1900, in which sentiment against foreigners again fomented into war. Then, in 1911, Sun Yat-sen began the great revolution in Guangdong Province, which would lead to the final downfall of the Manchus and the start of the People's Republic of China.

Before this period, China had been stable for six centuries, and almost no Chinese emigrated. But during the nineteenth and early twentieth centuries, when war, revolution, natural disaster, and opium took such a tremendous toll on the people and the economy, the first significant Chinese immigration came to America. These immigrants were part of a massive departure from China to many countries, and my father became part of this movement.

Before departing for the United States, my father gave his parents the dowry servants and pigs and left the beautiful furniture and household goods in their safekeeping. It would have been too challenging to bring furnishings to America. Anyway, there was always the thought that someday they would return to China and want them back.

I can only imagine my mother's consternation when she found that her husband did hard manual labor all day. He expected her to clean, cook, and sew alone in a small apartment in a foreign country where she didn't speak the language. Before this, she had been her mother's petted favorite. Her mother had delayed her marriage to keep her companionship that much longer.

Now, there were no relatives or friends to laugh and chat with, nor occasions to wear her pretty silks or gold and jade jewelry. She had come from a province with lush, tropical plant life and warm rains to a foggy, hilly Chinatown with hard, paved streets that covered up the earth. How her matchmaker had misinformed her! Yet, there was no turning back. She was married, and she could not undo that.

I do not remember my mother openly complaining about her altered circumstances, but she was often disheartened and homesick. Her sadness did not help her physical or mental health. It was as though her homesickness and unhappiness contributed to the natural weakness of her heart. Walking up steep flights of stairs to our apartment was a trial to her. Sometimes, she had to stop to catch her breath until her erratic heartbeat evened itself out.

In addition to the difficulties of her marriage, she and my father contended with the hostility of their adopted country. In 1920, shortly before I was born, there were reportedly about eight thousand Chinese living in San Francisco, with nearly four thousand more across the bay in Oakland. By far, this was the largest concentration of Chinese living anywhere in the United States at that time. However, this population was diminished by 60% from 1880 due to the Chinese Exclusion Act of 1882, which remained in effect until 1943.

In the early Gold Rush days in the West, Americans tolerated the Chinese. For instance, Judge Nathaniel Bennett of California welcomed Chinese and other recent immigrants in 1850 at the ceremonies marking the admission of California into statehood, saying, "Born and reared under different Governments and speaking different tongues, we nevertheless meet here today as brothers...You stand among us in all respects as equals... Henceforth we have one country, one hope, one destiny."

But by the 1870s, when harder economic times had hit, organized labor despised the Chinese for their willingness to work long hours for low wages, thus "taking" jobs from white people. Mark Twain described the situation in his book, *Roughing It*, in 1872:

"A disorderly Chinaman is rare, and a lazy one does not exist. So long as a Chinaman has strength to use his hands, he needs no support from anybody; white men often complain of want of work, but a Chinaman offers no such complaint; he always manages to find something to do. He is a great convenience to everybody – even to the worst class of white men, for he bears the most of their sins, suffering fines for their petty thefts, imprisonment for their robberies, and death for their murders. Any white man can swear a Chinaman's life away in the courts, but no Chinaman can testify against a white man. Ours is the "land of the free"— nobody denies that—nobody challenges it. (Maybe it is because we won't let other people testify.) As I write, news comes that in broad daylight in San Francisco, some boys have stoned an inoffensive Chinaman to death and that although a large crowd witnessed the shameful deed, no one interfered."

The Chinese Exclusion Act specifically excluded Chinese laborers' immigration to America. Only Chinese of other classes such as merchants, scholars, and students were legally allowed admittance. In practice, even those who fell into these classes were frequently mislabeled as laborers and denied admission.

My father was lucky. He was a citizen's son and, as such, was allowed in 1922 to enter the United States with his wife—only his status was a falsehood. My grandfather had acquired a citizenship document from a man in China who was returning there to settle permanently. More than likely, Grandfather had purchased the paper, for it would have been valuable. Pretending to be this man, my grandfather had entered the United States over a decade before to work. This same document later enabled my father to come to the United States as a citizen's son.

Father was doubly lucky in being able to bring his wife. Under the Exclusion Act, women were not allowed to enter the U.S. without family ties to a male in one of the permitted classes. Indeed, Chinese women had been subject to restrictions since 1875, ensuring that the Chinese in America were mostly a bachelor society who were allowed to work but discouraged from settling in the country.

It was not a matter of wanting to go to a hostile land far from friends and family to perform hard manual labor. The Reverend Henry Ward Beecher once lamented how difficult it was to convert the Chinese to Christianity due to the un-Christian treatment they received. He said, "We have clubbed them, stoned them, burned their houses, and murdered some of them, yet they refuse to be converted. I do not know any way except to blow them up with nitro-glycerin if we are ever to get them to Heaven."

Instead, with an economy at home weakened from war, opium, and natural disaster, immigration was one of few reliable ways to provide an income for one's family both here and back home. Chinese men like my father did not have the education to achieve a fair-paying post in China and were nobodies in America. However, working as laundrymen, chop-suey restaurant owners, or small grocery-store owners, they could send money home to support families. They had a chance to return to China with comparative wealth.

Loneliness, cultural isolation, and monotonous work led some to lose their earnings to gambling and prostitution. In a mostly bachelor society where Chinese American men sometimes outnumbered women by as much as 25 to 1, these were the usual temptations. In old San Francisco Chinatown, numerous alleys were known for gambling halls, opium dens, and brothels. Still, enough did well for themselves to continue the Gold Mountain story. What the Chinese at home did not always appreciate were the self-sacrifice and loneliness that overseas Chinese endured to return with this wealth.

2

A CHANCE TO GET AHEAD

Mother had a sister who also married a Golden Mountain man. Rather than settle in California, they had migrated east. Shortly after I was born, Mother's sister wrote from Detroit to encourage Father and Mother to join them there. Ford and General Motors were starting to boom, she said.

Indeed, by 1923, Ford Motor Company was manufacturing two million Model T Fords, having made just one million two years before. The price had dropped from $850 in 1908, when they first appeared, to $295 in 1924, thanks to improved mass production. The general industry's acceptance of these techniques led to similar cost-cutting by other manufacturers. In the 1900s, only the rich drove cars. Now, regular folks could drive too.

With the automobile's rise in popularity and affordability, there was a boom in factory workers in the Detroit area, with plenty of clothes to clean and wash. My Uncle Gee Taw had opened a hand laundry there and was doing a brisk business. There was certainly room for Father to open a laundry if he wished. Here was an opportunity to get ahead, be near family, and own a business. My father took the chance.

We traveled from San Francisco to Detroit by train. With Uncle's help, my father set up his first laundry shop in Highland Park, Michigan, the city of Ford's manufacturing plant. To conserve resources, he set up our living quarters in the rear of the laundry.

The layout was as follows: To either side of the front door were window cases, where my mother put potted plants. The customer would face counters divided by a small swing gate upon entering.

Behind this to one side was a long ironing table. My parents did not use the American-style ironing board but rather the Chinese-style ironing table, which was broader and longer. On the other side were a sewing machine and a clothes rack. On the rear wall were shelves with a curtained doorway in the center. Shelves on one side held piles of incoming dirty laundry. On the other side were clean laundry packages for customers to pick up. This part of the laundry is all that a customer would see.

Behind the curtain was the middle section of the laundry, which contained a drying room, another ironing table, a potbelly stove to heat about eight to ten irons, and a collar-pressing machine in later years. The washing machines of the time lacked a spin cycle. Freshly washed laundry still had to be wrung by hand or with a roller wringing device that had a bad habit of removing buttons.

My father sent out all the laundry we received in large sacks to a commercial washing plant. We then got it back clean and wet, ready for us to dry, iron, and package. To perform drying, he used the drying room, which contained rows of gas heaters all along the floor. Above the heaters were clotheslines where my parents hung the clothes. This drying method resulted in us living and working in a steamy environment.

Behind this ironing and drying area were our living quarters. My parents and I slept in a bedroom with two beds, a water closet, and a kitchen area where we kept our kitchen table and chairs, stove, sink, icebox, and coal-burning stove for heat. A metal tub hung from the wall and was brought down once per week and filled with hot water for bathing. That was the extent of our home.

My earliest memory is of toddling around in a walker and seeing Ba, as I called him (meaning Pa), folding and sorting clothes into piles. Collars were a separate piece of clothing from the shirt, and one attached them to the shirt with buttons. Sometimes Ba piled dirty collars on the floor, and then I tried to reach down and grab them. When I couldn't reach them from my walker, I would look up at Ba and cry in frustration, but then I would try again.

Ba rose as early as 6:00 a.m. to sweep the floor and set things in order. He then sorted, dried, ironed, folded, and packaged usually until eight or nine in the evening and sometimes later when there was a large volume of business. Store hours were Monday through Saturday, from 9:00 a.m. to 6:00 p.m. During these times, customers could drop off or pick up their laundry. Both my parents did laundry work, but Ba greeted the customers as he could speak some English.

On Sundays, they "rested," but even then, they usually sorted the bundles of laundry that had arrived on Saturday in preparation for sending it out to be washed the following week. In those early years, the business did so well that Ba soon hired a helper and opened a second laundry in Dearborn, where Ford had its engineering and testing facilities.

By the late 1920s, however, several incidents occurred that hindered our prosperity. First, other Chinese soon followed Ba's path, migrating to Detroit to open laundries and other small businesses. Many were also from the Kaiping District, and some even came from the same village. They directly competed with us for business.

Secondly, in 1927, Henry Ford completed the move of his manufacturing plant from Highland Park to River Rouge. Ba ended up closing the Highland Park location and replacing it with a laundry on Livernois Avenue in Detroit, and we moved there. There was also the stock market crash of 1929, which led to decreased spending.

Perhaps most importantly, a rapid succession of sibling births left my mother much incapacitated and less able to help my father. Sister Katie was born in 1925, followed by sister Jeannie in 1926. Next came sister Margaret in 1928. In between Jeannie and Margaret, a second stillborn child was born.

After Katie was born, Ma became seriously ill, and the physician advised her not to have any more children. She already had a weak heart and developed a weak liver and kidney. Homesickness, long hours of laundry work, childbearing, and childrearing aggravated her health. And then, after Jeannie was born, she was again so ill that my aunt, Ma's sister, who had not been able to bear a child and wanted one badly, took Jeannie to live with her. Still, Ma would not accept the idea of forgoing more children. More than anything in the world, she wanted to make a return trip home to see her family in China. To do that, she must first bear a son.

In her culture, people valued a son more highly than a daughter for several reasons. First, a girl was costly. After raising a daughter to adulthood, she would be married off to become a member of her husband's household. The bride's birth family would provide a dowry if they could afford one—the larger the dowry, the better the chance of marrying one's daughter into a well-to-do family. But in essence, every daughter born was viewed as an erosion of the family's ability to accumulate money, power, and status.

By contrast, parents expected their sons to care for them through old age. Once a son married, the family received the daughter-in-law's dowry, and the daughter-in-law would honor and care for her mother-in-law. Among other things, a daughter-in-law would bring her mother-in-law hot tea first thing in the morning and fetch her whatever she needed.

The colloquial term for a daughter was "a thousand pieces of gold." A friend or neighbor, for instance, inquiring about your daughter would ask about your thousand pieces of gold. To ask about your son, that person would inquire about your "million pieces of gold."

By association, a woman who gave birth to sons viewed herself as successful. A woman who gave birth only to daughters felt unsuccessful. Ma knew that her mother, with whom she had a close relationship, would have welcomed her home. But she knew that her mother-in-law principally valued her ability to serve the family by producing a son and heir. If she returned without sons, her mother-in-law would scorn her and accuse her before the villagers of "having no face," a traditional insult meaning that she would have no respect, honor, or social standing. So strongly did my mother feel this sense of inferiority that she could not bear to show her face to her in-laws until she had a son.

Of course, the result of much illness, childbirth, and childrearing was that Ma was less able to help Ba with laundry work, and physicians' bills mounted. The prospect of a trip home became even more remote, and Ba and Ma did not have a chance to break from work.

My parents would never have vacationed in the Western sense of the word by taking a trip to a resort or a place of natural beauty to participate in recreational activities. To them, a vacation meant a trip home to China to visit relatives and friends. There, freed from race consciousness and able to speak their native tongue among their people, they could have genuinely relaxed and felt at ease.

They would have liked to bring home exotic gifts such as scented factory-made soaps and stories of their foreign country. If they could have accumulated savings of even a few thousand dollars beyond their ship fare, they would have felt prosperous. They would have had the satisfaction of bringing home money and gifts to close family.

But as they could not take such a trip, they were like Westerners who could never vacation or go home to visit family and friends. Each workday, they pushed themselves hard, and the days ended in exhaustion. Ba's fingers flew as he wrapped and tied string around endless packages of laundry. Ma ironed countless white shirts. As the days passed, there was a growing sense of frustration with never getting ahead and never experiencing respect and status among their family and peers. As those early years passed, this was the position in which my parents found themselves.

3

LITTLE MONKEY

Even when she was ill, Ma had a gentleness to her manners and in her way of moving, which I admired, though I was a child. She had been a lady in China. Always I kept this in my heart, intending that someday, I, too, should be a lady and refined. In later years, she copied American hairstyles and fashion. However, in those early years, she dressed her hair in the Chinese manner by combing it neatly into a low bun.

One of her few luxuries was Coty's face powder. Then, as now, Coty's powder came in its distinctive box designed by Lalique with the powder puff pattern on a burnt amber background. Each morning after washing, she applied some to her face with a white powder puff, and I thought that was so lovely and elegant.

"Ma," I pleaded one day, "can I put some on?"

Ma smiled and held the powder where I could reach it. Plunging the puff deep into its container, I squeezed my eyes shut, then batted at my face, sending powder puffing around the edges. When I looked in the mirror, I saw two black eyes against a white, fluffy face. I was so surprised. I couldn't stop giggling as Ma wiped off the powder with a towel.

Feminine aspirations of elegance aside, I was a little girl of high spirits and energy whom my parents dubbed "little monkey." I liked to run, jump, swing, and do cartwheels, and I was always getting into trouble by being in the way or getting my dress and face dirty or banging into things. Usually, I played by myself outside the store because my sister Katie liked to sit and play quietly inside. You could dress her up, and after a few hours, she still looked the same.

Not so with me. I had only two toys, a red scooter, and a red wagon, and I nearly wore them out scooting and running up and down the street. I was only allowed to go up and down our one long block, so I was a familiar sight to the neighboring storeowners.

I also loved hopscotch. How many warm spring evenings were there when I played hopscotch until the sun went down? I played by drawing squares with chalk on the pavement. I threw a pebble onto the first square, then the second, and so on, always jumping over the square with the rock and then picking it up on the way back.

My indoor play was boisterous too. I loved to swing back and forth on the long roller handle of the collar-pressing machine, which was at the right height for me to reach up and hang from it when I picked up my feet. Ba always yelled at me to stop. If I didn't listen, he slapped me on the head. But it was so much fun that I would swing again when I thought I could get away with it. One day, I swung so high and so hard that I struck my backside against the potbelly stove behind me and burned both cheeks. How I yelped and cried. Then I stopped swinging from the collar-pressing machine.

Sometimes I jumped on my parents' mattress or swung from the headboard frame, which consisted of four posts along the back of the bed, all connected by a cross member at the top from which I swung. There were no box springs. Ba simply put a mattress over some boards on a frame. Every other Saturday, he took apart the boards and set up the bed for airing. Then I would lean the slat boards against the headboard between the posts to make a slide.

"Come on, come on," I would invite the others. Seeing how much fun I had, even Katie and little Jeannie, whom my Aunt sometimes brought to visit, tried to follow. Of course, the boards weren't too stable. Sometimes they slid out, and we fell with a bump. "Ouch!" But then we would look at each other and laugh and laugh. We didn't care. We had few toys and wanted to make fun for ourselves somehow.

Occasionally as a treat, Ba would take Katie and me to Chinatown when he had things to buy. Katie always wanted to go, but then she would be too timid to enter the stores. She was shy of strangers in general and especially of men. So-called married bachelors usually ran Chinatown stores. They worked in the United States but had wives and families in China. So wistful were they for family life that they loved for Ba to come by with his daughters for a visit.

"Hello, hello," the storeowners would say with a big smile. "Long time, no see. You should come to visit more often. How have you been?" But before we could go in, Katie would dig her heels into the sidewalk and pull at Ba's hand, wanting him to stay outside the store with her.

"No, Ba, no," she would cry.

"What is the matter, King Shu?" (That was Katie's Chinese name.) "We are just going in to get some vegetables."

But Katie would pout and dig her heels in again. So Ba would have to disengage himself and leave her anxiously waiting at the doorway. I then went in to enjoy the fuss that the storeowners made over me.

Quickly, the storeowners would bring out a coin or a cookie or a candy for me. "How big you are getting. And how pretty," they would say, thinking of their children at home. I would stand holding Ba's hand, beaming with pleasure, and eating my cookie or candy.

When Ma was too sick to care for us, Ba treated my sisters and me like a regiment. After rising early to sweep and pick up around the laundry, Ba would make a pot of oatmeal, then as we stood in line, he handed each of us a bowlful and a spoon. After eating, we lined up again, and Ba would use a towel dipped in hot water to scrub clean our faces and hands. He rubbed so hard that, afterward, we stood looking at each other, gingerly feeling our red faces.

Ba then took our pile of clothes and helped us step into our cotton dresses and sailor-collar sweaters that Ma had knitted for us. Ma made identical dresses and sweaters for Katie and me, so people often thought we were twins. Sometimes Ba was in such a hurry that he put our clothing on backward, and I might, for instance, end up with the sailor collar in the front instead of in the back. Once Ba got us clean, fed, and dressed, he could start his work.

Ba expected Katie and me to put on our cotton stockings and high-button shoes ourselves. Somehow, Katie would get hers on backward, then point at the bubble sticking up near her ankle and cry.

"Like this, like this," I would say, exasperatedly trying to show her how to fit the bubble part around her heel, but somehow she couldn't get it and kept crying. Then I couldn't stand it anymore and pulled her stockings off myself, with her squirming and fussing, and put them back on her the right way.

"There, see?" I said, showing her how the stockings fit smoothly on her legs. But the next day, the same thing would happen.

Still, for her femininity, Ba compared Katie favorably against me. After I came in from play, Ba would say to me, "Look at you! All dirty. Full of dust. Your hair's all messed up. Look at your sister."

I would look at Katie and see how pretty and perky and clean she looked. And I examined myself and saw how dirty and dusty I was. I felt bad because I wanted Ba to praise me too. But how could I keep from being me?

On the occasional Sunday when Ba caught up with his work, our family traveled by streetcar to Uncle Gee Taw's home and laundry on 12th Street in Detroit. Their living quarters were on the second floor of their building above their laundry. My auntie, whom I called Aye Yea, meaning an auntie older than my mother, had conceived a son, Kerwin, shortly after she took Jeannie to live with her. She always said that Jeannie had brought her this good luck and that Jeannie made a good "big sister" for her son. He was a year younger, and they grew up like siblings in my auntie's home, though they were cousins.

My sisters and I looked forward to these visits. If we arrived in the afternoon, Auntie served coffee with slices of bread. We children did not get coffee but were allowed to dip our slices into our parents' cups to get the flavor.

We enjoyed playing with Kerwin. He was artistically inclined and often sat drawing whatever he saw out the window, such as buses and streetcars. But he was also mischievous, which we girls found both troublesome and entertaining.

On one occasion, knowing how Jeannie feared insects, he took a broom filled with pill bugs and shook it on her so that she would scream. Another time, he tried to chase down his cat. The beleaguered cat ran underneath the stove and peeked between the curved legs. Kerwin then took a rolled-up newspaper, lit it on fire at a burner, and tried to force the cat out from one side. The cat dodged but wouldn't come out, so Kerwin ran to the other side, and the cat dodged again. We girls watched with big eyes. Finally, a grownup came in, grabbed the newspaper, stamped out the fire, and yelled at Kerwin to stop. The poor cat ran away to hide somewhere else.

Auntie cooked splendid dinners. Usually, she made a delicious soup, such as winter melon or bird's nest. Another favorite dish was steamed, tender white chicken, which we dipped in raw salt. Always there were excellent, crunchy vegetables, freshly stir-fried with soy sauce.

Sometimes, she served a dessert, such as candy or a cake or cookies that she had baked. At home, dessert was food that Ba frowned upon as being wasteful, so we rarely ate sweets and never had cakes or pies. On a rare hot day, Ba sometimes bought me a root beer, but then he told me that it was healthy because it was made from roots. Getting to eat a dessert at our Auntie's was another reason our visits were special.

For snacking at home, Ba left soda crackers in a jar, which we could eat whenever we wanted. One day, I didn't feel like eating crackers.

"Let's eat bread," I suggested to Katie, and she agreed. In those days, the bread didn't come sliced unless you requested it from the grocer. Then the grocer would remove the loaf from its package and put it into a slicing machine.

Taking an unsliced hunk of bread, I twisted it in half, giving half to Katie and keeping the rest for myself. Then we walked to the front of the store to sit on the sidewalk and eat. Soon, a large, hungry feral dog came. Pacing back and forth before us, he walked with his head high and his chest out. Katie began to whimper.

The dog bared his teeth, started forward, and knocked me over. I was so scared, I couldn't speak, but Katie was screaming and jumping up and down. The dog grabbed my hunk of bread and ran off. Now we both were crying and whimpering, and we ran inside. We looked at each other with scared, teary eyes, and then Katie tore her bread and gave me half. Together, we ate in the kitchen. Whatever our differences, we were always family.

4

GO WITH LIFE

Now Ba was a young man saddled with a large family, a sickly wife, and responsibility for two laundries. From the strain of long work hours, congestion in a small space, the monotony of work without a break, and the weariness of health and financial problems, Ba sometimes lashed out. Corporal punishment was generally accepted both in the United States and in China. But while I sometimes knew why I was yelled at or hit, often I didn't. I might just be standing somewhere, and he would impatiently slap at me as though I were an object in the way, and that was hard to bear.

Aside from the strain of a difficult life, there was another reason that my father hit me. He had learned this behavior from his mother. Grandmother had also been the wife of a Golden Mountain man. After marriage, she gave birth to my father at home in China. Shortly afterward, Grandfather left for the United States, leaving her at home to care for the baby and the house by herself. She understood that he would send money for her to live on, but as the years passed, this rarely happened.

An irresponsible young man in his early twenties far from home, Grandfather soon spent his earnings on gambling, prostitution, and opium. He had been the spoiled favorite of his mother, precious for having been born late in her life. Even before he left China, he had problems with opium and had begun to sell a portion of the lands he received from Great-grandfather to feed his habit. Left at home to eke out a living as best she could, Grandmother faced loneliness, loss of face, and poverty. In her bitterness, she lashed out at Ba.

For instance, at certain times of the year, when the weather was hot and humid, shrimp would rise in the village pond. Then all the villagers would rush to gather as much as they could. Grandmother's feet were bound as she had come from a well-to-do family. After marriage, she eventually unbound them out of a need to perform manual labor. Yet they were still deformed with some toes folded under, which caused pain in her feet and back. She could only walk slowly and not run.

Grandmother would send her little boy running down to the pond, and if he didn't bring back enough shrimp, she would cry and scream at him in frustration, yank his braided queue, and then beat his back with it. Once, she struck him so hard on the head that a permanent scar formed.

So Ba learned discipline and hard work at an early age but little about parental warmth and affection. At the earliest possible age, his mother put him in the position of caring for them both. When he turned fourteen, Grandmother borrowed money to send Ba to the United States to look after his father and find work to send money home.

Once Ba arrived in the United States, he worked hard during the day. He also took English lessons at the Catholic church in the evening to improve his ability to earn. He cut off his queue to look less foreign and bought Western-style clothing for himself. Ba did so well that he sent money home regularly and earned enough to send his father home. Grandfather was doing no one any good in the United States. Not until some nine years later would Ba return home to visit his family and marry the bride his mother arranged for him.

In my early years, my mother would also discipline me. "King Ying," she would say when I had done something wrong, "bring me the stick."

I would fetch a stick from a corner and bring it to her with a heavy heart. Then she would say, "Open your palm."

I would open my palm, and she would swiftly hit it once. It stung badly, and I would immediately recoil my hand behind my back. Then she would hand the stick back to me, and I had to return it to its corner with tears in my eyes.

The difference between Ma's hitting me and Ba's hitting me was that I always knew what I had done wrong when Ma hit me. The provocation might be slight, such as my making some little mess without cleaning it up properly or some other infraction, but at least I knew the reason.

One day, not long after Jeannie was born, Ba's frustration peaked. Pointing angrily to his baby daughter, he said to my mother, "Debt and more debt. And another girl. How will we ever get ahead? We should put her under a blanket and let her suffocate!"

I waited for the strain of Ba's anger to pass, but I did not believe that he would do what he proposed. I had heard other Chinese men say something similar in a blowing-off-steam kind of way. It was a terrible thing to say, expressing how little girls were valued, yet it was almost said as a kind of expression, upon which no one I knew had acted.

Infanticide has permeated almost every society of humankind since ancient times, particularly during periods of great economic hardship. In China, female infanticide goes back at least two thousand years. During the nineteenth century, China suffered from floods, droughts, famines, and locust invasions nearly every three or four years. Many peasants who were dependent on the land and the crops did the only thing they could think of to survive under these conditions—they killed their female babies.

There were no government benefits or charitable soup kitchens. Killing a son would have meant sacrificing one's future, whereas daughters were viewed as another mouth to feed. Desperation fueled by ravenous hunger led many to consider their survival as pitted against their children's survival. In saying what he said, my father was repeating the survival wisdom of his ancestors.

But Ma replied firmly and quietly, "No, Ho Sin," for that was my father's name, "go with life." And the words and the sound of her voice acted as a spiritual balm. Go with what life brings. Have faith. That was her meaning. Hearing these words of acceptance in the order of things, Ba's anger deflated.

He was a product of his time and circumstances. Sometimes in anger, he spoke the hurtful words of a culture that valued girls far less than boys, yet I do not think it was in him to murder. Each time a daughter was born to him, he was disappointed. Yet, as time passed, he cared for us in his way.

He took us for walks to the local park on Sunday afternoons and watched as we ran and played. Sometimes he played with us, swinging us around to make us laugh. He made sure that his sick wife got medical treatment even when he didn't know how he would get the money. And he worked hard to make sure that all of us were fed and clothed and clean. He never squandered earnings selfishly.

As for Ma, I believe that what she said was an affirmation to herself. Ba's statement sharpened her perspective. "Go with life." Indeed, life had turned out so differently from what she had expected, but she could try to accept what came and make the best of it.

5

LEARNING TO HELP

To save some of the expense of hiring a helper, Ba began to teach me household and laundry work. He started by sending me across the street to the A&P to buy groceries for our meals. He would give me some money and then coach me on what to say. The coaching went as follows:

"Now you say this," Ba would say. "'I want a loaf of fresh, sliced Wonder Bread.' Now say it."

"I want a loaf of fresh Wonder Bread," I replied hesitatingly.

"No . . . 'fresh, sliced Wonder Bread,'" Ba would correct.

"Fresh, sliced Wonder Bread."

"Now say the whole sentence."

"I want a loaf of fresh, sliced Wonder Bread."

"Now repeat it."

We spoke only Chinese at home, so my English was poor. Still, after I repeated the sentence a few times to his satisfaction, he would send me away to fetch an item or two. As my memory and speech improved, he sent me out for more groceries.

By seven, I could iron handkerchiefs and fold socks and underwear. Ironing was a real skill, and Ba didn't trust me to iron important clothing like shirts and pants. First, the irons, made from eight pounds of iron, were heavy for a child to wield. Secondly, they heated on a potbelly stove, and you had to judge when each was the right temperature by tossing drops of water onto it and gaging the sizzle. If the iron was too hot, I might scorch the clothing, and if I scorched it, then Ba had to pay for it. If it was too cold, I wouldn't burn the garment, but I couldn't iron well. Once the iron was cool,

I put it back on the stove and picked up another.

When Katie was old enough, she joined me in these tasks. We stood on milk crates to do the ironing. If the clothing was dry when we started, we used a mouth blower to sprinkle water. We did not have the convenience of a modern spray bottle. We used a mouth blower imported from China, a small, flattened metal pot with a lid filled with water. On one end was a tube, perforated with fine holes. On the other end was the mouthpiece through which one blew to cause the water to spray through.

I also ironed collars and then later used the collar-pressing machine, which consisted of two rollers through which I fed the collars to flatten them. Ma also taught me to use the sewing machine to darn socks. In those days, laundry service included not just cleaning but also repair of damaged clothing. If customers submitted a sock with a hole in it, they expected us to fix it. We also repaired small tears along the seams and other minor damage. Not all laundries did this, but this was one way by which we distinguished our laundry as superior.

Soon Ba taught me to take in laundry from customers, match customer tags with their packages, and make the change from our cash box. When a customer came in with her laundry, I would ask her to write her name on the laundry ticket; then I tore off the tag for her to keep. I would pile the laundry neatly on a shelf and lay the ticket on top.

When I became accustomed to this, Ba would leave me to tend the front part of the laundry while he worked at our Dearborn location. Once he returned, he would mark down the contents of each pile I had collected on the ticket. To identify which clothes belonged to which ticket, he wrote the customers' initials on a tag or a shirt, pants, or dress seam.

It is a testimony to the low crime rate of that era that Ba did not worry about leaving me alone in the front of the store for hours at a time. No one ever robbed us or appeared threatening to me. Indeed, people seeing a little kid standing on an orange crate to assist them were generally kind and thanked me nicely. Aside from laundry and grocery work, my other job was to wash the bathroom once a week. For this most distasteful of tasks, Ba paid me a nickel.

Outside the laundry, my whole world consisted mainly of the laundry's neighborhood. The end of the block was as far as Ba allowed me to go by myself. Our laundry was in a commercial district, and there were stores and businesses all up and down the street. Next door to us was an ice-cream parlor, and I used to walk by, wistfully smelling the sweet scents coming from there and seeing the people inside enjoying themselves. Once in a great while, when Ba had a better week of business than usual, he would buy me an ice-cream cone, and that was a great treat.

But by far, my favorite store was the corner drug store at the end of the block. Oh, they had such beautiful things on display. There were perfume bottles, jewelry boxes, and porcelain dolls. It was a favorite pastime to peer in the window and dream about owning a porcelain doll.

Once my wish almost came true. A visitor who had lived in Ba's village back in China looked us up when she and her husband moved to Detroit. As a gift to all of us girls, she brought a beautiful baby doll made of porcelain and dressed in pretty, lacy clothes. How my sisters and I admired and cooed over that baby doll during our guests' visit. She had blue eyes, long lashes, pink cheeks, and a cute little bonnet. But as soon as our guests left, Ba took the doll and stored it in the basement, saying that it was too beautiful to play with and that we would only get it dirty. How hard it was to swallow our disappointment when we saw that doll taken from us.

I thought I would try to save my nickels from cleaning the bathroom to buy something special from the drug store. I kept my coins in a jar for a while, but when Ba ran low on money, he would take the nickels back to buy coal for heating so he would not have to borrow more money from Uncle Gee Taw. I soon learned to spend my money when I got it.

I went to the newspaper stand at the other end of the block to buy

Sunday newspapers. The Sunday comics, or funnies as we called them, were a treat. My favorite cartoon was Jane Arden. She was the "world's greatest mystery reporter," glamorous and successful as an investigative journalist. The best part of the comic was the weekly Jane Arden paper doll with matching clothes. Each week, Jane had a new set of clothes in the latest fashion. Not only did I cut out the doll and clothes, but I used Jane's figure to trace, cut out, and color new clothes of my design with laundry wrapping paper. Jane got quite a large wardrobe that way. Someday I wanted to be fashionable too.

I never questioned the chores I had to do. I knew I was the oldest and that Ma couldn't do everything because of her poor health. I accepted that I needed to help and even took pride in doing so. Twice, however, my work got me into the worst trouble.

One day, Ma sent me to the A&P to buy groceries, but she had argued with Ba about what to buy for the evening's meal. Ma wanted pork, but Ba wanted fish. By the time I left, it wasn't clear to me what they had decided. Unsure which to buy at the store, I chose pork. When Ba saw what I had bought, he slapped me so hard that I flew back, and my nose bled. Ba felt that I disobeyed his authority as head of the household, but I bought pork because Ma was kinder.

On another occasion, after earning my nickel for cleaning the bathroom, I went to buy my weekly Sunday newspaper. I looked forward to cutting out the Jane Arden doll and making new dresses for her. As soon as I got home, I began cutting. But Ba thought I was making a mess on the floor. He told me to stop, and I did until he left the room. When I thought he was gone, I began cutting again. I didn't hear him come back, but I was again struck so hard across the face that my nose bled. I cried, wondering why he wouldn't understand that this was my pastime that made me happy.

6

GOING TO SCHOOL

Ba did not think that his daughters needed to go to school. In China, it cost money to send children to school, and poor rural families often did not send their daughters since parents felt that girls would only grow up to raise children, do housework, and not have much need to read or write.

Though my father had lived in the United States for over a decade, he lived in a kind of social isolation so that he understood little of American culture. He did not listen to the radio or read the paper often. He counted only other Chinese laundry or grocery men among his friends, most of whom were "married bachelor" immigrants. He had taken English lessons at a church. Yet, he knew only enough to be intelligible in his business transactions and rarely conversed with customers beyond the barest pleasantries of "Hello" and "How are you?"

He had limited interest in American politics. Instead, he often spoke with friends of the Chinese civil war between the Nationalists and the Communists and how he preferred Chiang Kai-Shek over Mao Tse Tung. Later, he spoke of the Japanese invasion of Manchuria, which began in 1931. Though he lived in America, his mind and heart were with China.

Fortunately for my sisters and me, the local police department did not agree with my father's old-country views on the education of daughters. Patrol officers seeing Katie and I sometimes at play in front of our storefront on school days, stopped into the laundry to confront my father.

"How many children do you have? And how old are they?" one

asked. When my father told him, the officer explained, "If you do not send your two eldest daughters to school immediately, we will fine you. The law requires that they begin school in September of the year they are five years old. Your oldest daughter is already over a year past that."

"But I don't have money to send them to school," Ba protested.

"Public school is free," the officer assured him. "Our taxes pay for it." The man gave my father the address of the local elementary school and explained how to register. And so, for the first time, Katie and I were allowed on our own to walk past the end of our block to Winterhalter Elementary School, which was twelve blocks away.

I was already late for starting first grade, but I had to start somewhere, so I was put in that class while Katie began kindergarten. We spoke little English. That morning, I learned a new word.

"Helen," the teacher called me, and I stood up. "Come here," she said, and I walked to her desk. "Take these papers and throw them into the wastebasket, please."

I didn't know what a wastebasket was, so I took the papers and hesitatingly walked back toward my desk. When the other students saw where I was going, they started to call out.

"No, no, there, there," they whispered and pointed toward the wastebasket in the corner until I finally got the idea and sheepishly threw the papers away amid giggles and whispers. That's how I learned the word "wastebasket."

My first homework assignment was a single sheet of paper, the front of which was illustrated with a smiling boy and his dog standing by a tree amid a landscape. On the back was a set of instructions, which began as follows:

1. Color the leaves of the tree green.
2. Color the trunk of the tree brown.
3. Color the dog a color of your choice, etc.

There were about ten instructions in total. Ba made me read

each of the sentences and repeat them about twenty times. Only he wouldn't let me follow the instructions. Coloring was "play," not work. How could coloring be homework? He thought it must be a reading exercise and was very proud when I could demonstrate how well I recited in English.

Aside from learning to read, write, and speak English, I began to be conscious of painful truths. Other children went home to regular houses. Why didn't we? I started to be ashamed of walking home past the blocks of houses and into the commercial district to the laundry where I lived. I would have liked to invite other children to play with me, but I felt too embarrassed to bring them to the laundry. I began to fall into the kind of social isolation in which my father had always lived. I vowed then that someday I would own a real home of my own and not live in the back of a store or other rented place.

Other children celebrated holidays like Valentine's Day, Thanksgiving, and Christmas. My family didn't. Valentine's Day was particularly trying. In preparation, the teacher provided us with construction paper, lace doilies, glue, scissors, and crayons to make Valentine's greetings for any of the other children whom we considered our friends. Katie, with her pretty femininity, received many such cards. I received few. How hard it was to walk home with Katie that day as she glowed from the happiness of so many valentines.

It was the same with our dance lessons. Each class prepared a dance from around the world for the school recital. Mine, for instance, learned a dance from Holland. Others practiced dances from different parts of Eastern and Western Europe. Each class took turns using the auditorium to rehearse.

"OK, boys," Teacher instructed us at the first lesson, "choose yourselves a partner." The lessons, of course, became another popularity contest, with the prettiest, most popular girls asked to dance first.

The remaining boys would then approach us remaining girls

with a grudging "Wanna dance?" to which we replied, "All right," gritting our teeth with humiliation.

In my case, there was more to my unpopularity than being shy or tomboyish. Prejudice against Chinese was common, and often on the playground, I had heard the taunt "Ching, Ching, Chinaman, sittin' on the fence, tryin' to make a dollar out of fifteen cents." I didn't even know what this meant, but still, I was humiliated by their sneering expressions and voices.

In the end, I wasn't allowed to participate in the recital anyway. I needed a costume to join, and Ba would not, or perhaps could not, buy one for me. When my class was called to perform, my classmates filed past me to the stage; I watched from the audience.

Yet my teacher and the school were kind and helpful to my sister and me in other ways. Shortly after we started school, an administrator came by our classes and asked if any children needed free tokens for hot lunches at the school cafeteria. Immediately, I raised my hand. There were no forms or applications required to demonstrate need based on income. The administrator took me at my word and gave me a set of tokens. I also asked for tokens for Katie.

We had previously walked the twelve long blocks back to the laundry as quickly as possible during our lunch break. We would scarf our hot lunch of rice with vegetables before hurrying back by the end of the hour. With tokens, we could eat at school.

On our first day at the cafeteria, we got in line, paid our tokens, and received a tray with a plate of lunch, a fork and knife, a napkin, and a drink. Katie and I had never eaten with a fork from a plate before. Always we had taken our meals of vegetables and rice, sometimes with meat, with chopsticks from a bowl. At breakfast, we ate our oatmeal with a spoon. We picked up our plates as we would have picked up our rice bowls at home and began to scoot food from it toward our mouths with the forks.

"Girls," Teacher approached us with a gentle smile, "let me teach you how to eat properly." We set down our plates with some embarrassment as the teacher joined us with her tray. "Now begin," she said, "by sitting up nice and straight to the table and opening your napkin to place it on your lap." Carefully, we opened our napkins and placed them in our laps.

"Leave your left hand in your lap and the plate on the table. Take a bite of food with the fork in your right hand." Teacher demonstrated; we followed her example.

"To slice the meat into smaller portions, put the fork in your left hand and take the knife in your right, slicing the food like so." A little clumsily, we practiced slicing.

Teacher continued until she had taught us the niceties of dining. She taught us to blot food from our mouths with napkins, to say "excuse me" when reaching across the table, and to fold our napkins neatly by the side of our plate when finished.

I was grateful to her for teaching us the American way of eating correctly. If she had not, I am sure we would have learned the hard way by being teased.

At school, I began to appreciate that the more I learned, the more the world opened to me. When I learned to read, I could interpret the signs on the store windows and read people's names on the laundry tags. I began to understand what people talked about on the street and in the stores. I learned songs that I could share with my sisters. One song, "Long, Long Ago," began:

Tell me the tales that to me were so dear
Long, long ago, long, long ago.
Sing me the songs I delighted to hear
Long, long ago, long ago.

Now you are come, all my grief is removed.
Let me forget that so long you have roved.
Let me believe that you love as you loved
Long, long ago, long ago.

Another song called "Bobby Shaftoe" went:
Bobby Shaftoe's gone to sea,
With silver buckles on his knee:
He'll come back and marry me,
Pretty Bobby Shaftoe!
Bobby Shaftoe's fat and fair,
Combing down his yellow hair;
He's my love forevermore,
Pretty Bobby Shaftoe!

I also learned new games, such as King of Romania. To play, one person, usually me, played the king. The other girls played young women, standing in a line opposite from me. As the king, I courted them by singing a song:

Here comes the king of Romania, Romania, Romania.
Here comes the king of Romania,
And I choose you for my queen.

During the song, I had to come up to the girl—one of my sisters—whom I picked as my queen. After I chose her, we skipped in a circle and then to my side of the room. Then I sang the song again and invited another girl. It was a simple, childish game, but we enjoyed the singing and the skipping, and it was something companionable to do together.

I also learned more about American culture and habits. This, however, brought me in more conflict with Ba. It was at school, for instance, that I learned the custom of celebrating birthdays. In traditional Chinese culture, only people who have reached an advanced age celebrate birthdays. Then it is they who give presents to their family and friends as a way of sharing the good fortune that has allowed them to advance to such a ripe age in prosperity.

But I wanted to please Ba, make him a little happy, and make him like me more and hit me less. I knew that his birthday was approaching. I wanted to get him a present. But how? My nickel from cleaning the bathroom wasn't enough to buy anything of value, and I wanted to get him something special.

I thought of the laundry stored on the highest shelf. After a time, when a customer did not pick up his package, we removed it from the lower shelves and stored it on the topmost shelf, hoping that he would someday return to claim it. There was one package that I knew with certainty had been there for years. It was stored high in a corner behind other packages.

One day, when Ba was out, I climbed up there and brought it down. When I opened the package, I found a bundle of all different types of clothing. But right on the top was a crisp, starched handkerchief, folded up nice and tidy.

I took this out, rewrapped the remaining clothes, and put the whole bundle back on the top shelf in its corner. The handkerchief I carefully wrapped in paper and hid away. When the expected day arrived, I brought the gift out from its hiding place.

"Happy birthday, Ba," I said, handing him my little package.

Ba squinted his eyes in suspicion, looking ill-tempered and tired. It had been another long and exhausting day. Opening the package to find the handkerchief, he sharply asked, "Where did you get this from?"

"I . . . I got it from the oldest of the unclaimed laundry packages."

Ba slapped me and said that I was never to do that again. I knew then that it was no use trying to explain that I understood that the handkerchief did not belong to us, that I knew that it was dangerous to climb to the top shelf and that it was not his custom to celebrate birthdays. But none of that had been important when I so much wanted to do some little thing to make Ba happy. Why could he not see that also?

On another occasion, the school administrator came to our class. "Are there any children," she asked, "whose families could use some help for the holidays this year and who would like to receive a basket of Christmas food?"

Immediately, I raised my hand to ask for the basket. How exciting, I thought. I told Katie about it on the way home, and she was excited too. I hoped that Ba would be pleased that I had got us a basket of food. In any case, it would be so lovely to have a special supper.

On Christmas Eve day, a volunteer parent came to the laundry. "Merry Christmas, Mr. Yee. From all of us at the school to your family, we wish you a happy holiday."

Ba was dumbstruck as he inspected the great basket. It was decorated with green and red bows and was filled with canned cranberries, bundles of yams and sweet potatoes, loaves of fruit and nut bread, and a whole smoked ham.

"Thank you," he began slowly, "but what is . . ."

"Ba," I began to explain in Chinese, "I got that for us. Someone from the school came by and asked if any of us needed help for the holidays and would like to receive a basket of food for Christmas. I said that we would like one. Aren't you glad?"

Ba's face became hard and pinched looking. The man again said he hoped we would enjoy our holiday, but Ba did not reply. At last, the man attempted farewell and hesitatingly walked out the door.

Ba turned to me, saying, "Now you listen to me. We do not take charity from anybody. We take care of ourselves. Do you understand that? We take care of ourselves!" He was so angry. He did not hit me, but I felt struck. And underlying his anger, I sensed his profound loss of face, deep bitterness, and shame at not being able to comfortably provide for his family, no matter how hard he worked.

There are statements that our parents make that shape our lives. I never forgot what I felt, having tried again to please my father and having failed. I never forgot his words or his fierce pride. They burned through me, and afterward, independence became my driving force.

I would later take great pride in being strong, surviving, and caring for myself. But though I was proud, I was also hurt by my father's failure to see and return my affection. Independence became a sometimes painful path.

It has sometimes meant, like my father, driving myself relentlessly even when I needed to rest. It has sometimes meant not admitting defeat when doing so might have freed me to pursue a more fruitful path. It has sometimes meant helping others and not accepting help for myself. Independence, like all qualities, must be taken in moderation, or it becomes a tyranny in itself.

Even so, I did not tell Ba that our lunches were also a charity, or else he would not have allowed that either. I let him believe that the school provided lunch to all children. So Katie and I continued to eat at the cafeteria.

7

THE GHOST IN OUR HOUSE

On December 26, 1931, my mother gave birth to her fifth daughter. Before that, Ma had given birth to yet another stillborn child, so this was her eighth pregnancy and delivery. So disappointed was my father in the arrival of another girl that he gave her a boy's name: Ding Ping, the name of a great Chinese general. By giving my sister this name, he hoped to improve his future luck for having a son. As with his other children, he asked the physician to suggest an American name.

"However," he said, "make it an easier name to pronounce this time. Margaret is too long and difficult to say." That is how my youngest sister was named May.

My mother was also disappointed. The birth of another daughter meant putting off a return trip to China that much longer. She began to be more depressed and ill. She frequently went to the hospital, sometimes staying there for days to treat heart, liver, and kidney conditions.

Sometimes she woke me at night. "King Ying, please," she would say, handing me an ointment to massage her back or neck because she was sore from illness and too much lying in bed. Other times, she sat up alone and cracked pumpkin and winter melon seeds and saved the kernels on a plate. In the morning, presenting a plate piled with seeds, she would say to my sisters and me, "These are for you."

At that time, it was not possible to buy pre-shelled seeds from the store, and winter melon seeds were particularly challenging to crack without shattering the kernel. How many sleepless hours went into the shelling of so many seeds? Ma, in her reserve, never hugged or kissed us, but by such a gesture, she demonstrated her affection.

When she felt too ill to cook, she directed me from her bed to prepare the meal. "King Ying, help me get out the pot for cooking rice." I would get the pot out from its cabinet and show it to her.

"Fill it with rice up to the middle of your middle finger." Then I would fill the pot with grain as directed.

"Rinse the rice twice, and then fill the pot with water up to the height of your knuckle." In this way, she taught me to use two parts water to one part grain to prepare the rice. Step by step, she instructed me until I had cooked the whole dinner.

At other times, when she was too sick even to direct me, Ba would prepare a dinner for us, tired as he was. It was generally a rather dull sort of bachelor supper, perhaps of boiled vegetables and rice. Still, it was something to eat until Ma felt better.

Now Ba had a friend whom he called Gong Gu, Gong being his given name and Gu meaning "bigger brother," which was a term of respect in deference to his being older than my father. Gong Gu was a bachelor who had grown up in the same village as Ba and now owned a small store in Detroit's little Chinatown. Having no wife or children, Gong Gu liked to visit us on weekends to chat with Ba and play with my sisters and me. When we visited him in Chinatown, he always brought out cookies and candies for us.

One night, Gong Gu called to say, "Ho Sin, my relative Quan is in the hospital. He has been in an accident, and he is dying. He and I don't know how to speak English to the people at the hospital. Can you please come to interpret?"

Holding the phone, Ba turned to explain to Ma what had happened. But Ma, looking at the clock and also seeing that it was storming with snow outside, was afraid and said, "Three o'clock in the morning? You don't want to go out there in the middle of the night. Don't go. Don't go. Just tell him you can't come." So Ba didn't go.

Later that night, the phone rang again. As Ba went to answer it, Ma stood to look out the window at the trees whipping back and forth in the wind and snow. Though she had never met him, she saw a man whom she believed to be Quan standing in the storm. At that moment, she knew he had died. As it turns out, Gong Gu was on the phone informing my father of Quan's death.

My mother's grief, when she heard, was unbounded. She cried miserably, repeating over and over to Ba, "I should have let you go. I should have let you go. Only it was three o'clock in the morning, and I hated to let you go. It's all my fault. I should have let you go and translate. It's all my fault!"

She wept herself into a fever until she could cry no more, so bitterly did she blame herself. Her bitterness and depression went on for days and weeks. Finally, her mental health, already weakened from prolonged illness and homesickness, began to break.

One evening, after my sisters had gone to bed, Ma rose from the kitchen table and walked outside the laundry. She stood for a while as though lost among the passersby and just staring out at the street. When she walked back in, her face and her bearing were changed.

"Hello," she said. "It's Quan." Ma spoke as though she had just come in for a visit, but there was something in her expression that was distant, as though she didn't see us or was in a trance. I watched her, amazed and transfixed. I didn't know what to make of her and couldn't speak.

Ba spoke her name, or, rather, he addressed her in the old Chinese manner by calling her King Ying ga Ma, meaning "Mother of King Ying," a customary way for husbands to address their wives. If they had had sons, he would have called her the mother of their eldest son.

Ba then took her hands and pinched her fingers near the nails, trying to bring her out of her trance with pain. But Ma did not respond and continued as though she were Quan. However, after a time, Quan faded, and she became Ma again, quiet and depressed, seeing us again, but remembering nothing of the incident. And we did not speak of it to her.

Over the next several months, Quan came and went in Ma. Whenever Quan was in her, he raised the hair on my spine, so eerie was it to see my mother's face and bearing transformed. I became a little afraid of her then.

Ba drew illustrations on red paper of frightening men with chubby cheeks and chubby arms, crouching bare-chested, each bearing a knife menacingly. He hung them over the door, hoping to prevent the spirit of Quan from entering. I hated those drawings. I don't know if they scared the ghost, but they scared me. Ba also consulted the elders in Chinatown.

"It is a spiritual matter," one said. "You must take her to a sacred place."

"Yes," agreed another. "Take her to a Christian minister in one of the churches. He should help you if anyone can." This elder told my father of the Central United Methodist Church, not far from our home by streetcar.

For the sake of his wife, and for the first time in my remembrance, Ba spent money a little frivolously. He let Ma go to the beauty parlor, where her long, straight hair was cut short and styled in finger waves according to the latest American fashion. He allowed her to buy a fashionable dress and hat for herself and new hats for my sisters and me so we could all go to church.

Oh, how excited I was to get my hat, made from peach-colored felt. I loved to wear it for as long as possible. It also pleased my mother a great deal to dress up her daughters, put on new clothes, and see how lovely her hair looked in the mirror. Making herself beautiful and wearing pretty clothes had been among her pleasures when she was young, and it had been so long since she had any reason or means to do so. The whole act of putting on new and fashionable clothes was a spiritual refreshment for all of us.

Then we all got on the streetcar to go to church. Leaving the laundry for someplace new felt like an adventure and a tonic to our spirits.

We did not understand much of what the minister said once we got to the church. My mother especially had the least knowledge of English of any of us. There was something about a carpenter god who liked children and wanted us to be like children. We had to leave a garden, but he kept another garden for us in heaven if we prayed to him. Much was lost in translation.

Still, my mother understood that this was a place where people gathered to commune with God and receive spiritual healing. The church was beautiful and peaceful, with high gothic arches and stained glass. Such an interior was so different from our spartan, steamy laundry. The minister and the choir wore colorful, flowing robes. The people were warm, friendly, and welcoming. These in themselves had a curative power.

The minister preached in a thrilling voice at every service, "You are accepted! You are forgiven!" Ba translated, and my mother wept quietly.

From then on, we went to church on Sundays. At first, we children sat with our parents in the sanctuary. But after a time, we were directed to classrooms to attend Sunday school. As the months passed, Quan came less and less often to visit us. Sometimes Ma still fell into quiet depression, and then Quan appeared again. But after a while, he did not come anymore. The elders had been right. Ma healed, and her physical and mental health improved.

8

ON SEX EDUCATION

On hot summer evenings, I sometimes liked to take my stool and sit just outside our shop door to watch the world. I watched the cars that passed and the people who walked by. I decided which cars and fashions I liked best and tried to guess what people were thinking or feeling by their expressions.

It was the early 1930s, and women's fashions were transitioning from the flapper styles of the 1920s to the longer, more fluid styles of the 1930s. Hemlines were starting to drop toward the ankle, and dress waists were returning to a more natural waistline. Dresses had slightly full skirts, soft, squared-off shoulders, and decorative necklines, often with wide scallop-edged or ruffled collars. Ladies wore their beret or pillbox hats at an angle and sported shoes with round toes and wide, thick heels. Men wore suits designed to create the image of a broad torso with squared-off shoulders stuffed with wadding or shoulder pads and sleeves tapered to the wrist.

One evening, a well-dressed, laughing young couple came toward me down the street. They ran trippingly into an entry alcove nearby. As the business was closed, I couldn't imagine what they wanted to do there. I leaned forward a little on my stool and turned my head in their direction. I could see that the young man had the young woman pushed against the door and was kissing and holding her passionately. I had never seen anything like this before. With a child's curiosity, I leaned further forward on my stool, craning my neck to see them.

I was like that for so long that I aroused the curiosity of my father inside the store. He came out to see what I was looking at. When he saw, he slapped me across the head and yelled at me to come inside.

"If I ever catch you doing anything like that when you grow up, I'll kill you," he yelled.

I cringed, and running inside with my little stool, I promised myself, "When I grow up, I will never let anything like that happen to me."

Of course, I didn't know that what I was doing was wrong, so I felt the hurt of his anger all the more intensely. What I did not realize is that I would never have seen such a scene if I were growing up in Ba's native village. Ba might admire American material wealth, but much of American behavior was shocking and unprecedented in his experience.

When he saw American women on the street half-nude in their sports clothes, it seemed indecent. When he saw men and women embrace and kiss openly in public places, he thought of it as animal behavior. American wives were unreliable because they sometimes divorced their husbands. There was no such thing as a woman divorcing her husband in China. In every way, as far as Ba was concerned, Chinese women were morally superior to American women.

But I was growing up in America, so it was hard to reconcile what passed for normal all around me with my father's different cultural values. I began to have a confused idea of what love meant and how to get and give it. There was the Chinese idea of doing everything possible to ensure your mate's prosperity and success with the hope that feeling and emotion would follow. There was the Western idea of pursuing romantic love first with its physical affection, roses, and valentines and the trust that prosperity would follow if the love were "true."

I received no explanation of the birds and the bees or childbirth. When my mother was pregnant, I was never even aware of when she experienced labor pains. Periodically, a doctor carrying a great black bag would simply show up. Then I was (and, later, my siblings were) hustled away to my aunt's home to stay for a day or two.

When I came home, there was a new baby.

"Ba, where did this come from?" I asked when I first became conscious of these things.

"Didn't you see the doctor come to the door with his black bag?" Ba would ask. I remembered the bag and nodded.

"When the doctor comes, he brings a baby in his bag for us."

For years, I believed this until I was old enough to realize that this didn't make sense, but I still didn't know how we had gotten the new babies.

Years later, when I was about twelve years old, I was sitting on an armchair and absently decided to hook one leg over the arm of the chair. Ba slapped me and told me to never sit like that with my knees open. Of course, this made me profoundly modest about something I had never considered before. Ever afterward, I sat and even slept with my ankles crossed.

9

THE COMING OF THE LANDLORD

On November 24, 1933, Ma gave birth to a son. Not quite eight months pregnant, she went into premature labor and, on the advice of her physician, gave birth at the hospital rather than at home. Ba named my brother Shew Min. The doctor named him James. He was born slightly sight impaired but was otherwise healthy and whole.

The year that followed was perhaps the happiest and healthiest of my mother's married life. At last, she felt that she had status. She began to think of returning to California, where she had a brother, and to China to share her "birth-of-son happiness." Her heart still bothered her, but she now worked among us like a real mother where before she had frequently been bedridden.

Her improved health, however, did not alleviate my father of his financial worries. The enormous debt accumulated from so many past hospitalizations and doctor's visits still weighed on him, and money was hard to come by in the Great Depression. Sometimes he got behind on his bill paying.

In the summer of 1935, the landlord of our Detroit laundry announced that he planned to evict us to rent the building to someone else. But where could we move our home and business on short notice with little cash and poor credit? Ba did not immediately hit upon a plan.

The longer we stayed, the angrier the landlord became. One day, the landlord came and shouted at my father in a great fit of rage, "You're gonna move out by tomorrow, or I'm gonna come down and kill you. You understand that? I'm gonna come down and kill you!"

"What did he say?" Ma asked in alarm after the landlord had left.

"He said he's going to kill me if we don't move out by tomorrow."

"Oh," said Ma, turning white. "What are we going to do?"

Ba didn't answer. He was worried, but he didn't believe that the landlord would kill him.

Ma, however, took the threat literally and seriously and began to panic and fret over what would happen if the landlord killed or injured my father. There were stories of Americans having done such things to Chinese people in the past. What would she do with six children, two in diapers, without my father? Already, we were in such debt to Uncle Gee Taw.

As might be expected, Ma slept with difficulty that night. She tossed and turned and frequently woke in misery before trying to sleep again.

As was his custom, Ba rose early to sweep the laundry. By then, Ma had fallen into a troubled sleep, but when he put away the broom and dustpan, the broom fell, and Ma woke with a start. She put on her robe, got up to look for Ba, and found him in the front ironing. She was tired, frightened, and not in her right mind, trembling with fear. She looked expectantly at Ba, but he said nothing and continued his work. Not knowing what to do, she took up clothing and began to iron.

In the early-morning light, she saw the figure of a man coming to the door and trying to open it. Perhaps it was a customer or a tradesman. We never did know. Ma leaped back in fright, her heart stopped, and she fell to the floor.

"King Ying! King Ying!" Ba yelled for me, and I ran to the front of the store. Now Ba was not in his right mind. I found him hunched over my mother, trying to open her mouth. He grabbed a pair of scissors off the ironing board and tried to pry her clamped teeth open with them. Then he took a glass of water and poured it into her mouth, and the water dribbled out the side.

"King Ying," he said, "you stay here with your Ma while I go across the street to call a doctor." We were moving, so Ba had disconnected our phone. He had to use the payphone in front of the grocery store. When the doctor arrived, he declared my mother dead. She was thirty-two years old.

My sisters and baby brother still slumbered. I roused the older ones and brought them to the front to see Ma before paramedics took her away. Only Jeannie was not present, for she was living with my aunt.

"Ma died this morning," I said, and my sisters looked at me with disbelieving faces. I am not sure they were old enough to understand death, or perhaps we were all too shocked. In any case, it was strange that none of us cried. I know that my first thought was, *What will become of us now?*

10

A SLOW BOAT TO CHINA

In retrospect, I believe that Ma knew that her time on earth was short. It is strange, but she called me to talk with her a few days before her death.

She appeared healthy, but she said, "King Ying, I have something important to say to you."

"What, Ma?"

"If anything should ever happen to me, and your father doesn't treat you and your sisters right, you should try to get help from the authorities, like the police. Don't let yourself get separated from your sisters and brother. Always keep yourselves together and take care of each other."

Of course, I didn't like to hear such a thing, and it was strange that she should say it now that she was well and at home with us. "Aren't you feeling well, Ma?"

"I think so, but . . . well, you never know. I just wanted to say that to you." A few days later, she died, and I could not help but believe that she had a premonition of what was to come.

Ba moved my sisters, brother, and me to my aunt's house while he set about moving our possessions out of the Detroit laundry and still tried to manage the one in Dearborn. He wrote to his mother in China about our circumstances, and she advised him to come home and get a new wife. She would make the arrangements with a matchmaker. Ba agreed that he needed to do this. Race issues aside, what American woman would marry a man with six children and live with him in a laundry? There would also be the issue of dating and courtship, which were utterly foreign to him.

For a time, Ba spoke of putting all of us in foster homes or a home for orphaned children, and I worried that what my mother feared about our being separated would come to pass. But then Uncle Gee Taw offered to loan him more money, and they devised a plan for Ba to bring us all back with him to China. There, we could be kept together cheaply until he could bring us back to America.

In December 1935, we took the train from Detroit to Seattle and then to Vancouver. Ba could not afford to buy tickets in the sleeper cars. For five days and three nights, we sat on wooden benches facing each other and tried to sleep sitting upright with a one-night stay in a hotel in Seattle along the way. Toward the end of our trip to Seattle, Ba complained of an odor.

"King Ying," he barked, "your feet smell bad. Change your socks." It was true that I hadn't been able to clean myself for a few days, so I changed my socks, tucked my feet under, and tried to stay away from the others, but still, Ba complained of the odor.

When we got to the hotel in Seattle, Ba found that James had a load in his diaper, and May had peed in her pants. These were the causes of the stench. Auntie had been taking care of us, and Ba was not yet used to caring for babies. In the hotel, we all cleaned ourselves and changed our clothes after the several days spent in cramped quarters.

Then in Vancouver, we boarded a Blue Funnel Line freight steamship, so named for its blue funnels from which steam emerged. As we got on the ship, I looked back to the land and thought about how Ma wasn't coming with us. I thought about how she was still in Detroit and that we were leaving her. I thought about how she had yearned for so long to take this trip and about how badly she had wanted a son so she could return home without reproach. Finally, she had her son, but she would never have the joy of putting him into her mother's arms.

"Ma is still here," I said to my sisters in a shaking voice. "We are leaving her behind." Seeing my tears, my sisters began to cry too. The impact of our loss and our mother's loss struck us. I thought of how lonely she must be without us, and we were so young to be without a mother. I was just twelve, Katie was ten, Jeannie eight, Margaret seven, May four, and James two.

During our short time with our mother here on earth, we hardly saw her when she was not subdued and depressed. When she appeared to be gaining in health and happiness, at last, we had lost her.

Ba had booked accommodations for us in steerage class, which consisted of rooms filled with bunkbeds, all surrounding a central mess dining hall. There was a community bathroom. All of us were in a single room with four bunks on two walls. Ba, Katie, Jeannie, and I each got our own. Ba then pushed together two armchairs to make a bed in which Margaret and May slept together. James took turns sleeping with the four of us in the bunkbeds.

Ba found a place to wash James' and May's dirty diapers every day. He never apologized about mistaking the stink of their dirtied diapers for the smell of my feet, but he had learned to be diligent in changing them frequently.

At mealtimes, we ate in the great mess hall at long tables. In between, my sisters, brother, and I managed to entertain ourselves with such activities as children who are accustomed to making do without toys contrive.

Sometimes we walked through steerage class and stopped at rooms where people had left their doors open. We would say hello and ask where they were going and where they had come from and engage in other childish prattle. Sometimes we sat in our room and made up stories or sang songs. Sometimes we took turns swinging around some poles or counting stairs as we climbed them. Other times we played with chairs, pushing them together to make a tunnel to crawl under or lying on our backs on the seats with our legs hooked over the chair back. And sometimes, I climbed up the long flights of stairs to the deck to look out upon the ocean. But my sisters would not join me in this as they were afraid to venture far without Ba being with us.

I believe my sisters and I were the only girls on the ship. Most of the other passengers were Chinese men working in America while sending money back home to their families in China. Now they returned to China to retire, visit their families, or find a bride. For most of them, it had been many years since they had seen Chinese girl children, and they thought we were so cute that many of them opened the crates of apples and oranges that they had brought and gave us some.

We stopped at many ports in Japan and northern China before arriving in Hong Kong. Dockworkers removed a portion of our freight at each port and added new cargo. This was long before the days of containerization and automated removal of containers onto waiting trucks. Instead, at each port, groups of men attached great hooks and clamps to each crate and raised the loads by a pulley, and then an operator swung them onto the ground. The operator then hoisted loads onto the ship from the ground, which were manually arranged and settled into place. This process was time-consuming, so we spent four to seven days at each port. Our journey took forty-two days from Vancouver to Hong Kong. Truly we had taken a slow boat to China!

In Hong Kong, we waited two days for the arrival of a river junk boat that would take us to my father's village. We stayed in a hotel, and while my father went to take care of some business, my sisters, brother, and I stayed in the room and kept each other company.

There was a button on one of the walls, and baby brother James liked to push it. This caused a woman from room service to come up and inquire about what we needed. When she found that we were Chinese-Americans whose mother had died and whose father was returning to China to seek a new wife, she waited for Ba to return. She offered to marry him on the spot.

Ba thanked her but said that his mother had already made arrangements for him through a matchmaker at home. I could not help but feel sorry for the young woman and wondered what circumstances prompted her to offer herself in such a way with so little inquiry.

The junk boat journeyed up the Pearl River from Hong Kong to our village for one day and night. There were no private sleeping quarters as there had been on the steamboat. Instead, we slept with the other ship's passengers in one great room on the floor with ropes hanging in rows above our heads. At the end of each cord was a heavy metal hook onto which passengers hooked their belongings. So as we slept, bundles, packages, and hooks swayed and creaked over our heads.

I thought again of how pleased and excited my mother would have been if she were with us. As for me, I could not help but observe that conditions on the Chinese junk were more primitive and uncomfortable than conditions on the Canadian steamship. I wondered what further privations we would soon endure.

Just as we arrived at our destination in the morning, James dirtied his diaper. Hastily changing him, Ba wrapped the dirtied diaper with layers of old laundry wrapping paper and tied it up neatly with sturdy blades of water grass. He left it hooked onto one of the ship's ropes.

Unfortunately, this looked like a neat bundle of laundry or some other item of importance. A fellow passenger who thought he recognized my father from the village unhooked the package and tried to catch up with us to return it.

"Ho Sin! Ho Sin!" he called, but neither my father nor any of us heard him as we were too far away. However, as he was eventually going to the village, he kept the package. Upon arrival there some days later, he kindly returned the bundle to my father, saying, "You forgot this on the boat." What could my father do but thank him?

When we arrived, a considerable portion of the village came out to gawk at us and followed us in a mob to my grandmother's house. Many of them had seen Chinese men dressed in the American style as they returned from the United States. This district was impoverished. Any family who could save enough to send even one son, father, or uncle to the United States, Singapore, or the

Philippines to earn some money to send home did so. Almost none, however, had ever seen females dressed and groomed in the Western style. This was long before the days of television. Moreover, not even radio or popular magazines were available in this remote place.

"Their hair, their hair," an elderly woman remarked as she stared disapprovingly at our short, bobbed styles. "It sticks out and pokes the earth god." It was immediately apparent that where we had been foreign in the country of our birth, we would also be foreign in the land of our heritage.

In the village, all women dressed similarly. Unmarried girls wore their long hair in plaits. Married women wore their hair in a bun, often decorated with flowers. Both girls and women wore loose trousers with Chinese-style high-collared jackets with sleeves that reached either above the elbow or the wrist. Their boxy clothes, constructed of a fabric called "leung sah," meaning cool, breathable fabric, differed primarily in the colors they chose. Leung sah is a stiff fabric that doesn't cling to the skin. Combined with the boxy shape, the clothes kept the wearer covered but as cool as possible in the tropical climate.

In Western nations, society had begun to see women's legs some fifteen years before. Even in Hong Kong, women of fashion wore long silk dresses with slits that revealed their legs. This was still unheard of in the village. Our legs seen below the hem of our knee-length dresses were the cause of much comment.

When we got to Grandmother's house and went in, the mob still peered in at the door. What struck me was that no one stood directly in the center of the doorway. They piled on each other on the edges of the door, wishing to keep protection from our strangeness.

However, we did nothing more compelling than meet and greet our grandmother, uncle, and aunt and began to unpack and look about us. The crowd started to disperse until just one little boy stood at the door. Finally, he hissed at me through the doorway, "Are you wearing any pants under there?"

"Of course, I am," I said, blushing and thinking of my underwear. "Hmph," said the boy, and he ran off.

11

A NEW HOME, A NEW STEPMOTHER

Grandmother Yee Jung Shee was a thin, tiny old lady, a little under five feet tall, dressed in black and wearing an embroidered headband across her forehead to keep her head warm. Uncle Ho Huang, my father's brother, was a well-built, handsome, and beautifully dressed young man, some six feet tall with a look of intelligence unfortunately spoiled by an ill-tempered expression. He dressed in elegant sandals and a Chinese coat of rich, embroidered silk with frog buttons in a row down the front and trousers perfectly tailored to fit him. He cut such a different figure from Ba, dressed in his khaki slacks with a collared shirt and whose small stature demonstrated the effect of poor nutrition in childhood.

Uncle's wife, my aunt, was a pretty young woman. Where Uncle was sulky, Auntie was shyly conversational and greeted us warmly. Uncle and Auntie's home was across the footpath from my grandmother's house.

Grandmother had treated Uncle very differently from my father when they were children, lavishing him with love and attention as he grew. Why my grandmother should prefer Uncle to my father was never clear to me. Perhaps it was because my father was associated with that time of her life when she had been desperate and hungry. In contrast, Grandmother gave birth to Uncle after her husband had returned after a long separation.

When Grandfather died in his fifties, Uncle was Grandmother's only companion. By then, she was more financially secure, thanks, in significant part, to my father's hard work. Ba had sent money home for Uncle to be married and to buy a house in the village. Now, however, Grandmother treated her two sons with equal deference.

Grandmother gave us her home to live in while she slept in Second Granduncle Yee Jeong Nug's house nearby. My grandfather was one of three sons, of which he was the second. The third son had died in childhood. His parents afterward adopted a son, as was often the custom when families lost a son to disease or accident. This adopted son, our second granduncle, had gone to the United States some time ago to seek his fortune and left his home in my grandmother's care.

Early each morning, Grandmother returned from Second Granduncle's home and spent her days among us. Also living with us was our servant, Tieu Hall, who had been part of our mother's dowry. She had been a girl when my mother married. Now she was a young woman, and she helped to care for us.

Conditions in our new home and the village were depressing to one accustomed to modern conveniences. We had lived poorly in Detroit, yet we at least had indoor plumbing, electricity, a flush toilet, and a telephone. In the village, we stepped back a hundred years to an impoverished peasant mode of living.

The entrance to the village consisted of two concrete walls, about six feet long, separated by a heavy wooden beam. Inscribed Chinese characters read Tai Ting Pong[1] , meaning "Big Well Village." Our well was not large, yet it was larger than the wells of villages near to us so that we had some distinction among our neighbors because of it.

Near the entrance to the village was the outhouse, which consisted of a sizable wooden shed built over a pit. Heavy boards laid across the hole, so users stepped out upon two parallel planks

---

[1] Tai Ting Pong represents the Cantonese Sze-Yup dialect pronunciation. In Mandarin, the village is called Da Jing Bang or Dajingbang, which is how one will find the village on a modern map.

and squatted to do their business with a stench rising from below. At appropriate times of the year, the village men would dig out the contents and spread it around the rice-paddy fields as a fertilizer.

To use this facility, I would stand outside the door and clear my throat, "Ahem," to announce my presence. If anyone were within, he would also ahem to preclude my entering. I would then wait outside until the person exited. If no one responded, then I entered straight away. As for soap for washing, there was little, and it was hard to come by. What was available was rough and felt as though it had grains of sand in it.

To the right of the outhouse, as you entered the village, were rows of houses built on similar floor plans. Most were duplex homes in which two families shared one building. Our three-room structure of red clay had a ceramic tile roof, the corners of which sloped upward in the Chinese style. Our family and another family had the rooms at either end for our exclusive use. We shared the center chamber as a living room.

The room's layout for our personal use was as follows: To one side of the door were two beds behind a curtain. One was the sizable, red-painted bed with an embroidered canopy included in Mother's dowry. Aside from embroidered silk, the bed was covered with a gauzy cheesecloth-type fabric to keep out mosquitoes and for privacy.

Perpendicular to this bed was a wooden platform covered with straw mats, where we children slept all together. Near the door were ceramic urns for rice storage along with oil-wick candles, which only dimly lit the room at night but created large shadows.

To the side of the canopied bed and against the far wall from the door was my mother's teakwood washbasin stand with the porcelain washbasin set into it, and next to this was a knee-high chamber pot with a wooden lid. Throughout the room were baskets for storage. Each of us had a small basket for storing our few clothes. In all, I had only two sets of clothes, one that I wore and one as a change.

An oval metal tub hung on one wall. We periodically took this down and filled it for bathing. A wood-burning cook stove stood on the other side of the door. Beneath each of two burners was a little door for feeding in the fuel of dry branches, rice stalks, and wood shavings, and to the side of the stove was a worktable. Our table for eating stood in the center of the room.

A wood box with a screen door for perishable food storage hung from the ceiling near the dining table. There was no refrigeration, so the box simply protected food from flying insects and animals.

To one side of our shared living room hung an altar where we honored our ancestors. Above it were red, rectangular strips of paper inscribed in brush calligraphy with the names of our forbears. My mother's name was the newest addition. Food, wine, candles, incense, and oranges sat on the altar's shelf. Oranges, with their bright color, were associated with happiness. They were used ceremonially as gifts to friends or relatives or in stacks as decoration around the home. When gifting oranges, one always gave three, six, or nine as these were lucky numbers.

Pigs and caged chickens slept in this room at night. In later years, James sometimes cared for a neighbor's ox when they were away, and then he brought the ox into the living room at night and allowed it to sleep under our altar. Also in this room was a wooden pounding device mounted on a hinge, which we used to polish rice. Below it was a bowl into which we poured unpolished grain. We then pumped the foot of the tool, causing the head to rise and fall, pounding the rice until husks separated from the grain.

Opposite the altar was a hole in the floor into which we poured dirty dishwater and bathwater. These flowed into a central trench, which extended down the length of the footpath. Above this area, the roof was open so that fresh air could circulate, and rainwater could eventually dilute the dirtier water. The Kaiping District is in a tropical area, which is generally warm, so it was possible to leave the roof open in this way without being cold at night.

Toward the end of the rows of houses were newer houses where wealthier villagers lived. These were larger and sometimes made of brick, which was costly compared to red clay. Villagers could harvest red clay for free from the land.

Wild star-fruit trees were to one side of the houses, and the village well was beyond the houses, a stone structure some ten feet deep. It was possible to drop in a bucket and haul up drinkable water during the rainy season. However, in the dry season, water ran so low that it was not possible to collect water by tossing in the bucket. Children or servants went down the well to hold the bucket carefully on its side to skim the thin layer of cleaner water floating above the mud.

They were able to perform the descent and climb by bracing their feet and hands against the sidewalls of the well and slowly edging themselves down and up the shaft. Someone at the top of the well would haul up the water while the child waited for the well to recharge. The person at the top would lower the bucket again, and the skimming process would continue until sufficient water was collected. The unevenness of the stonework gave one moderate hand and footholds to climb up and down. However, it was still quite tiring, dangerous, and frightening. Once the villager had hauled up the wooden buckets of water, they would carry these on each end of a bamboo pole balanced across the shoulders.

Beyond the rows of houses was an altar shaped like a short stove, where villagers came to burn candles and incense during prayer to the local earth god, protector of our village.

Each village had its earth god. Other deities belonging to the so-called Taoist pantheon, such as Laozi, founder of Taoism; Guan Yin, Goddess of Mercy; and the Eight Immortals, were worshiped in the temple on a hill not far from our village. Monks kept their living quarters near there. Aside from this type of Taoism, the villagers' beliefs also encompassed elements of Confucianism, as evidenced by family altars.

Beyond the well and altar were the meeting grounds, a small open field for feasts and celebrations, such as wedding banquets or the spring and moon festivals. For wedding banquets, villagers sat on the meeting grounds around large circular mats of bamboo. Ten people could fit around each mat.

At the end of the village, beyond the meeting grounds, was a pond edged with stands of bamboo. In this pond, villagers fished, caught shrimp, swam, watered their oxen, and cleaned laundry. To one side was a large community garden where each family had a plot for growing vegetables. Partly surrounding the village were the rice-paddy fields. Each family had its plots among these fields as well.

All inhabitants of the village had the same surname, Yee. Young women who married left to live in their husband's community, while young men who married brought their new brides to live with them in Tai Ting Pong. Once married, women kept their maiden name but added their husband's surname and the title "Shee" to indicate being married. For instance, in my mother's case, she was born Fong Bo-Ling, Fong being her family name and Bo-Ling her given name. After marriage, she became Yee Fong Shee, which means Mrs. Yee, nee Fong. The family would still call her Bo-Ling, and her full name would be Yee Fong Shee Bo-Ling, meaning Mrs. Bo-Ling Yee, nee Fong.

In our case, Grandmother made arrangements with two matchmakers so that Ba could select between two potential brides from neighboring villages. The eldest candidate was twenty-one. After meeting her briefly, Ba settled on her with the thought that someone taking care of six children at once should be as mature as possible.

After Ba selected his bride, the two families negotiated the terms of marriage. The bride's family was to provide a dowry, which was to include such things as linens, furniture, kitchenware, and servants. In return, the groom's family would pay for the wedding feast. They would also provide the bride's family a cash sum and a certain number of wedding cookies to be shared among them.

The value of the dowry might be roughly equivalent to the cash paid. However, sometimes, if parents particularly valued their daughter, they might give her dowry possessions of a higher value.

According to what the families negotiated, the number of wedding cookies given might range from hundreds to well over a thousand. About a week before getting married, on an auspicious day chosen from the astrological almanac, the groom's family representatives would bring the cookies and money to the bride's village. They would present the cookies to her parents in a stacked set of black, gold, and red lacquered boxes.

Upon receiving them, the bride's parents would convene their friends and relatives for a bridal going-away tea and cookie party. The representatives from the groom's family would stay through this party. At the end, the bride's parents would present a set of gifts for the groom and return some cookies and a little money. Traditional gifts were a new wallet to hold his money, a new pair of pants, and a belt. Returning some of the cash and cookies meant that the exchange was complete. In the days following, the bride's mother would prepare packages of the wedding cookies to give to each of the family's relations.

In addition to the going-away party, the bride had to participate in a series of confessional gatherings with her unmarried female friends and relatives. The purpose of the confessionals was to rid the bride of any spiritual malignancy that she harbored so she could enter marriage with a clean heart and soul. The gatherings occurred over a series of days. On each day, the bride kneeled on her bed, facing the corner wall with her head bowed and holding a handkerchief over her face. Her guests sat behind her a short distance away, also covering their faces and sitting with bowed heads.

On the first day, the bride would scold her parents for all the unfair and unkind things they had done to her as she was growing up. After each statement, she would sob in the form of ritual crying while holding the handkerchief over her face. The group would then also respond with ritual sobbing. The bride continued until she had rid herself of all resentment toward her parents.

On the next day, she would state all her regrets. Again, after each statement, she would engage in ritual crying with her handkerchief held over her face, and her guests would cry in response. On the third day, she would apologize to all those she felt she had hurt. Again, there was the ritual sobbing. Villagers believed that the bride was spiritually cleansed and prepared to enter marriage at the end of this process. On the final day, she blessed her parents for all they had given her. This was the custom of our region.

When my father's wedding day arrived, Grandmother sent my sisters, brother, and me to our neighbor's home. As reminders of my father's first wife, she considered it unlucky for us to attend the new bride's wedding. As with Mother's wedding, there was a procession through the village, which began when an honored elder lady greeted and welcomed the bride and her matchmaker at the village entrance. She started the procession, followed by the bride and her dowry.

But where my mother had been wealthy, our stepmother-to-be was poor. She was not carried in a sedan chair but walked through the village behind the honored elder. Red silk veiled her face, so the matchmaker cupped the bride's elbow to assist her in walking. She did not come with servants, furniture, jewelry, or embroidered silks. Having returned with many daughters and without wealth, my father no longer commanded the type of valued bride my mother had been. Still, there was food for feasting, including meat, fish, and fowl, teacakes, and other goodies, all provided by the groom's family by tradition.

Although the bride was poor, she was healthy, accustomed to hard work, and able to read and write well as her mother had been a schoolteacher. In many ways, she was better suited to my father's station in life than my mother had been.

By custom, the procession ended at the home of the groom's parents, which, in our case, was where we lived with Grandmother. There, the wedding tea ceremony took place before the groom's parents and elder relatives. As the bride had left her family to become a new member of ours, none of her family was present. Only two female servant representatives came to ensure the bride's safe arrival at her wedding and to witness, on behalf of the bride's mother, that the ceremony took place.

The bride and groom kowtowed three times to my grandmother and other family elders and served each elder tea. The honored elder lady stood by the bride to facilitate the making and serving of the tea. Each elder drank from the teacup, blessed the union, then returned the cup with a lucky red envelope filled with a gift of money. Grandmother and other relatives also presented the bride with gold and jade bracelets, necklaces, and earrings, the traditional bridal gifts. Women had limited property and inheritance rights, so jewelry was the primary form of feminine financial security.

Following the ceremony, the bride went directly to the bedroom of her new home to await her husband's return later that evening. The honored elder lady kept her company, procured food for her, and advised her on matters of matrimony for the remainder of the day until her husband returned. In the meantime, the groom, with his adult male relatives and friends, went to the meeting grounds to begin the feast celebration served by a person hired for the occasion. Female relatives remained at home in the parlor to eat and visit before returning home to care for their houses and offspring.

Of course, the village men loved their feast days. They would usually prolong the groom's eating, talking, and drinking until late at night. They sought to get the groom as drunk as possible before he returned home to his bride. Aside from its celebrative purpose, drunkenness also served to diminish the groom's inhibitions in being intimate with a woman he had met only briefly or sometimes not at all. Upon the groom's return and entrance into the bedroom, the elder lady would rise and leave. The groom would then lift the silk veil to look upon his trembling bride's face, sometimes for the first time.

The day after the wedding, my siblings and I returned home to meet our new stepmother. We called her Seam, meaning Stepmother, as we could not address her as Mother. Our birth mother, it was presumed, lived on in the afterworld, and it would have been disrespectful to address another by her title.

Seam was extremely surprised when she saw all of us. Seeking to allay an anxious bride's fears, her matchmaker had told her that my father had only three children. She appeared to count our number repeatedly after we walked in. However, as nothing could change the fact of our existence as six children, she quickly swallowed her dismay. She attempted to collect herself and held open her arms to baby James, picking him up and fussing over him, perhaps to hide any further awkwardness.

We all greeted her, introduced ourselves, and gawked a bit overly long, trying to take in the fact that this young woman, just nine years older than me, was our new stepmother. We did know that our mother could not return to us and that we must try to make the best of our situation, so we attempted pleasantries.

"Your wedding day went well?" one of us asked hesitantly.

"Yes, very well. Thank you."

"We hope you will be happy here."

"I am sure we will be happy together."

There was leftover feast food, teacakes, and other goodies piled on plates throughout the house. We children eyed them, wistfully hoping to taste some. To our delight, after introductions, we sat down together and shared from among these treats our first meal as a new family.

12

OF FARM AND SCHOOL WORK IN A KAIPING VILLAGE

By tradition, after the first month of marriage, Seam's mother-in-law, our grandmother, allowed her to go home for a day to visit with her parents and siblings. Grandmother sent teacakes with Seam as a goodwill gesture from our family to hers. But after this post-wedding visit, it was a long time before Seam was allowed to revisit her family, and she was only allowed to go at Grandmother's discretion.

Not long after their marriage, Seam and Ba had a great argument with Grandmother, who demanded more money from Ba for herself and Uncle Ho Huang. She also felt that Seam should be more deferential, cater to her needs, and serve her more. Elder women were demanding of their daughters-in-law. They expected them to act as their servant.

But Ba sided with Seam. He couldn't see how she could care for his mother and take care of six children along with household and farm chores. Moreover, he was already in debt back in the United States and couldn't spare more money for his mother and brother.

Ba decided to move us into town temporarily until tempers cooled. He bought a beautiful white chow dog with a curly tail to guard us and keep us company. People generally left their doors open during the day and only closed them at night before sleeping. However, Ba always had a habit of closing the door earlier, and one evening he forgot that our dog was still outside. When the dog returned home late in the evening, he began to paw at the door.

Ba hollered down the stairs, "Go away! Go away! We don't want anything."

At that time, however, if you didn't keep your pets in a safe place, people sometimes stole them for food. When Seam opened the door in the morning, she found the dog with a bloodied head, apparently from a bludgeoning attack. It appeared that the dog had successfully escaped his assailant, but now he was not in his right mind.

He went berserk, chasing a cat down a drain and then running through our house like a mad dog, yelping and foaming at the mouth. All of us were scared and screaming, but Ba managed to corner him into one room and lock him in. Seam then paid a man to kill the dog and take it away. The following day, we saw this man selling dog stew in the street.

Ba bought us a new dog. This one was black, and Ba named him Dewey, after prominent Republican Thomas E. Dewey, who had gained national prominence as a special prosecutor against organized crime in New York. Ba later supported him in his unsuccessful presidential election bids against President Roosevelt and President Truman. The Republicans were supporters of the Nationalist Chinese under Chiang Kai-Shek, whom Ba favored over the Communists. Ba also bought us a cat, which he named Knowland, after California Republican Senator Bill Knowland, also a supporter of Chiang Kai-Shek.

Not long after we moved into this flat in town, there was a flash flood. We lived on the second floor, but water began to creep up the stairs. James, who was quite little, thought this was exciting and crept under the porch to collect water in his bucket, shouting at us to hoist the bucket up after he had filled it. He then went down to look at the water on the stairs. Fortunately, I walked a little way behind to look after him, for suddenly he fell into the water. He did not yet know how to swim and began to thrash and float away. There were ledges on either side of the staircase. Quickly straddling the stairs by stepping onto these ledges, I reached down and yanked James up by the hair. He was scared and a little injured but, fortunately, not much the worse for wear.

We did not live long in town. When tempers had cooled between Ba and Seam and Grandmother, we moved back into Grandmother's home in the village. In June 1936, three months after his marriage, Ba returned to the United States, leaving his wife and children in China while working at the laundry business again. He was to send money for our upkeep and would also work to pay his debt to Uncle Gee Taw until he could afford to bring us all back to the United States.

After her wedding, Seam set about the daily business of our life. It was spring, and working with neighbors, she began to plant vegetable seeds and seed sweet potatoes in our plot in the community garden. On nearly a daily basis, she also emptied urine from our chamber pot into a bucket, diluted it with water, and ladled the mixture over the vegetable plot as fertilizer.

Seam also cared for the pig we shared with the neighbors and our chickens and ducks. During the day, Seam allowed the pig and fowl to walk freely outside the house. At night, however, she would call them, and recognizing the sound of her voice, they returned to our home. The pig slept in the living room over the hole in the floor leading to the trench, where it was cool and moist. The chickens and ducks she shooed into coops, which she also stored in the living room.

Seam began the work of preparing our rice paddies for planting. Heavy rains fell from March through June. Sometimes if the rains started early, one could harvest two rice crops per year, one in June and one in September. In these cases, the September harvest tasted best. Usually, however, there was just one harvest in September, and Seam prepared to this end. Neighbors helped her do her paddy work, and she helped the neighbors do theirs.

We ought to have had a good deal of our own land. Great-grandfather Yee Bill Mo was a scholar who had accumulated wealth in nineteenth-century California. He did immigrant translation work with one of his two wives, Yee Shee Leong, an English-speaking Chinese American. He later invested much of his savings into Chinese real estate. He accumulated many rice paddies, some of which should have come to my father. As my father had never had a loving relationship with his parents, he had looked to his grandfather as a role model. He had great respect for his work ethic and pursuit of education.

Unfortunately, my grandfather had sold some of the lands years before to feed his opium habit. Grandmother later signed over all of what remained to Uncle Ho Huang, who proceeded to sell the properties for cash. By the time we arrived, all our family lands were gone. Seam used some of the money that Ba had given her to buy new tracts of land. Ultimately, however, these were not sufficient to feed our family for a whole year. To get through the end of the year before the next harvest, she would later have to buy more rice at the grocery store in town.

Rice paddies are flat tracts of land with earthen sidewalls for water control. The paddies of our village were on hillside terraces, and we did our paddy work as follows: Once spring rains flooded the rice fields, weeds sprang up fast. Seam and the neighbors would then push a wooden plow through to eliminate weeds. A few villagers were fortunate enough to have water buffalo to help with this work. Immediately after plowing, villagers drove oxen fitted with a wooden tool through the fields to create furrows for planting.

Then the planting of rice sprouts could begin. Rice sprouts are regular rice that has been allowed to sprout into a grass carpet about six inches high. To plant sprouts, Seam would carry a basket of sprout carpet, pull off tufts, then push them a little over an inch deep into the furrows. Consistently pinching off just the right amount quickly and efficiently was a skill, as anyone who has ever tried to separate tangled sprouts can attest.

Water flowed through the paddy like a languid river. A series of dams controlled water movement, some where the water came in and some where the water came out. Wooden boards and the earth itself controlled the water. If more water was needed, Seam repositioned a board or mud so that more water came in or else less water flowed out. Knowing how to maintain the correct water depth and flow was an art.

The rice sprouts would grow into young plants a few days after planting. These plants would then be left to grow for three to four months until they flowered, matured, and turned a light brown. Villagers flooded the fields during all this time, or the rice wouldn't grow properly. They also continuously pulled weeds to maintain the proper flow of water.

If insufficient rain fell to keep the paddies flooded, water was diverted from the pond to the paddies by canals. A cupped paddlewheel pumped the water. The spokes of the paddlewheel had perpendicular rods. A man would climb onto a rod, then step up to the next rod extending from the next spoke. In this way, the wheel would begin to turn, and the cups would collect water from the pond, then splash the water down to the canal propped on a large rock.

Once the rice turned light brown, villagers drained the water. When the field was dried and the plants became a hay color, the paddy could be harvested by hand with a sickle knife.

Once the villagers finished harvesting, everyone gathered to thresh the rice to separate the grain from the straw. If the harvest was in September, the seed head, being drier, separated more easily from the stalks. Threshing was more difficult if the harvest was in June, for the weather was still wet. The seed heads, being greener and more robust, were more challenging to separate from the stalk.

We threshed the rice by beating the stalks against the inside of a three-walled enclosure until the heads fell off. The grain heads were then gathered into bamboo trays and left to dry in the sun. Once dried, we removed the husks by grinding the grain heads between stone wheels, the top wheel having a handle that we could use to turn the stone.

Finally, at home, we all took turns polishing the rice with our pounding tool to remove the bran from the grain. Seam fed the bran and husks to our pig. The rice straw she used as fuel for our stove. Once we harvested the rice, we then used the paddies to grow different crops that were less water-intensive, such as sweet potatoes.

However, to tide us through until our first harvest, Ba had left sufficient funds for Seam to buy food from the nearby town. Seam had a relative who owned a grocery, and she always went to his store to buy our provisions.

Seam also went to the altar by the meeting grounds twice a month to pray and make an offering. She asked the earth god for the blessing of a plentiful crop. All offerings were in sets of three, such as three dishes of food, three sets of utensils, three bowls of rice, and three cups of white wine. She also made offerings to our ancestors at the family altar, praying especially to my mother for her blessing and assistance as she strove to continue Ma's work in our family. Mother's photograph, surrounded by flowers, sat on the altar.

She set Jeannie and Margaret to help her in the fields. As she had sufficient funds, she enrolled Katie and me in school. We went to a school called Song Jook, meaning Double Bamboo, located between our village and a neighboring one. Song Jook would not allow us to attend in American clothing, so Seam bought us Chinese clothes.

My Chinese pants were full and long and worn by folding one side over the belly, then the other, tying a cord around the waist to hold the pants up. I pulled up the pants until the hem hung at my ankles. I then tucked the rope ends to keep them from dangling. In this way, I could wear the pants without growing out of them for a long time. Over the pants, I wore a loose Chinese jacket with frog buttons. The buttons snaked from the center of my neck to my right shoulder and down to the right armpit. The coat covered the rolled pants at the top.

Outside Song Jook School was a playground. Every morning, we gathered there with the other children until a teacher came out to lead us in calisthenics. I had not yet mastered the method of tying up my pants, so during the jumping exercise, they suddenly fell. I was profoundly embarrassed as I hurriedly pulled up my pants. However, the other children did not jeer or laugh at me. They only continued their calisthenics, looking sideways at me with surprise and amused expressions. After this, I tied my pants on very tight.

We spent most of our day learning to read and write the Chinese language. We especially practiced our calligraphy. If a dot or a dash was off, the character might have a whole different meaning, so it was vital that our writing be precise. We also learned math up to the level of introductory algebra.

While Katie and I went to school, Jeannie and Margaret labored in the rice paddies. Workers wear tall rubber boots in modern-day rice-paddy work to protect their feet and legs, but my sisters did not have this luxury. Instead, they sank knee-deep into hot mud and emerged with leeches attached to their legs. They were about the length of a finger and swelled wide when gorged with blood. Jeannie and Margaret were constantly peeling them off with disgust as soon as they found them, fearing that they would bore inside of them.

In the paddies, they hand cut rice, which they collected on the pathways between the paddies. When they had enough to make a sheaf, they tied the stalks together with rope. Once they had two sheaves, they stuck a bamboo rod through one and then the other and lifted the rod onto their shoulders with the weight sagging from each end of the rod. They carried this to the temple, halfway between the field and our house. There, they stopped to rest before bringing the load the rest of the way home. They were so small and thin to be bearing such a burden. Afterward, they returned to the paddies to cut more rice. Eventually, Jeannie complained so much about the leeches that Seam excused her from the harvesting work.

Katie also did limited rice-paddy work after coming home from school. However, she always preferred, and was usually assigned, house cleaning and cooking and sometimes going to the well for water. As they got older, May helped gather vegetables, and James collected shrimp from the pond for Seam to preserve with salt. As for me, it was not long after I started school that I became ill with malarial fever. Flooded rice paddies were frequently a breeding ground for mosquitoes, which at that time were controlled neither by pesticides nor by the raising of rice-paddy fish to feed on mosquito larvae.

Sick with the flu-like symptoms of malaria, I would push myself through each day at school. I then came home exhausted and aching with fever and little appetite and mostly slept until the following day. After my long sleep, I would feel slightly refreshed and push myself through another day at school or at least part of a day. Sometimes I was too weak and couldn't attend, but I tried to make myself go if at all possible.

Sometimes I would think I was getting better. However, after several days or longer, I would relapse, and the fever, suppressed appetite, and weakness would return. All of us siblings took our turn with malaria, but it clung most tenaciously to me and, secondly, to Margaret. As a result, I seldom worked in the fields.

After a time, as Ba continued to send money for our support, Seam allowed Jeannie, then Margaret, to attend school. All of us were eager to learn. Education was a privilege for which our family had to pay. Always there was the specter of funds possibly running out. So if we could go to school, we felt lucky and worked hard to learn as much as we could as fast as possible, and we helped each other with memorization and testing. We so much wanted to learn. We did not want to be ignorant.

If a student was the top scorer in their grade, they won a scholarship to attend school for free in the next term. If a pupil was the second or third highest-scoring student in that grade, they paid only half or two-thirds of the tuition, respectively. Seam paid for the first term for each of us. Then she set an expectation that we should each reach and stay in our grade's honor roll to reduce the family expenses.

Margaret worked hardest to win scholarships of all of us, forcing herself to study even when she was sick with a fever. She wanted so badly to receive an education and didn't want to lose her chance because of Seam's temper or a shortfall in Ba's income. She was the fourth daughter, so her tuition would be the first cut if funds began to run thin. She burned the midnight oil, staying up to study by the light of a wick burning in a dish of oil.

For her efforts, she won scholarships for multiple terms in a row. Once, however, when she came in third, and Seam was late in paying tuition, the schoolmaster would not let her go home to eat as punishment. By the end of the day, she was famished and lightheaded.

Eventually, Margaret received the distinction of leading the school's honor guard, which meant she drilled the guard in their marching and deportment. It was an honor but also a demanding responsibility. When dignitaries visited the school one day, Margaret led the guard in a marching exercise. It was a hot day, and, unfortunately, Margaret had her period. In the village, women had only squares of rough straw paper tied on with string as feminine protection. Margaret was sore and exhausted by the time she was through with marching and standing at attention for hours in the heat.

Though she received all these honors, Seam liked to tease Margaret about how she followed orders. Margaret always tried to accommodate everyone in the family. She ran all errands and did whatever chores were asked of her conscientiously and without complaint, taking requests for help from almost any of us who made demands upon her. Because of this, Seam dubbed her Ngow Ngall, meaning Crazy Margaret. Seam said, "You don't know when to say no," but Margaret's heart was in the right place as she sought to attend to each of our cares and concerns.

Katie and Jeannie also won scholarships. Jeannie was good at test-taking and could memorize a great deal of information shortly before a test and do well. Katie, by contrast, won awards through a long and detailed review of her texts and many times finished first in her class. In the long run, it was Katie who retained knowledge of Chinese better than Jeannie. Only I did not win scholarships due to unrelenting illness. Seam, however, continued to pay my tuition for two full years.

Among us, Jeannie was most social. She did not have the feminine demureness of Katie but outgoing friendliness instead, which attracted friends she went to visit and who came to call upon her. They played mahjong for small stakes. When Jeannie lost more than she won, she set Margaret to keep a lookout for Seam while she snuck away a cup or two of rice to pay off her debts. At first, she had set Katie as a watch, but Katie was one who always felt guilty about breaking the rules. As soon as Katie saw Seam coming, she burst into tears and made a full confession. After that, Jeannie only used Margaret as her lookout.

Once Seam did catch Jeannie stealing from the extra rice set aside for our New Year's celebration, but quick as a flash, Jeannie looked up with an innocent face.

"Oh, Seam, I was stealing rice to make a special supper for your birthday in a few days."

Seam softened and said she thought this was very considerate. I do not know whether Seam believed Jeannie. This fib may have so amused her that she decided to let Jeannie go through with the act of making the dinner.

As to village social life for unmarried girls, a building was set aside as a meeting place. Here, girls could relax and chat after their day's work. Usually, they sat together crocheting, knitting, or embroidering linen in preparation for their wedding day. It was also here that older girls explained to younger ones about menstruation. Often the girls stayed in the house overnight to sleep, enjoying the companionship of their friends as a change from staying with their families.

Once a girl left for marriage, she was allowed by her in-laws to return once or twice a year. Recently married girls often spent a portion of their return time visiting their younger friends in the girls' house. Then everyone would gather, eager to hear stories about married life. Marriage, which involved leaving all that was familiar and dear and becoming subject to a new husband and mother-in-law, was something we all feared. We always hoped to hear happy stories about marriage. Or if stories were unhappy, we wanted to know how the young woman managed and coped.

The only rule of the house was that each girl should bring some food to share with the others. However, Seam would not allow my sisters and me to take food for this purpose. Jeannie, however, had a friend who so much wanted her to come that she snuck extra food out of her house and gave enough to Jeannie so she could attend.

As for Katie and me, we went to the unmarried girls' house a few times without food. When it was time for dinner, we would pretend that we weren't hungry and turn into bed early. After a while, however, we felt too embarrassed to go repeatedly without any contribution. It was hard to lie awake in the sleeping area, smelling the scents of dinner and hearing the laughter and conversation without participating. So we stopped attending. I never learned about menstruation from the older girls, and I learned very little from the young women how they managed their married lives.

13

THE GAMBLER

Not long after I came to the village, I learned the cause of Uncle Ho Huang's ill humor. Uncle was a compulsive gambler. Like all gamblers, he lost more than he won. All the affection that Grandmother had kept from Ba came alive on the birth of her second son. She had lavished Uncle with her love and attention. Grandmother provided him with the best food, clothing, and education, neglecting the one thing that would have brought these gifts to fruition. She omitted the gift of discipline.

Uncle learned to be clever but not good or useful, playing petty tricks or cracking jokes at others' expense. He learned to manipulate his mother's affections so that she could deny him nothing. Uncle was bright, handsome, and charismatic. Whenever he had dealings with others, he came away with the better end of the bargain.

As he grew older, he developed a sense of entitlement. Manual labor, he felt, was beneath him. He began to drink, play the part of the playboy by making chauvinist remarks, and gamble. And his gambling became pathological. Like his father, the opium user, before him, he lost self-control, hopelessly following the addict's pursuit of the brief, intense highs of winning.

His game of choice was pai gow, an ancient Chinese betting game, something like poker but played with Chinese dominoes, also called tiles. Whenever he had money or anything of value to gamble, Uncle walked in the morning to the gambling house not far outside our village, and he did not return until it was starting to become dark. When he lost, he was like the most foul-tempered drug addict.

When he came home after losing, he would beat his wife and

throw and smash objects. Once, Auntie had set the table with dishes of food. Immediately, he took a bowl filled with food and smashed it into her face, saying that her complexion was too dark and ugly. Sometimes he threw dishes out of the window. More than once, when I was sitting outside, I had to duck from bowls flying toward our house.

He wanted revenge, and he stopped at nothing to acquire cash to feed his habit again. He took his wife's gold wedding jewelry and sold it to pay his gambling debts. He set his wife to borrowing money from their acquaintances. If no one would lend to her, he beat her again. Once when he was gambling, he literally lost his shirt.

When he won, which was seldom, he rose to an elevated, almost manic mood. But he was restless. He had money, but he didn't pay down his debts. Instead, he would buy himself beautiful clothes and shoes. And he could only think of winning more and of trying to gain back what he had lost, as though it was others who owed him money.

He began to badger Grandmother for money. If she wouldn't give him any, he beat her too. Once, we saw Grandmother with two black eyes. She said that she had walked into a shelf. He got her to sign over the properties that Great-grandfather intended to pass on to him eventually. Even before he owned them, Grandmother would have allowed him to work the land to grow and harvest food, just as Seam worked on Ba's rice paddies. Instead, one by one, Uncle sold each tract until all was gone.

Then Auntie didn't have anything left to feed herself, her husband, or her daughter. Grandmother began to steal grain from our rice urns on their behalf. In this, Jeannie became her accomplice as she felt compassion for our aunt and young cousin and was afraid of their going hungry. When Grandmother came to steal rice, Jeannie saw what she would do.

She asked, "Do you want me to watch out for Seam?"

Grandmother didn't answer. She hesitated with a pained expression suggesting shame and not wishing to corrupt her granddaughter. But Jeannie knew the answer. While Grandmother scooped rice from the ceramic urn, Jeannie watched for Seam. Thanks to Seam's hard work and Ba sending money home regularly, we had plenty of rice.

Because of his gambling habit, Uncle had years before coerced Grandmother into signing over to him both the lands intended for him and my father, without Ba's permission. Uncle then sold these to feed his habit. In all this, my father did not have any redress. He had never actually owned the land, so he could do nothing.

As for Auntie, culturally, a man's wife was his property. One might have complained to the police in a big city but not so in the village. There were cultural pressures that influenced most people to conform to an acceptable code of behavior. Yet people rarely interfered in what they considered another family's business. After each beating, Auntie would cry great sobs. Then she would be quiet for a while, and then she would gather herself to continue the day's business. She conversed with us like a regular neighbor across the way, commenting on the day's weather or other inconsequential matters. She could do little else, and perhaps she feared that any complaint might make her life worse.

Once there was a young woman from our village accused of adultery. As punishment, she had to walk with a sign around her neck and a rope around her waist. A man walking behind her held the cord. Throughout the village, she had to repeat, "I am an adulteress! I am an adulteress!" while villagers pelted her with stones or other objects. I often wondered afterward why the man she had an affair with didn't also have to walk through the village.

Auntie's daughter developed epileptic fits. Possibly this was due to a blow to the head from her father, which is sometimes the cause of epilepsy; however, I never saw this happen. I only know that suddenly, without warning, my cousin's body would go stiff, and she would collapse on the ground, foaming at the mouth with her body twitching. After a time, she would seem to fall asleep. When she awoke, she remembered nothing.

Grandmother believed herself powerless to control what she had wrought. She was always sad and never smiled. She sustained conversation with difficulty as her mind wandered off into worrying thoughts. Her husband had mistreated her, having abandoned her to care for my father alone and without resources. Now the son on whom she had bestowed her great love was worse. She told us two mountain stories.

She said, "Once there was a man who set his goal to move a mountain. Day after day, month after month, and year after year, he worked steadily. And pebble by pebble, rock by rock, gradually, he moved that mountain." This story was to teach us that no goal is too large if we are willing to work for it.

She continued. "Once, there was also a man who had piles of money as big as a mountain, but he spent lavishly. Soon the peak was cut deeply. One day, it was gone down to the last coin." This story was to teach us that if we only spent and didn't save, even a vast amount of money could dissipate. By these stories, Grandmother hoped to prevent our becoming like her husband and son.

On numerous occasions, authorities arrested Uncle for stealing and jailed him. Then Grandmother began to sell my mother's beautiful teakwood dining furniture and send Seam or Auntie to bail him out. However, years later, long after Grandmother died when I was in my early twenties, Uncle was again arrested for stealing and put into jail. Desperate for anything that he could sell to pay his gambling debts, he had taken a sizable coil of wire, which was in the process of being used for a public works project. He was caught and sent to jail in Toy Sheung, some four or five miles away.

Auntie and Seam would not bail him out. The government did not feed convicted criminals. Prisoners had to rely on their families to bring them food. None of our family would bring Uncle food.

Shortly after Uncle went to jail, Auntie gave birth to a second daughter. Now she was alone with an infant, a husband in prison, and almost no resources left to feed herself or her family. Auntie bought a special kind of rice paper from a store in town. This paper came in squares with a golden square printed in the center. Villagers burned this paper to represent sending gold and money to their ancestors in heaven.

Auntie took squares of the golden rice paper and soaked them in rice whiskey. She put these over her infant daughter's face. The vapor from the whiskey made the baby calm and sleepy. Once the baby fell asleep, Auntie wadded up the paper and put it in her baby's mouth, and covered her mouth and nose. The baby couldn't breathe anymore. Auntie sent her baby to heaven with gold in her mouth.

After this, she took her baby to the Pearl River and set her baby into the water, letting the river carry her away. With her elder daughter, Auntie left the village. For a long time, we did not know what had become of her. However, one day, someone told us that they had seen her living many miles away. She explained how she had walked and walked the many miles until she came to this place. There she met a fisherman whom she married. She also sold vegetables in the street to make ends meet.

Uncle died in jail. He was thirty-three years old.

14

BABY GIRL, SERVANT GIRLS

Some eleven months after her wedding day, Seam gave birth to a daughter in February 1937. She named her Fay-Thleem. As we were not living in the United States, Ba did not write to send his sixth daughter an American name. (Many years later, when Fay-Thleem came to the United States, she asked our sister May to suggest a Western name. May had a good friend named Wanda. She suggested this name to Fay-Thleem, but she was unsure of the spelling, so she wrote "Wanna." Ever afterward, Fay-Thleem went by Wanna.)

All of us sisters enjoyed caring for Fay-Thleem. She was a baby doll come to life for us, and she was also much loved by Seam. While Seam worked in the vegetable garden and rice fields, each of us took our turn playing with her, feeding her, holding her, and bathing her until Seam came home to care for her herself.

When she began to eat solid food, we started by feeding her rice, which is easy for babies to digest. To keep the rice from falling off the spoon before it all got into her mouth, we first took the rice into our mouths. We shaped it into a solid mound with our tongues before feeding it on a spoon to Fay-Thleem. We tried hard not to waste a single grain.

As for baby waste, it was the custom among villagers to feed the stools of their infants to village dogs. Dogs are well known for sometimes eating the excrement of their puppies or other animals, and they are not naturally averse to feces as humans are. Noting this behavior, villagers dressed their babies in crotchless pants. Then when a villager saw her baby about to defecate, she simply held the baby away from herself with the legs up and let the stools fall to the ground. Next, she would call upon the family dog to take them away. The dog performed the additional service of wiping the baby's bottom clean by lapping it with his tongue.

"Doo-doo ga-gai! Doo-doo ga-gai!" Seam would call. As soon as she shouted, our dog, Dewey, would merrily come trotting from wherever he had been with his tail wagging. Of course, infant stools were not the only food that Seam fed to Dewey. He also ate our table scraps but always came trotting most quickly when Seam called "doo-doo ga-gai," as though he looked forward to a special treat.

Now Seam had seven children to care for besides doing housework and fieldwork. Though my mother came with two dowry servants upon her marriage, each, in her turn, had received offers of marriage. As was customary when servants became of age, Grandma had let them go to be free and married, paying for a small wedding for each in thanks for faithful service.

Grandma purchased a new servant before our arrival out of the money that Ba sent her. I call her a servant, although she was something between an enslaved person and an indentured servant in that Grandma bought her, probably from her parents. The girl earned no wages but only room and board and was not free to leave us of her own choice. She was not even allowed to retain her given name. When a girl was purchased, her new mistress renamed her. My mother, for instance, had named one of her servants Choon Gill, meaning "delicate spring." A servant's only hope was that when she came of age, her mistress would set her free to marry, as was customary.

Grandma named her new servant Gill Hall, meaning "delicate or sensitive goodness." Gill Hall was round-faced with a pleasant expression, close to me in age though a little older, and well skilled in the domestic chores required of her, such as food preparation and laundry cleaning. After our arrival, her workload significantly increased to encompass caring for Grandma and helping Seam take care of our large family.

Neither Seam nor Grandma sent her to school, and they expected her to help with the heavy work: gather firewood for our stove, fetch water from the well for us, and do other chores. However, Seam otherwise treated her respectfully and did not scold or hit her. Gill Hall ate her meals with us and played among us, and her genial disposition in the face of a significantly increased workload won for her genuine gratitude and special favor from Seam. In this way, I grew jealous of her.

It was the custom among women of the village to crochet pretty fingerless gloves and decorative shawls for themselves and sometimes their daughters for special occasions or walking into town. After making herself a set, Seam began to crochet another from pale green yarn. I watched her crocheting and thought how beautiful the gloves and shawl would be. I so much hoped that Seam was crafting them for me. As it turned out, she gave the set to Gill Hall.

That struck a nerve in me. Any token of Seam's approval and affection would have meant a great deal to me. It was natural for her to feel warmth for an impoverished girl who helped her with the most demanding tasks. However, I still resented what appeared to be favoritism in my eyes. My sisters and I also worked hard at school, even through illness. Why didn't Seam also reward us with gifts?

I picked a fight with Gill Hall. To dry clothes, Seam lashed together two sets of three bamboo poles to form tripod stands. She then used the two tripod stands to support one long bamboo pole for the hanging of clothes. I ran out of the house, grabbed the drying pole, and chased after Gill Hall until she finally turned around and grabbed the pole opposite me, and then we pushed and shoved at each other back and forth. I didn't even know that I had this in me. Still, all my hurt and resentment fueled me, until after much pushing and shoving, and after Seam yelled at us to stop, we both stopped and walked back home in stony silence.

Years later, I learned to crochet the stitches that Seam had used to make the shawls and gloves so I could make such pretty clothes for myself. But I never did. It hadn't been the clothes that were important as much as the meaning behind them.

In retrospect, I do realize that I didn't have it the hardest. Gill Hall lacked connections and education. Burdened by her heavy workload, she eventually appealed to a neighbor whether she knew of any man looking for a wife. Our neighbor had heard of a Mongolian who recently came from the north to seek a wife in our poor southern province. Why a northerner should be seeking a wife in our area was unclear. Perhaps he also had limited means and considered that the bride price in our district was likely to be less than in the north. Or maybe he was seeking an inexpensive second or third wife.

Gill Hall seized this opportunity to escape her servitude and ran away to be married without so much as a wedding gift or celebration provided by our family. Whether happiness resulted from this elopement, I cannot say.

With Gill Hall gone, Seam began to think of obtaining a new servant. It was customary in our village for all families to eat their dinner at about the same time. During that time, begging families or single begging men would walk through the rows of homes singing songs or reciting rhymes then asking for food handouts. Sometimes these people were homeless, but usually, they did have a simple house like ours; however, they didn't have enough to make ends meet. Sometimes they did not even sing or recite but simply came to the door to beg for food scraps or leftovers.

Seam would occasionally pass out a little rice or some vegetables, and sometimes she didn't. But there was one begging family who began to come by and who had three daughters. One of these daughters always had a cheerful disposition and a big, wide smile, and she was endearing in her expressions and bearing. She was also very appreciative whenever we gave her food. She was about our age, and we began to look forward to her coming.

Poor families often sold their daughters when they couldn't

make ends meet. It was a better solution than putting them to death, and when the girl grew to adulthood, she was almost always allowed to marry and be free. Seam made the girl's family an offer for her. At the same time, she spoke gently to the little girl.

"Would you like to come and live with us?"

The parents responded similarly, saying first that the price was acceptable but then gently asking their young daughter if she would like to be part of our family. Slowly, the girl nodded her head. Whenever she came to our house, we gave her food, and she didn't always have food with her parents. Seam and the girl's parents set a date and a time for delivery. The girl spent the interval preparing to part from her parents and sisters.

However, before the appointed day, Seam suddenly grew concerned about spending so much money and declined to buy her. Instead, she recommended the girl to a relation of ours who was also looking for a servant. So, to our disappointment and the little girl's, she went to live with that other family. They named her Sun Yee, which means "flowing beautifully."

I was not as poorly off as our servants, nor was I least favored among my siblings. Among my sisters, May was most questioning and stubborn. Because of this and because she was the youngest of the stepdaughters, Seam favored her least. When May came of age to attend school, Seam skipped over her and sent Fay Thleem instead. May did not go to school until much later and received only two years of formal Chinese education during all her time there. Schooling was a privilege, not a right, after all.

May became sensitive about being left out or slighted. She took to studying herself in the mirror and fastidiously grooming herself, frequently combing her hair and wetting red gift papers to get the dye on her cheeks and lips. Seam scolded her for playing at harlotries, but it pleased May to beautify herself and appear older. As a game, she and her friend from down the lane shouted raucous insults at each other from the doorsteps, imitating the elderly married women who did the same.

As for James, he was nearly littlest among us, yet Seam favored him most for being a boy. However, none of us resented it or even thought twice about it as this was the common custom of our culture. If there was only enough to buy one serving of meat, then this went to James, and the rest of us ate only vegetables and rice.

Margaret was usually the one sent to the market to make the purchase. The seller would wrap the meat in leaves bound with blades of water grass. On the way home, Margaret would hurry along the path, holding the little packet close to her body lest a person or animal should attempt to steal it. When James had finished eating his meat, he would give the remaining bone to one of us sisters, and we took it as a treat, taking turns chewing off the scraps and sucking out the bone marrow.

On another occasion, a duck, which Margaret had raised from chick to adulthood, was ready to be butchered. Ducks didn't always reach maturity. Sometimes they fell prey to disease or predators such as field rats.

Seam announced, "Because Margaret has successfully raised this duck, she will get a select portion."

Margaret eagerly sat up in anticipation of her treat. Seam, however, used chopsticks to pick off a duck claw and gave this to Margaret as her reward. She allowed James to take as much as he wanted from the remainder. Poor Margaret sat with her duck claw, sucking whatever juice and edible food she could glean from the skin and bone.

Seam then took portions for herself, Fay Thleem (whom she favored), and Grandmother. Grandmother gave her entire part to Uncle Ho Huang's family. Seam then cut five small equal portions to be shared among Katie, Jeannie, Margaret, May, and me. From these, I, as the eldest, had first pick, then Katie came next, and on down to May, who always had the last choice. The rest Seam stored away to eat on another day.

James was playful and a real boy. He jumped into the village pond over and over and paddled about until he had taught himself to swim. He especially liked to paddle to a depth where he could do handstands at the bottom of the pond with his feet sticking out above the water and waving in the air. Villagers disposed of dishwater in this pond and washed laundry and babies' bottoms there too. It's a wonder that he didn't acquire any disease worse than the occasional fever and cold.

Being older yet close to James in age, May took it upon herself to look after him. He was someone smaller whom she could care for and protect. Once per year, Seam issued each of us one pair of wooden sandals, and if they wore out before the year's end, we had to go barefoot.

Once when an older boy was picking on James, May grabbed a bamboo rod and tried charging the boy. Not the least intimidated, the boy charged back, scaring her, so she dropped the rod, then took off running, and he gave chase. May lost one of her sandals somewhere in the long pursuit and never found it. For the remainder of the year, May walked with only one sandal.

15

OF SUPERSTITION, MYTH, AND FESTIVAL

We marked the passing of time by the rise and fall of the sun and tracked our days on a lunar calendar. Each season had its festivals and myths. There was the autumn moon festival, a holiday born of ancient legend, which falls on the fifteenth day of the eighth lunar month or about mid-September on the Gregorian calendar. Then, the moon was brightest and roundest, and legend said that one might see the lady of the moon. In the evening, we gathered with other families on the meeting grounds to enjoy the soft lunar glow. For the occasion, Seam, along with other women of the village, prepared homemade moon cakes, traditional pastries filled with sweet black beans.

Throughout China, there are many versions of the moon lady legend. The one that Seam sang to us told of a corrupt and uncaring high official whom no one liked. He thought only of his pleasure. He kept many concubines and coveted immortal life. He paid a mysterious medicine man to make for him the elixir of everlasting life. However, the high official's prettiest concubine learned of his plans. Wishing to escape her degrading servitude, she made love to him when he came home until he tired and fell asleep. She then swallowed the elixir and left.

When the high official awoke to find his elixir gone, he sent an army to chase her. However, as no one liked him, the soldiers didn't search too hard, and the young woman ran fast. Gradually, as the elixir took its effect, her steps grew lighter and lighter until her feet lifted off the ground, and she floated to the moon to live forever. Her figure is most visible during the full moon. The evening when the moon is brightest is the occasion of her festival. Although families celebrated together, it was a festival primarily for women, for the softly glowing moon, waxing and waning, manifests feminine yin energy. By custom on this evening, my sisters and I, along with the other young women and girls of our village, brought out large wooden bowls filled with water and draped with translucent silk. By positioning the dish correctly and peering into it, we could glimpse the veiled figure of the Lady of the Moon. Legend said that upon seeing her, a young woman or girl, like the moon lady before her, could express a secret dream and hope to have it fulfilled.

The moon festival was also for couples, for it was pleasant to sit together gazing at the full moon and eat the delicious moon-cakes, sometimes with rice wine. Even if the couple could not be together, they could still enjoy the night by watching the full moon at the same time and thinking of each other. Women such as Seam, alone in the village while their husbands worked abroad, gazed longingly at the moon as they sang their moon songs and ate their moon-cakes. We children sat with Seam, swaying as we sang:

We praise the moon so bright.
We praise the moon so shining.
Every year we praise the moon,
We grow wiser and wiser.

This text is a rough translation. The song is more beautiful in Chinese, for the words have a singsong, rhyming quality.

My sisters and I remember other festivals including the maiden's festival, which fell on the seventh day of the seventh lunar month. This was a day when unmarried girls, ordinarily kept under discipline, were allowed to run wild. In our village, this generally meant that bands of girls would form raucous night-raiding parties. They would steal vegetables or potatoes from the fields or some of the shrimp cultivated in the pond. Afterward, they would gather at the girls' meeting house to cook all the stolen food into a feast and eat and talk and laugh late into the night. By custom, no one pressed charges about the stolen vegetables, potatoes, and shrimp. Still, the following day, there was usually much complaining about the damage done.

Perhaps the most ancient holiday was the dragon boat festival, celebrated on the fifth day of the fifth lunar month. Dragon boats are narrow racing boats with a prow carved in the shape of a dragon's head and a stern carved in the form of a dragon's tail. According to legend, on the fifth day of the fifth month in 277 BC, the patriotic poet Chu Yuan drowned himself because his king would not take his advice. As a result, enemies conquered the kingdom. Chu Yuan's admirers rowed dragon boats to the place where he drowned. To pay their respects, each threw into the water a dumpling prepared from sweet rice wrapped in bamboo leaves.

Only once, shortly after Seam and Ba's marriage, when we lived in a town near the Pearl River, did we have a chance to see a dragon boat festival. There were many dragon boats on the river, each with a team of rowers. As soon as each race started, musicians along the riverbanks beat on great drums, creating a thunderous pounding that set all our pulses to racing. Everyone along the banks shouted and cheered for their favorite team. The goal was to row to a certain point on the river. Upon reaching that point, each team dropped its dumplings into the water. This tradition honored Chu Yuan and all those consumed by the river in drowning accidents or floods.

However, by far, the most important festival was the spring festival, or Lunar New Year. We celebrated New Year's Eve through the fifteenth day of the first lunar month. Spring festival represented a chance to clear away the old and outworn and make a fresh start both physically and spiritually.

In the weeks leading up to the festival, we cleaned and swept the house, Seam purchased our new clothes for the year, and she paid off her debts if she could. Every home in the village had strips of heavy red wax paper printed with auspicious poetic couplets on either side of the front door. Those among our neighbors who could afford it posted fresh calligraphy at this time of year.

On the day before New Year's Eve, Seam rose early to go to the market and do all her shopping for the New Year's meals. This was the busiest day of the year at the market, for every family had a wife or daughter doing her holiday shopping. Seam would buy fresh fish, dried root vegetables, edible flowers, seaweed, flour for making pastries, spices, brown sugar, salt, oranges and tangerines, lychee nuts, coconuts, and winter melon candies, as well as incense and candles for our altar.

We spent the remainder of the day and a good part of New Year's Eve preparing dishes for the New Year's feasts. In our first year in the village, we shared a pig with one of our neighbors, who slaughtered it on our behalf. When we got our share, Seam cut the bulk of it into pieces, steamed it, and then preserved with salt what she wasn't going to use immediately. She stored the preserved meat in our food basket, which hung from the ceiling so that rats couldn't get to it. Then she set aside the remainder for our holiday feast.

Seam herself slaughtered our chicken. The poor chicken would be innocently pecking around her feet in the kitchen when suddenly she would snatch it up, bend its head back, and slit its throat. I wished she would warn us of when she was going to do this because I hated to watch it, but she never did. She herself was calm.

As soon as the throat was slit, Seam drained the blood into a waiting bowl. When finished, she poured it into a pot of boiling water, at which point the blood congealed into a kind of gelatin cake. We could eat this at any time and not save it for feasting.

In addition to meat dishes, Seam prepared dim sum or tea cake delicacies, such as steamed pork buns and deep-fried sweet flour dumplings, some filled with pork, shrimp, and chestnuts, some with coconut, sesame seeds, and honey, and others with sweet bean paste.

When we finished our chores on New Year's Eve, we bathed and washed our hair, then prepared to eat the New Year's Eve meal to close out the old year. Legend said ghosts rose to earth on this night, so every family member must be present for the meal. Anyone missing might become a ghost himself! After the meal, we all went outside, and James and other boys played drums and performed traditional lion dancing. Also, the boys and men lit firecrackers to drive away evil spirits and greet the new year. Deafening noise engulfed the village.

Before sunrise, we had to make an offering and prayers to the earth god, protector of our village, for peace and prosperity in the new year and protection against evil. Seam rousted Margaret for this purpose. She would give Margaret a tray prepared with food, incense, gold paper, and firecrackers to carry to the village altar in the pitch dark of a new moon night. If she were fortunate, someone would have worshiped before her, and there might be candles still glowing so she could find it more quickly in the darkness.

Margaret would set out the tray of food before the altar in token of offering our food first to the earth god before consuming it ourselves. She then lit incense that her prayers might rise to heaven with sweet scents. Next, she burned the golden paper to represent sending money to our ancestors. She concluded by lighting a few firecrackers to vanquish the last of the old ghosts and evil spirits before the sun shone upon the new year.

Before returning to bed, however, she had to make an offering at one more altar, designed to restore the proper flow of chi (life force energy) to our village. Several Taoist branches of study are concerned with the flow of chi and how it affects our wellbeing. Acupuncture is one example. Feng shui is another. Where acupuncture has to do with the flow of energy in one's body, feng shui relates to the flow of energy within the environment. The belief is that the quality of one's environment has subtle but profound effects upon one's physical and mental states and, consequently, one's health, relationships, and even prosperity.

There is feng shui having to do with the proper arrangement of furnishings in one's home. Then there is geographical feng shui, which involves the appropriate placement of buildings in the environment. Houses in Tai Ting Pong looked out upon an open space. We considered this critical to a good flow of chi and, consequently, essential to the wellbeing of the village.

There were perhaps many logical reasons for this belief. For instance, a village with a hill or mountain at its back and open space in front of it could see enemies approaching at a distance and more easily defend itself. But, also, the ability to view the free, uncluttered, natural environment could restore the spirit. Chi flows through all living things, running water, and fresh outdoor air.

Unfortunately, one villager disregarded these principles and built his house smack in the middle of the open space, disrupting the view and flow of chi for all other villagers. Villagers constructed an altar between their homes and his, making offerings to restore the balance of positive energy. It was to this altar that Margaret went to make her final offering before returning home to bed.

Once New Year's Day broke, and we all had risen, Seam gave each of us children a lucky red envelope containing a coin. This was the only time of year when she gave us money, so we were excited about it, though the amount was small. One year, after the spring festival was over, I went to a seller of crispy cooked lima beans in the market. He had little piles on the table before him, and my coin was enough to buy one, so I paid him, and he scooped the beans into my hands. I ate them on the spot. Another year, I spent my coin on a few pieces of candy, which we children had nicknamed the "cat doo-doo candy." Notwithstanding its unfortunate appearance, it was delicious. Again, the seller scooped the candy into my hands as I brought no bag with me.

New Year's Day was customarily austere after the meat-heavy meal and loud celebration of New Year's Eve. By tradition, we ate only vegetable dishes all day. It was a time for staying at home with family and finishing preparations for the feast that would come the following day. Seam said that whatever we did on New Year's Day was an omen for the rest of the year. We must wear clean clothes without tears or holes, and we must speak only kind and seemly words.

With our limited means, it was sometimes hard to make sure that each of us wore clothes without tears, and Seam had little faith in our ability to get through a whole day without speaking inappropriately or lapsing into sibling bickering. She practically forbade us to talk at all unless it was essential.

In the evening, we dined on a New Year's stew called Jai made from root vegetables, edible wood fungus, dried lily flowers, translucent rice noodles, a kind of soy pasta, and a hair-like dried seaweed, all cooked in a chicken broth thickened with rice flour. The seaweed was called fat choy, which sounds like the words for "good fortune" or "prosperity," so its use in the New Year's stew was symbolic.

On the evening of the second day of the New Year, we again ate a feast, this time to welcome the new year. We spent part of the daytime preparing the last holiday dishes, such as diced sweet potatoes cooked in a broth of brown sugar. Once we finished cooking, Seam placed our food on a platter before our family altar. There was a slab of steamed pork and a whole cooked chicken, with an entire green onion stalk in its beak, including the roots and shoots. There was also a whole fish, including the head, fins, and tail, and a cooked pair of sprouting arrowroot bulbs to represent new life and growth.

She also set out a bowl of oranges and tangerines, including their leaves and stems, the platter of dim sum, three bowls of rice, three sets of chopsticks, and three cups of rice wine, along with narrow candles and sticks of incense set into a bowl filled with sand. Everything placed on the altar had to be whole, for, with all good things, there is a beginning and an end, and we must be complete as we enter the new year. It wasn't proper to offer a fish or chicken without a head or a plant without roots. Although we couldn't afford a whole pig, we presented our slab of pork with the skin and fat still attached to keep it as whole as possible.

After lighting incense and candles, she called upon James to honor our ancestors on behalf of the family. For good or ill, we are a product of our ancestors. Their eyes are upon us even after death, and their spirits have the power to harm or help us according to how we honor their memory. James held his hands in prayer and bowed three times. He then poured each cup of wine from left to right before the altar. Now the meal could begin.

I thought it strange to eat food that had first been sampled by ancestral spirits. Even so, the pork was the best I have tasted in my life since the meat was so fresh, and the pig had fed on a diet of rice bran and other nutritious foods. For dessert, we ate lucky oranges and tangerines. Seam placed the lychee nuts, coconuts, and winter melon candies in the center of the table. However, we reserved these for guests visiting later in the week. We children could eat whatever of the candy and lychee nuts remained after the festival was over. In sum, this was one of the few times of the year when we had many good things to eat.

During the first five days of the spring festival, we were not to bathe, sweep, or clean. If crumbs fell to the floor, we picked them up by hand. Using a broom at this time would sweep away all the fresh good luck. Bathing would similarly wash away good luck. Instead, this was a time to eat well, reflect on the past and future, and remember friends and family. On the seventh day of the festival, we visited and received friends and family. Seam packaged oranges and candies for James to deliver to the homes of our relations. The eldest sons of these families brought similar gifts to our family. The celebration officially ended on the fifteenth of the month with the waning of the moon.

Aside from festival customs, we had everyday customs as well. To the extent possible, given the smallness of our home and our limited means, Seam attempted to order our home environment according to feng shui principles. For instance, we never pointed either the head or the foot of our bed toward the door. In this position, one was carried from the house upon death. All brooms and cleaning equipment must be kept from sight, for though we used such tools to clean away staleness, they might also sweep away good fortune if left out. The front door, made from two panels, was broad and tall, and we left it open during the day to welcome prosperity. We kept this area clean out of respect to the door gods, represented by calligraphy on red paper attached to each door. We did not place knives upon the stove as this would offend the stove or kitchen god, the deity installed in each home by the great emperor of the universe. He watches over the comings and goings of the inhabitants.

As a child of America, I dismissed most of these sayings as so much nonsense. However, I had to admit that whatever the reasons, when all the principles were applied, the result was an orderly home, comfortably and aesthetically arranged. Though each superstition and tale was expressed differently across China and even within the same village, everyone knew about the stove god and the moon lady, and everyone celebrated the spring festival.

Just as there were many dialects but only one written language, our festivals, legends, and even superstitions gave us common ground with Chinese across the nation.

16

WAR

A little over a year after our arrival, the Second Sino-Japanese War began in July 1937. This war was primarily between the Republic of China and the Empire of Japan. It resulted from a decades-long Japanese imperialist policy to expand its influence to secure access to raw materials, food, and labor. Some scholars consider the Second Sino-Japanese War to be the beginning of World War II. It was the most significant twentieth-century Asian war. It resulted in between ten and twenty-five million Chinese civilian casualties and over four million Chinese and Japanese military personnel dying from war-related violence, famine, and other causes.

Initially, the Japanese scored major victories, capturing both Shanghai and the Chinese capital of Nanjing in 1937. The assault on Nanjing in December 1937 ended in the so-called "Rape of Nanjing," three months of atrocities that included massacres, arson, rape, looting, and indiscriminate bombing. Some Japanese writers have estimated that the Japanese executed as many as three hundred thousand Chinese soldiers and civilians.

The Chinese, under Japanese rule, suffered greatly, and food shortages were prevalent everywhere. Ultimately, the war sapped the Nationalist government's strength while allowing the Communists to gain control over large areas through the organization of guerrilla units. Thus, the Second Sino-Japanese War was an essential factor in the eventual Communist defeat of the Nationalist forces in 1949. The exact number of dead from this war may never be known, but it was the bloodiest theater of the

Pacific War.

As children in a small village, global power struggles were beyond our knowledge or comprehension. There were no television, radio, or newspapers to inform us. We only knew that we were under attack by the Japanese and that life had become rapidly dangerous and desperate. Every morning, Japanese Zero planes flew so low over our fields that we could see the heads of the pilots, especially as they tilted their planes to observe us. Sometimes we could see them laughing at us. Sometimes a brief spray of gunshot rained down to intimidate us.

In later years, the Japanese ordered their soldiers to live off the land. They would occasionally come out of the mountains demanding food and animals. When this happened, we villagers tried to hide.

My friend Ming, for instance, would hide under her bed, holding onto the rungs underneath so that a rod passed beneath would not detect her. Once, however, her brother didn't hide fast enough and was caught. The Japanese ordered him to hold down a chicken wire fence so that the soldiers could pass through. He was scared witless and afterward ran into the first open house that he saw. A few soldiers followed him to the house and stole the chickens that they found there.

In later years, as the Communists took advantage of the weakening of the Nationalist forces to gain power, mail grew unreliable so that not all of Ba's letters came through. If Seam received them, often the money was stolen. With this loss of income, the Japanese taking our food, and the reduction of our lands due to Uncle's gambling, we didn't have enough money or crops to last through the year. Our family had to devise new means to survive.

My mother, when she married, had come with a great deal of gold and jade jewelry and still received more from my father's family on her wedding day. As she had so much, she gave each of her daughters and son one gold necklace and one gold bracelet as gifts upon our birth. All this time, though Ba was in debt, he respected his wife's jewelry and never asked her to sell it, nor did he take any from his children.

During our return trip to China, Katie, Jeannie, Margaret, and I carried a portion of the jewelry in pouches around our waists. Ba thought that we children would be less likely to be searched or mugged. After Ba's marriage, Seam dug holes in the mud walls and the floor to hide all these treasures. But as the years of war passed, with little food and income and the price of groceries soaring, Seam began to dig them out of the walls and remove them from the hole in the floor. One by one, she sold our mother's jewelry to buy food for the family.

To supplement her income from the gradual sale of our jewelry, Seam bought locally manufactured clothing in the nearby town. She would then walk all day and night to the City of Chung Hing, which was not yet occupied by the Japanese, and trade the clothing for rice at a profit.

During these times, Katie, who had always preferred housework to outdoor work, was left to cook for us and care for James. Seam would entrust a certain amount of rice and tell Katie in how many days she would return. Katie would have to divide the rice into tiny portions to make it last for all the time that she expected Seam to be gone.

However, sometimes there was simply not enough, and we were all hungry. Then Seam took advantage of her position to pinch more than her share for herself and Fay-Thleem. After we had all gone to bed at night, she would creep to the bed where we children slept and feel our eyes. We lay still and pretended that we slept, for we were raised not to question or defy a parent.

But I do not know how or why she could think that we remained asleep when she then lit an oil-wick candle and began cooking rice with slices of sausage. There was no wall between our bed and the cookstove but only a curtain. When she had finished cooking, she woke Fay-Thleem. Together they ate at the table while my siblings and I lay hungry, smelling the sausage and rice.

Once when Seam went to the outhouse before eating, Jeannie snuck from our bed, moved dishes on the table, and twirled the pot on the stove so that the handle faced a different direction. Then she hurried back to bed. She hoped that Seam would think that my mother's spirit had moved these things so that she would feel guilty. Seam took care on the first and fifteenth of the month to honor our mother and ask for her blessing. But when Seam returned from the outhouse, she either did not or chose not to notice. The ritual of late-night eating continued.

If there wasn't money to buy vegetables while Seam was on one of her selling expeditions, Margaret and May searched for edible weeds. As the land became more barren farther afield, they began to pull out the tough weed roots. When these were gone, they sometimes dug again, trying to get any strands that might be left.

Jeannie was most fortunate among us during this time as her godmother, Lay Ling Soon, was the person who served the wedding feasts for the village. Usually, she had money and food and would share some of her food with Jeannie when she came to visit. Jeannie also had a good friend from a wealthier family, and sometimes she also gave Jeannie food to eat out of her family's supply.

Once when Margaret and May were out on one of their foraging expeditions, they passed by someone's house and heard laughter. A family was playing cards and laughing about the outcome. They invited Margaret and May to join them. The girls decided they would join in for just one hand as they knew that their siblings were hungrily expecting them. However, they began to have fun, and the game and the laughter were a welcome respite from their worry and care. One game became two, then three.

"This will be the last game," they kept saying, but then the game would end, and they were enjoying themselves so much they decided to play "just one more." In this way, time flew by. Suddenly, they heard a commotion outside.

Someone was yelling, "The Japanese! The Japanese have shot

someone!"

When they ran outside, they found that it was Katie. They had stayed out so long that Katie had ventured out with a neighbor named Gee Jeong Hu, who was knowledgeable in herb lore and able to recognize edible weeds. Whatever Gee Jeong Hu picked, Katie picked also.

In our area, Nationalist soldiers were fighting against the Japanese. Often when Margaret and May were foraging for edible weeds in the fields, they could hear bullets flying between the Japanese soldiers and the Chinese Nationalists in the nearby hills. But they had grown so accustomed to this that they no longer paid any attention. They made a game of looking for the weeds and walked and skipped in a leisurely, confident manner, and no harm came to them, for they were only children at play.

Katie, however, was afraid at every moment and tried partly to conceal herself by walking in an irrigation ditch. She kept looking about her and over her shoulder to see if the enemy was nearby. She looked for edible weeds and called out for her sisters along the way, but Margaret and May were involved in their game, and they did not hear.

What Katie feared came to pass, for she behaved so sneakily and suspiciously that a Japanese soldier, wondering what she was up to with her head bobbing up and down in the irrigation ditch, shot her. Gee Jeong Hu ran for help. She happened to run into Jeannie's godmother, Ling Soon, who, upon hearing the news, ran stooping onto the field and, putting Katie on her back, crawled out on her hands and knees. Katie held on tight with her arms around the woman's neck and shoulders and her injured leg dangling behind her until Ling Soon had crawled with her to safety.

Katie was lucky. Not only did Ling Soon risk her life to save her, but also the bullet shot clean through the flesh near her knee and did not hit bone. Much of the village then gathered around Katie in a great commotion, but Ling Soon went to pick medicinal herbs. She applied a wet poultice of these herbs tied on with a cloth.

Afterward, she devised a sedan chair by running two bamboo rods through the arms of a chair. Villagers carried Katie to a local camp of the International Red Cross, where there were better medicines to treat the wound.

Margaret felt guilty and cried. "It's all my fault. I shouldn't have kept playing cards."

But Katie had good fortune. The Red Cross knew how to treat her wound, and it healed without infection. Since then, when my family has seen Ling Soon at a celebration, we make a point to speak to her and pay our respects. We will not forget her bravery.

17

THE LONG ILLNESS

To live in the village was to live steeped in superstition. We lived close to the earth and were dependent upon and subject to her fickle nature. Such closeness wove mysticism around our everyday lives. We sensed nature's goodness from the warm rains that fell to nourish our rice crops, in the whispering of the breeze through the stands of bamboo, and the beauty and shade of the tropical trees. But we also suffered greatly from floods, plaguing insects, and disease. Our survival was only partly in our hands, so we could not but feel the influence of fate.

After two years of intermittent struggle with malaria, I became so weak that I lost the power to walk. Seam called in an elder lady to inspect me. This lady said that my illness was spiritual. When she heard that I had a stillborn older brother, she cited this as the cause of my sickness.

"Her older brother," she said, "has reached an age of maturity and desires a companion. He makes King Ying sick so that she will join him in heaven. You must find a suitable bride for this brother so her illness will pass away."

Seam consulted a matchmaker, who found another family with a stillborn daughter about my brother's age. They decided to match my brother with this girl. Seam constructed paper dolls to represent my brother and the bride. She also made paper furniture, paper food, and paper money. She held a formal wedding procession, carrying all these artifacts from the village entrance to our house, with the matchmaker in attendance. At the end of the wedding ceremony, she burned the paper dolls, money, furniture, and food to send them to heaven. I did not heal.

Another elder lady called to inspect me said that I had the monkey disease because of my drawn face and bonelike limbs. She offered to practice so-called ancient medicine upon me. Seam consented.

The elder lady lit an oil candle. She would burn the evil spirits out of me. Seam held me down, screaming, while the lady used the live wick to char circles on my ankles, sides of my knees, upper thighs, above my breasts, and on my forehead between my eyebrows. To this day, I bear the physical scars of this treatment, though, fortunately, they have faded from my face. I did not heal.

I was not the only one to suffer from the elder ladies' strange notions of cures. When James suffered from childhood earaches, Seam poured either rusty water or rice whiskey in his ears. She made him lay his head sideways on the table to hold in the water. After a time, he flipped his head over, and she poured the rusty water or whiskey into the other ear. Perhaps this was the cause of some loss of hearing he came to suffer. I also received this treatment and am hard of hearing too.

On another occasion, Uncle Ho Huang contracted a common skin ailment called the coin rash, so named for causing a rash in the shape of red circles around the neck. The elder ladies said that certain caterpillars caused these hives and advised the application of ox manure. Now fresh ox or cow manure does have medicinal benefits. For instance, while it is still hot, it can be applied as a poultice to a boil to draw out pus. However, Uncle's wife, my aunt, couldn't find fresh manure and applied old ox droppings to Uncle's neck instead. Manure that has been sitting for a time develops worms.

Soon, Uncle felt something crawling around his neck and ears. Glancing into a mirror, he suddenly shouted and began clawing at his throat and yelling at his wife to help him remove the dung.

As for my case, Seam next called upon monks from the temple on the hill for assistance. Two of these monks came to my bed dressed in long-sleeved brown robes with shaved heads. Around my neck, they put a necklace of red paper tags on which were marked characters meant to cast a healing spell. They strode around the house, shaking a bell-shaped object that wobbled, though it made no sound. They tossed rice in the air around my bed and chanted strange words that meant nothing to me.

Still, I did not heal. All I had was plain malaria, but the villagers knew nothing of the cause or the cure. Those who grew up in the village from birth tended either to die young or else grew immune to many such diseases. I also suffered from dehydration and beriberi, a disease caused by a thiamine deficiency in the diet and little heard of in the Western world.

Once I became bedridden, Seam put me on a strict diet of steamed, salt-preserved fish and white rice without water, fruit, vegetables, or other grain or meat. Polished white rice, which has had the bran removed, is without thiamine, one of the B vitamins. I do not know what beneficial response Seam expected. Perhaps she thought this diet would purify me. She put my siblings under strict orders not to give me water or other food as these would be "bad" for me. If I didn't eat my salt fish and rice one day, she would give me that same food again the next rather than cook fresh fish and rice for me.

Freshly steamed salt-preserved fish has a sharp, fishy odor and taste that only custom and hunger render palatable. However, this was nothing compared with salt-preserved fish cooked several days before and left out to sit. My whole body ached for water and the bread I remembered eating in Detroit. Sometimes I refused to eat, but then Seam gave me nothing else, so with revulsion, I would eventually swallow a little of this same food week after week.

Occasionally, she provided a strange supplement to this diet. She would search for the fattest, healthiest chickens and cats she could find and follow them until they defecated. She would then take their stools to deep-fry them and feed them to me. She believed that the essence of their health and vitality might be in their excretions, and she sought to pass these qualities on to me in this way. Fortunately, I did not know what I had eaten until after she had fed me.

I should soon have died altogether from dehydration if it had not been for my sister Margaret. I begged for water from all my sisters, and none would give me any because they were obedient to our stepmother, who told them that water was bad for me. Margaret alone snuck me a cup.

She held up my head while I drank. How good that water tasted! It was pouring life into my body. As soon as I had finished, Margaret hurriedly wiped out the cup and put it back in its place lest Seam should catch her. By sneaking water to me, she kept me alive.

Beriberi has a crippling effect on its victims, affecting many systems of the body, including the muscles, nerves, digestive system, and heart. To this day, I suffer from heart palpitations, which my physician believes may be related to my childhood malnutrition.

My limbs grew limp and lifeless, my stomach bloated, and I could no longer turn myself or sit up. Sometimes Seam would change my position. Margaret said that I looked like a snake because I was so painfully thin, and my only way of moving was to slither from side to side. During this time, while Seam and my siblings spent their days at work and school, I stayed home alone.

One day, a snake did come into the house and coiled under my bed, and I didn't even know it until Seam came home. She grabbed the snake by its tail and swung it above her until she reached the pond. There, she hurled the snake into the middle. On another day, a dog crept under my bed to have her pups. The stench of blood and placenta was horrible while I lay there, but there was nothing I could do until Seam came home to clear them away.

Sometimes we all suffered from bed bugs, which fed on our blood at night. In the morning, we awoke to feel the hard, swollen welts left on our skin, which itched. Usually, however, as soon as these appeared, Seam would take our bed apart to clean it and let the straw mats stand outside in the sun and fresh air. This process usually cleared the bed bugs for a time.

Sometimes we would get worms. We could see them moving under the surface of our skin. Then Seam would lance the skin with a needle and pull the worm out with the tip. However, when we got too many, and Seam couldn't get rid of all of them, they would eventually go away on their own. Perhaps these were roundworms, which people catch by drinking water from ponds infested with larvae. The worms mate and grow in the stomach and eventually burst out through a blister on the skin.

The worst was the open sores on my body that wouldn't heal. Some were bedsores, and some, I believe, were the result of biting insects leaving small wounds that festered and didn't improve. The sores would swell with pus, then break, ooze, and develop a hard, glue-like coating. Then pus would build up again, and the process would start over.

At night, winged cockroaches about an inch long crawled over my body to feed on the oozing wounds. If someone lit a candle, they would scatter immediately. But I usually perceived their presence in the morning by how my wounds appeared reduced to a lower level of the skin, which left the lesion more sensitive. The sores on my hipbones where they chafed against the straw mat were most painful.

In recent years, some of my relations have returned to our old home in Tai Ting Pong and have brought their children to see how we lived.

I cannot. This memory is too dark.

All my sisters suffered from these wounds from time to time, though I had them the worst, and Margaret had them the second-worst. We were malnourished and not healthy enough to heal our bodies properly. Once, Margaret got a sore on the back of her knee that was so painful she could not walk for a time until it healed.

In this way, I passed nearly two years from age fourteen to sixteen. Often, I feared that all was lost. Yet a candle inside of me somehow kept burning. I had a will to live. Over and over, I said to myself, "Someday, I will return to America, and I will eat bread and butter." It was as though I knew what I needed to heal myself. Wheat bread, made from whole-wheat grain, contains B vitamins.

Over and over, I promised myself that I would claim my little slice of happiness in this world before I left. My mind and my spirit were still intact, though my body suffered. I refused to let my life end this way. I knew that Seam kept our perishable, leftover food in the screened cabinet, hanging from the ceiling. When she was out one day, I slithered snakelike from my low platform bed down to the floor and across the room. However, once I was under the cabinet, I could not stand up. I tried and tried, but I ended by lying there, exhausted. Hopelessly, I stared at the food basket hanging over my head until Seam came home, picked me up, and put me back in bed.

Sometime later, however, during a holiday, Seam brought home a sugar paddy cake. She hid it on top of our stored rice, then covered the urn with its lid again. Unlike Ba and Ma, Seam regularly observed all holidays by preparing extra food and sometimes purchasing special foods when she could afford them.

As for me, it had been a long time since I was allowed to eat any special foods or even any foods that were different from my salt-preserved fish and rice.

"Please," I said when I saw Seam storing the paddy cake away. "I would give anything to have just one bite of cake." I had gotten it into my head that if I could eat just a small piece of that sweet cake, it would help me get well.

But Seam repeated that it was not allowed and would be unhealthy for me. Soon, she and all my siblings left for the day. I lay there dreaming about the paddy cake, feeling almost that I could taste it. After a time, I gathered all the strength that I didn't know I had. I slithered slowly and painfully off my bed and over to the urn nearby. I pushed and pushed at the lid until it had just opened enough for my bony hand to go in and pick up the cake. I took one bite, and I put it back.

This day was the happiest of my life during those long months and years when I was bedridden. Part of me didn't expect that I could make it to the urn, but I did. Part of me didn't realize I had this much will, but I did. Part of me didn't expect that eating cake would make any difference. But I felt suddenly light and happy. Because I could do this, I believed I would get well.

Unfortunately, Seam did not see things this way. When she came home to find her dessert spoiled with a bite taken out of it, she grilled me about it. I wouldn't admit I had done it, but she didn't believe me and told my siblings that I had spoiled the cake.

Moreover, after two years of my being bedridden, Seam had at last given up on me. There is a board that every family kept in their homes for carrying out relatives who died. Our family's death board had last been used to carry out my grandfather when he died years ago before our arrival. But the week before I ate the cake, Seam had laid me out on the unpadded death board with the thought that I would soon be gone.

Yet a few days later, a miracle happened. I could hear Seam talking outside with some ladies.

One said, "Why don't you mix some *hom pei* (rice bran) with water and see if she'll eat that?" *Hom pei* was a rough food, usually thrown out to the pigs, but nutritious and filled with B vitamins. This remedy was the simplest yet recommended, but where the other treatments spoke only to the spirit, which was already strong, this spoke to my body, which was weak. I never learned the identity of this woman. I only heard her voice, yet she saved my life.

The boiled *hom pei* smelled so good that I ate the whole bowl that Seam gave to me. Seeing that I ate it, she gave me more and then some more.

As the days passed, the more I ate, the stronger I became. I began to move and to turn myself. Seam took me off the death board and put me back in bed. After some weeks, I could sit up, and she began to hold me under my arms to practice standing. And then something amazing happened.

One day, Seam propped me up on a chair at our kitchen table, where I could look out the door at the footpath. Suddenly, a neighbor came running up.

"Somebody's at the gate! At the gate," she said. "They've got a letter for King Ying!" A letter always caused excitement, and since the war had begun, they came less frequently. My whole family ran down to the gate. After a time, through the door, I could see Seam and my siblings hurrying up the path with my letter. Suddenly, my whole body felt light. I stood up.

But I had forgotten that I was not able to stand up. I was more spirit than substance then. I fell forward on my face and my knees. My family rushed in to pick me up and set me back in my chair. I was flushed and teary with excitement. My sisters opened the letter and began to read. It was from Uncle Phillip, our mother's brother, who lived in California.

"Dear Helen," it read, "We heard you have been sick, and we are worried about you. We hope you are getting better." The letter went on with many kind thoughts and wishes for me, and inside was some money! This was the best, luckiest day of my life. I had never received a whole letter and some money just for me.

Seam soon took care of the money. Every cent was needed to buy food for the family. Still, I knew it had been there. And I knew that someone halfway around the world had thought that I was important enough to send me their kind wishes and thoughts and that money. How fortunate that this, of all letters, should make it through the sometimes unreliable wartime postal system. I took this as a great omen of hope. The more I thought about it, the better I felt until I sat there glowing with happiness. From that day forward, I continued to grow stronger.

18

FOUR DUCKS AND A SUITOR

Whenever Seam had time, she helped me practice walking by holding me under my arms. I practiced on my own in-between times by holding on to tables and furniture like a baby just learning to walk for the first time. The irony was that the stronger I became, the more Seam allowed my diet to be varied, further improving my health. I was still painfully thin and had a bloated stomach, but I was no longer at the brink of death.

For two years, I had not left our house. Now, at last, Seam helped me walk from our house to the pond and back. At first, I kept feeling my knees buckle underneath me. However, I gradually developed some muscle in my legs again and could walk on my own. The sun shining on my face, the people at work in homes and fields, the animals snuffling and pecking the paths, and the children at play were all things I had not seen for so long except as they passed by the door of our home. It was a frightening world with war raging, uncertain prospects, and the threat of new diseases, yet somehow, it was a precious world, and I still wanted to be a part of it.

Seam brought home four duck chicks from the market at about that time. As soon as I saw them all in their baby black down with bright yellow spots quacking up at me, I asked if I could care for them, and Seam consented. Daily at dusk, I searched for frogs by the pond and by any water in our rice and vegetable fields. I took our net and a sack with a round frame opening and lid. As soon as I saw something move or leap by the water, I would pounce with my net, open the cover, toss the frog in the sack, and snap the lid shut. I used the lidded bag instead of a rigid container as it was harder for the frogs to jump out again from the soft sack material.

When I had caught several, I brought them home and had them sliced into small pieces to feed to my ducks. A field rat swallowed one of the chicks, but the other three grew strong and healthy on their diet of frog meat. Like our chickens and pig, the ducks were allowed to forage on their own during the day. Then, Seam called to them at dusk, and cheerfully they came waddling and quacking back to the house, where she shooed them into their cage. We stored this cage in the living room near the hole leading to the trench.

Seeing me about the village, a matchmaker came to our house and approached Seam regarding my prospects. An older gentleman she knew of, aged forty-two was looking to procure a young girl as his wife. Sixteen was the customary age for marriage. No doubt, I should be financially well settled compared to our present situation, and it would relieve Seam of a mouth to feed. Wouldn't this interest Seam and be to her advantage and mine?

But when Seam presented this case to me, I burst into tears. The thought of being paired with an "old man" to live out my days in a Chinese village terrified me. I cried and pleaded, "Please, please, don't let this happen. I would be so unhappy. I want to return to America. I'm not ready to marry, and I don't want to marry an old man. Please, please, I don't want to! Please don't make me!"

I had no clear concept of sexual relations between men and women. From being severely underweight, I had not even begun to menstruate, nor did I have an idea of what it was or why it happened. Though some of my sisters had begun, they never spoke of it and were so discreet that I never had cause to inquire. Nonetheless, the idea of having any sort of physical relationship with such a man was horrifying. I had not fought with my entire soul to live through starvation and malaria to come to this end.

Seam listened and was sympathetic. She was not inclined to make me do what I was dead set against, though it was in her power, and the thought of one less mouth to feed was appealing in a time of desperation and war. However, it had not been so long ago that she had been an anxious bride. She put off the matchmaker by saying that she would consult with my father. She would write a letter and wait for a reply, which would take time.

To my immense relief, some weeks later, Ba agreed by letter that I should not be married in China. He wished for all his children to settle in the United States. Moreover, now that I was sufficiently recovered from my illness to walk, he decided I should be the first to return to the United States. He rightly believed that the improved climate, food, water, and sanitation would further improve my health.

Four years had passed, and Ba had nearly paid off his debt to Uncle Gee Taw for the hospital and physician's bills that my mother had racked up from much illness and childbirth. Now he sent $250 for my return passage along with a coat in the American style for me to wear on the long ocean trip home. It was 1939, and the coat had a substantial longhaired fur collar, which, small as I was, made me feel as though my head was half-swallowed.

Seam wished for me to be as strong and healthy as possible for the trip home. While I was out one day, she killed one of my ducks, stewed it with herbs, and served it for supper, intending it as a strengthening treat.

However, I was so dismayed and surprised at the loss of one of my ducks. I had tended them so carefully and come to see them as pets, or more than pets. After my long illness, they were an affirmation of life. I had fed them, watched them shed their down for feathers, and laughed at their waddling antics. I was sad when one fell prey to a rat. At first, I refused to eat.

"That was my friend," I said.

Seam, however, insisted. She had prepared a special treat for me. Was I going to be ungrateful and picky? Moreover, I was far too thin and needed more health and weight for the journey. She would not brook further complaints or objections. At last, with a heavy heart, I swallowed a few bites.

Out of the money Ba sent, Seam purchased a new set of clothing and underwear, along with rectangles of the rough compressed straw paper that we used as toilet paper for solid waste. She packed these into a knapsack for my trip.

"Soon, you will need these," Seam said, referring to the rough straw paper.

"What do you mean? What for?" I asked, gathering that she alluded to some purpose other than their customary use as toilet paper.

"You will know when you need it," she said without looking at me directly.

I was confused, and Seam would not say more. Of course, she intended the thick rectangles for use as sanitary pads. To use them for such a purpose, women usually folded the corners at either end and attached strings to secure them about the waist. But I knew nothing of this. Mystified as to the meaning of Seam's hinting, I assumed that she meant them only as toilet paper. As toilet paper was now scarce and expensive, I thought she was generous to include such an ample supply in my knapsack.

With my clothes purchased and packed, I was ready to leave. Seam hired a guide to take me down the Pearl River to Hong Kong, where an uncle would meet me. I now felt a mix of emotions. I was sad to leave my siblings, excited to be going to America, scared of what the future might hold, and hopeful that my guide was a good and trustworthy man. However, with final goodbyes to my sisters, brother, and Seam, I set out on my next journey.

19

A SKILLFUL GUIDE AND AN ENGLISH GENTLEMAN

My guide bought tickets for us to travel by the same river junk boat that had first brought me from Hong Kong to the village. There was the same shared sleeping room with hooks dangling from ropes attached to the ceiling.

"Find a spot on the floor and go to sleep," the guide instructed me. Already there were people onboard who had staked out their floor space. They were lying down with their belongings next to them or hanging from the hooks above. So I found a spot and lay down to rest, using my knapsack as a pillow. We had hardly begun our journey when the guide returned from wherever he had gone.

"Get up! Get up!" he yelled. "The Japanese!" Japanese Zero planes were suddenly flying low overhead, apparently observing our boat. Other passengers also jumped up, scrambled to gather their belongings, and began to run onto the deck. My guide also ran out, yanking me behind, and flagged a nearby river man on his punt.

"Boatman, come here," the guide yelled. "Take us to the riverbank. We'll pay you money!"

Other passengers were also seeking means to evacuate the ship. But hearing my guide shouting at him with an offer of money, the man on his little punt drew close, and we quickly descended a ladder on the side of the junk and hopped in. The punt was a small, narrow boat with a few benches and a small shelter against the rain at one end. The riverman navigated by using a pole to push off the riverbed first on one side and then the other.

Once we were on the punt, the riverman, at my guide's instruction, brought us to the banks of the river, where we hid under cover of overhanging tree branches and bushes. Being so young, I was not scared but only excited. I had seen Zero planes so many times before. They were almost a regular part of life now, yet I was still glad that my guide had brought us under cover. The planes roared and swooped overhead but did not shoot. After a time, they departed.

By this time, the junk was some way down the river. My guide instructed the man to follow the boat until we caught up with it. He then paid the man some money, and we hopped onto the ladder on the side of the riverboat and climbed back on. Again, I laid myself down to rest, though I could hardly sleep at first after our adventure. At length, however, I did sleep, and the remainder of the night passed without further incident, or so I thought. By morning, I had contracted a case of head lice, which I suppose resulted from sleeping in close quarters with others who suffered from the condition.

In Hong Kong, my guide searched the crowd at the dock for someone who might also be searching for me. We were looking for Uncle Gee Lum, Seam's brother. We did not know what he looked like, and he did not know what I looked like, but at last, seeing each other looking about, we asked if he was Uncle, and he asked if I was King Ying, and in this way, we found each other. The guide relinquished me, and Uncle brought me to the home he shared with his mother as he was young and not yet married.

My step-grandmother was a schoolteacher, and she had an educated, soft-spoken manner of communicating. Where Seam was tall and big-boned, she was slender and of moderate height for a Chinese woman. She wore her hair in an elegant chignon and dressed in black pants with a black floral top, which was tasteful and suited her. After being there for a day, she observed something jump from my hair.

"Lice," she said and called Uncle. Uncle worked at the bus

station, so he brought home a cup of gasoline from work, applied it to my hair, and instructed me to leave it in overnight. The smell was disgusting, but it did get rid of the lice, and a day or so later, I was able to wash my hair. The shampoo did not come as a liquid but as a solid block infused with tea leaves. I shaved off a chip, boiled it in water, and then used the resulting liquid to clean my hair, which worked well and left my hair clean-smelling and shiny.

At Seam's request, Uncle purchased a blanket for me. He chose one of sturdy, camel-colored wool with brown stripes, and seeing that I still wore wooden sandals, he also bought me a pair of shoes in the Western style.

"When you go to the United States," he said, "it won't be proper to walk around in those sandals." So he bought me a pair of black Mary Jane pumps. They were my first pair of heels. I practiced tottering in them for a while before putting them away in favor of my sandals.

Each morning of my stay, I awoke to the sounds of salespeople walking along the streets and shouting up at the windows. "Porridge for sale! Porridge for sale," they would say, and then they would name the price per bowl. If you got up and waved from the window, they came to your door, and you could buy cups for breakfast. The sound of many wooden sandals clicking along the pavement was also loud.

As I had little to do during the day while Uncle worked, I began to sit on the steps in front of his apartment to watch the world. If I got up quite early, I sometimes observed that people without homes slept in our doorway, which was startling as I had never seen such a thing.

But mostly, throughout the day, I watched the masses of people walking by in their wooden sandals. They usually wore the traditional wide pants and Chinese tops, but a handful sported smart Western-style suits and dresses. Rickshaws carried well-to-do individuals. Occasionally, there was a car.

There was also an Englishman dressed in a suit, tie, and riding boots who performed survey work with a tripod. He was tall with receding brown hair in a widow's peak and, of course, stood out from everyone around him due to his height and appearance. Seeing me observe him for a time, he asked his interpreter to say hello and ask me my name.

Before his interpreter could speak, I replied, "My name is Helen." The man was surprised.

"My name is Mr. Hattan. How is it that you understand and speak English?"

I told him my story of how I was born in the United States but lost my mother four years ago. I explained how my father had returned home to get a new wife and left us in the village to keep us cheaply until he had paid down the debt caused by hospital bills.

"And now," I said with some pride and excitement, "the debt is nearly paid, and my father sent money, so I can be the first to return. Soon, I will sail on a ship to San Francisco."

Mr. Hattan appeared moved by my story and perhaps by my appearance, which was still gaunt for one so young so that he could likely guess at the hardships I had suffered in the past four years. He discovered that I was just sixteen years old and traveling by myself and hadn't a clear idea of what the future held for me. For the remainder of the week, whenever he came out to the street to perform his work, he always greeted me and exchanged kind words.

Uncle soon took me to the ship's company office to purchase my ticket for passage to San Francisco. "Oh, I'm sorry, but we haven't got any tickets left," the clerk replied. "Why don't you try back in a month?"

Uncle was very surprised at this and hesitated but said at last, "Well, King Ying, I guess you'll just have to wait then."

The following week when Mr. Hattan came again to work on our street, he was a little surprised.

"Why haven't you left on your journey yet? By now, your uncle ought to have been able to procure a ticket for one of the ships that have left."

"The man at the ticket office says there aren't any tickets left for a month." At this, Mr. Hattan's face darkened.

"Helen, please bring your uncle to see me when he comes home. I wish to speak to him."

When Uncle came home, I introduced him to Mr. Hattan. "Mr. Gee," he said, "please allow me to go with you to the ship's ticket office. I believe I can be of assistance."

So we returned all together to the office the next day. Mr. Hattan took my money from Uncle and told the clerk that we required a single one-way passage to San Francisco in the steerage class. Immediately, the clerk gave Mr. Hattan a ticket for a ship sailing in the following week. England ruled Hong Kong, which was then her colony. The clerk did not dare to play games with an English representative.

"Thank you! Thank you," my uncle and I exclaimed. "I guess the clerk wanted a bribe," Uncle said, "only I didn't realize it."

Without Mr. Hattan's kindness, I might have left much later or not been able to leave at all. Then who knows how different my life might have worked out? For months after I left Hong Kong, Mr. Hattan and I exchanged letters as he was concerned about my welfare and continually wrote to ask, "How are you?" "What are you doing?" and "How are you keeping yourself?"

When my Great Aunt Mary, wife of my grandfather's youngest brother who lived in San Francisco, bought me a dress in the Western style, I had my photograph taken in it and sent it to Mr. Hattan, and he sent me back some photos of himself. In one, he is dressed in a suit and tie and standing with his interpreter as I remember him. In another, he appears in white Bermuda shorts, a short-sleeved shirt, knee-high socks, and sandals. I put these photos in an album in memory of his kindness.

20

ANGEL ISLAND AND THE KINDNESS OF A STRANGER

In December 1939, Uncle Gee Lum brought me to the dock in Hong Kong to board the ship dressed in my Chinese pants and shirt, fur-collared coat, and Mary Jane pumps. There was no gangway, and passengers had to board by climbing a metal ladder, which was leaned against the top rail of the ship and supported by the deck below. I was still unused to walking in heels, and no sooner had I begun to climb the ladder than my heel caught on a rung and snapped off, falling to the deck below.

"Ai," Uncle exclaimed as he caught it. I descended back down the ladder to the deck, and quickly Uncle looked about for assistance. Flagging down a passing tradesman, he borrowed a tool and used it to hammer my heel back onto my shoe. Putting the pump back on, I then climbed the ladder again as carefully as possible. I successfully boarded the ship this time, where I waved to my uncle below.

I was sailing aboard the *President Cleveland*, a passenger ship that was part of the American President Lines fleet. Five other women and I shared a room with bunkbeds on opposite walls. My roommates were generally queasy most of the two-week trip and spent much of their time in the room. But I am not one to get seasick, so I spent most of my days walking up and down the decks, looking out to sea, and observing the other passengers. I made the acquaintance of the ship's engineer, who invited me to see the engine room. It was a steamship, and in the engine room, giant brass pistons pumped up and down loudly.

When we arrived in San Francisco, immigration officers boarded our ship to cross-examine us. When I said my name and that I had emigrated from Vancouver via Seattle, the officer examining me said, "I see no record of your emigration. Do you have a passport?"

My eyes widened, and my heart raced. "No," I replied.

"Without proof of citizenship, we cannot admit you to the United States," the officer said. "Stand over there until we can take you to the immigrant detention center."

"What happens there?" I asked.

"If you can't establish proof of citizenship, you may be deported."

I felt faint. Had I made this journey across an ocean for nothing? What could I do now? I had the address of one of my mother's relatives in San Francisco, but how could I get a message to him?

I then noticed a crowd of Chinese gathered around the ship's cook. He was Chinese, and many other detained Chinese were begging him to take messages ashore to their relatives for them. The cook was sympathetic. He had endured this process himself once, and he agreed to help all his countrymen as best he could.

"Sir," I pleaded, "I am being detained. Would you kindly take a message to my uncle in Chinatown?"

"I will."

"Thank you," I replied, giving him my uncle's address.

Here was another instance in which my fate depended on the kindness of a stranger. I gave the cook the address of my mother's cousin, Uncle Fong Bing Sheung, who went by "B. S. Fong" on his business correspondence. He had a business in Chinatown and was president of the Chinatown Chamber of Commerce. His vocation was providing legal assistance to the Chinese regarding immigration matters, and his wife was a notary. If anyone could help me, they could.

In the meantime, I was deported to Angel Island on a tiny motorboat with hard wooden benches. The sea was rough and tossed the little boat up and down, so my rump hardly made contact with my seat before I bounced up again. The boat bruised my backside badly by the time I arrived at the island. There, I was to await my records.

Angel Island is in the middle of San Francisco Bay and was the home of the Angel Island Immigration Station. Between 1910 and 1940, the Angel Island Immigration Station was routinely the first stop for many immigrants crossing the Pacific. During the years of its operation, hundreds of thousands of immigrants from around the world came through. However, whereas some immigrants passed through Angel Island in a few days, the average detention time for a Chinese was two to three weeks and often several months. A few had been on the island for nearly two years. This detention was due to the Chinese Exclusion Act of 1882, which continued during all the years of Angel Island's operation.

Chinese, who were not citizens, were required to pass difficult entry hearings, which often lasted two to three days. Inspectors interrogated applicants about the smallest details of their house, village, and family. Then a family member of the applicant was also interviewed to confirm the answers. It was vital to answer questions such as "What are the names and occupations of neighbors in your village lane?" the same way as your relative who had responded to the same query. Failure to do so could result in deportation. The last resort was an appeal to a higher court and an indefinite stay on Angel Island while awaiting a decision. Inspectors presiding over each case had broad discretionary power in determining the fate of each applicant.

Isolated as Angel Island was, immigration officials regarded the location as ideal. They could easily limit communication, enforce quarantine, and prevent escape. The barracks usually housed about 250 to 350 people. Immigration officials separated men and women and Chinese, Japanese, Koreans, and Europeans from each other.

Upon arrival, I was assigned a bed in one of the women's barracks. These barracks had three narrow bunkbeds on each side of the room for a total of six beds in one small space. At the end of the sleeping area was a small bathroom. Strung across the beds were lines for drying and storing laundry, for there were no closets. After an official had escorted me to this room, he locked the door behind me. My new roommates told me that we could not leave until mealtime.

"My name is King Ying," I said, "or Helen."

My roommates introduced themselves.

"I am a citizen. I don't expect to be staying here long," I said.

The women exchanged knowing looks. One said, "There are some women here who have waited two years for their paperwork to clear up. Some have had to go back to China. You'll be lucky to get out in a month."

At this, I was scared and fervently hoped that the cook would keep his promise to deliver my message to Uncle.

At mealtime, our keepers unlocked the door and spoke tersely. "Time to go to the dining room."

We stood and walked out double-file on the narrow sidewalk to the mess hall. I followed the other women.

The place looked like a prison to me. Everywhere there were locked gates. In the mess hall, a stew was served cafeteria-style in bowls on trays. After eating, we were escorted back to our barracks and locked in our room again.

Fortunately, the cook had been true to his word and delivered my message on the same day that he got it. Since my uncle specialized in immigration matters, he knew just what to do. As soon as he heard, he went to Western Union to wire for my papers. The next morning, a worker brought me to a room where officials interviewed me.

"To verify your identity, we are going to ask you some questions. What is the name of your father's brother?"

They were referring to my Uncle Ho Huang. Only I didn't know his name at that time.

"I have never known his name. I simply call him Yea Sook, meaning Second Uncle."

Fortunately, they asked me a few other questions about my family, which I could answer. Also, my papers had arrived and appeared to be in order. Combined with my English-speaking abilities and perhaps the straightforwardness of my answers, the officials were satisfied.

"Everything appears to be in order. You are free to go."

21

TWO AUNTS

A round this time, I began to believe that a guardian angel was looking out for me. As difficult as my life had been, someone had always appeared to prevent my falling into the worst straits at critical moments.

There had been Margaret, who gave me water when no one else would. There had been the village woman who suggested that Seam feed me rice bran when I lay on the death board. My Uncle Phillip's letter and money arrived at a time of war to give me hope. There was Mr. Hattan, who helped me buy a ticket to get out of Hong Kong. And there was the ship's cook, whose willingness to deliver a message allowed me to enter the United States. Each was a freely given act of kindness, which meant all the world to one who had nothing. I began to believe that if I always tried my best and kept up my hope, somehow I would be all right. And so, with much trepidation but a hopeful heart, I looked forward to the next phase of my life.

I contacted Uncle B. S. Fong by phone, and he agreed to pick me up. Immigration officials packed me back onto the little motorboat with several other newly released immigrants, and we boated over to a pier in San Francisco. As we approached, I could see a group of people waiting, looking out expectantly and presumably hoping to catch the first glimpse of their approaching relative or friend.

When I disembarked, a plump man approached me. He looked like a small Chinese version of Alfred Hitchcock, with a round belly and face and a settled, sway-backed posture. In America, he was a typical, overweight, middle-aged businessman. In China, we would have said he looked prosperous. He dressed in a suit with a pocket watch and chain.

"Hi, King Ying?" he asked.

"Uncle?" I replied. We had never met, but Uncle picked me out as the only person my age on the boat.

"How was your trip?" he asked.

"Fine, thank you," I replied. "I didn't get sick. I got to tour the engine room."

"And how is your health? I heard you were ill."

"I'm ... fine. Much better, thank you."

"Good. Well, your father has made arrangements for you to stay with your Great Aunt Mary. She lives not far from here in the city. I'll drive you there."

Ba had written to Great Aunt Mary to ask if I could "stay awhile." He hadn't specified how long "awhile" was to be, but Great Aunt Mary had nonetheless agreed. I was immensely relieved. I had been anxious aboard ship about where I would stay and what I should do upon my arrival. Uncle B. S. Fong presently drove me to Great Aunt Mary's home, dropped me off, and bid me goodbye. It would be some time before I saw him again.

Great Aunt Mary was the wife of my grandfather's youngest brother on my father's side. The first thing I noticed about her was her feet. They were very much arched up and foreshortened relative to her height. Once upon a time, she had been the daughter of well-to-do parents in China who had bound her feet. But on coming to America, the realities of her new life quickly set in. She soon understood that the Golden Mountain offered opportunities to work but not wealth. So she unbound her feet and took work in a sewing factory. She worked long hours and came home in the late evening after her children had eaten supper.

She dressed in a sport-collared button-down shirt with an attached skirt and wore small high heels to fit her still-little feet. Because she wore heels on deformed feet and the hills of San Francisco were steep, she usually walked with her rear end stuck out behind her. She would trot up and down the slopes with rapid, mincing steps.

I simply called my great uncle Cheung Gwong, which means "Great Uncle." Specifically, "Cheung" indicates a great uncle younger than my grandfather. Cheung Gwong was a mysterious figure to me. He left for work early in the morning and came home late at night, often after most of the household was asleep, so I rarely saw him. He was tired and quiet when he returned and mainly kept to himself or with Great Aunt Mary. He didn't even appear in various family photos scattered about the house. All the time I lived there, I never learned what he did for work or even his real name.

They lived in a second-floor flat near Clay and Powell Streets with their son, Henry, and daughters, Lily and Barbara, whom we called Bobbie. Great Uncle and Great Aunt shared one of the bedrooms. A second bedroom was reserved for Henry, though he was away at college and came infrequently. Lily had the third bedroom. However, she was engaged to a dentist and often gone in the evenings. Bobbie, the youngest, slept on a sofa bed in the living room, which she had to open each night. Because there was nowhere else to sleep, I slept with Bobbie on the sofa bed.

Great Aunt Mary was devoutly Catholic. Every morning, she put on her black wool coat with the fur collar and her black felt hat and took me to St. Mary's Catholic Church by 7:00 a.m. Most of the mass was held in Latin, so I understood little, nor did I partake in communion as this was not my faith. However, I examined the church and observed the people. After my absence from the United States, I liked to see how people dressed and behaved then compare them in my mind to the people of our village.

Most of the parishioners were Chinese Americans who lived in Chinatown. Many of these churchgoing Chinese adopted Western clothing and, to some degree, Western habits. They were more likely, for instance, to stand in line, to let a lady go first, and even to open a door for a woman. Much of the Asian style and behavior remained in the rest of Chinatown. Older women from the villages, for instance, often wore baggy pants with flower-print vests over plain quilted jackets with high Chinese collars.

These were the sorts of women who still behaved in the old village way. For instance, at the grocer's, they would not stand in line. They simply crowded around the cashier. As soon as space was available, they would throw their vegetables onto the counter then barge forward with their purses open, ready to pay. They did not hesitate to push their way through the crowded, narrow aisles. If there were spots on the fruit, they asked for a discount. With its bustling, hustling, elbowing, and bargaining, the Chinatown marketplace resembled the New York Stock Exchange more closely than a typical American grocery store.

The older men of this ilk often sat on planter ledges or benches along the sidewalk or in parks. They smoked cigarettes and talked. If an attractive woman walked by, their expressions changed little, but they followed her with their gaze and paused in their smoking. If these men appeared with their wives, they walked in front, and their wives walked behind.

Old world views were evident among workers as well. Once, when I dined in a Chinatown café, I found a small insect in my soup. When I called the waiter's attention to it, he replied scornfully, "You want another bowl of soup? I'll ladle it out of the same pot."

I couldn't tell if he thought that, by village standards, I was wasteful in complaining about so small a matter as an insect in my soup. Or maybe he felt that young women shouldn't be so self-important and demanding. Perhaps he meant both. In any case, genteel civilities were not a part of the village culture. Villagers lived hard and sometimes bitter lives and tended to speak their minds bluntly, which was, at times, refreshing—but usually not.

After mass, Great Aunt Mary and I returned to the flat for a bite to eat. Then Great Aunt Mary went to work, and Bobbie and I went to school. Bobbie was close to me in age, though a little younger. Because her parents lacked time for her management, she played small tricks on me and was never reprimanded. Mostly they were innocent pranks, like misplacing my things and putting them where I would not expect them.

Somehow, I didn't mind. In part, I was so innocent that I didn't always perceive the pranks played on me. In part, I was too grateful for a place to stay to complain about a member of the household. And in part, to have a companion close to me in age was a real pleasure despite the minor pranks. There was no money for entertainment like movies or shows, so we talked a great deal over dinner and in the evenings.

Bobbie explained the meaning of the monthly bleeding, which began after I arrived. I was sixteen years old, and no one had explained menstruation to me. I changed my underwear repeatedly, but soon I asked Bobbie about it.

"Bobbie, I don't know what's the matter with me," I said worriedly. "I keep bleeding into my underwear."

"Oh, don't worry," she explained quietly. "It's your period. We get it every month. I'll show you how to keep it from getting onto your pants." She gave me one of her sanitary belts and a set of napkins and explained their use. My reserve in speaking of such matters prevented me from further inquiry into the cause of this bleeding. However, I was relieved to know that I was not injured or ill.

I enrolled in Francisco Junior High in the North Beach District. The last time I had attended an American school, I was in the sixth grade. Now I entered the ninth grade due to my age. I enrolled in the usual English, math, and science subjects, along with sewing and gym. I had an aptitude for academics and did well in most of my classes, despite the gaps in my education. In gym class, however, I was regularly reprimanded for poor posture. I had a distended stomach from malnutrition, and sit-ups and other exercises did not make this go away.

"Stand up straight. Tuck in your stomach," the gym teacher would bark. But no amount of tucking in my stomach could prevent my belly from bulging. Moreover, I was not skilled in the usual sports, having neither previous experience nor natural ability. We all dressed in the standard women's physical education uniform, which resembled bloomers with a blousy top. I tried to play baseball and basketball with my classmates in these clothes.

I played terrible baseball. I couldn't hit or catch at all. I tried hard to play basketball as I thought this was the more exciting sport, but then I injured my arm and played that poorly too. By the end of the year, I received As and Bs in all subjects, except an F in gym.

I made a friend, Louise, who chummed around with me. We took a sewing class together. She already knew how to sew a little, and I didn't at the time. I remember her saying, "You hold your scissors wrong. That's why your material isn't straight." So it was Louise who showed me how to cut fabric properly. We each sewed the class apron, and I got an A in this subject. The class and working with Louise sparked an interest in fabrics and sewing. However, though Great Aunt Mary worked in a sewing factory, she did not own a sewing machine, so I could not pursue my interest.

Shortly after I arrived, I used my limited Chinese writing skills to compose a sort of kindergarten letter to Seam, telling of my safe arrival and whereabouts. However, I did not receive a reply. Nor did I receive any message from Ba. Despite the kindness of Aunt Mary and the companionship of Bobbie, I felt alone. Often, I would lie in bed at night, thinking of my situation and feeling sad.

A year of my life passed in this way until Great Aunt Mary spoke to my Aunt Emily, the wife of Uncle B. S. Fong, to say that she could no longer afford to keep me. She hadn't heard from Ba about his plans for me or whether he planned to claim me.

This conversation was a revelation. I had not considered what a financial burden I was to my aunt or that Ba was not sending any money to her for my upkeep. With a heavy heart, I began to consider that somehow I must find means to provide for myself— only I hadn't a clue how to do that. Fortunately, Aunt Emily agreed to take me.

Uncle B. S. Fong and Aunt Emily owned a building with three

flats on a side street in Chinatown near Stockton and Clay Streets. They rented the top flat to Aunt Emily's brother. They rented the middle apartment to non-family members, and they lived in the lower flat with their four children: Florinda, Matthew, Albert, and Wilmer.

Albert was away attending Stanford University but came home during breaks and sometimes on weekends. All the children were well educated and well-spoken with a straightforward friendliness, which bespoke self-confidence. Albert eventually became a doctor, Florinda a chemist, and Matthew a minister. Wilmer became director of the Chinatown YMCA and then represented the YMCA in China.

I shared a bedroom with Florinda, but I had my own bed in this home. Furthermore, Aunt Emily couldn't stand the coat Ba had bought me with the massive fur collar that swallowed my head, so she bought me a new one more becoming to a young woman. Finding that I owned only one pair of shoes and two outfits I alternated wearing, Aunt Emily also bought me a new dress, socks, and shoes.

I came to admire Aunt Emily a great deal. Her children's confidence, friendliness, and accomplishments spoke well of her. Besides this, she made the most of her talents. She worked in her husband's legal assistance business at 749 Clay Street, acting as a notary and assisting clients with immigration issues and letter writing. Often, an immigrant wished to compose a letter to his family at home but lacked the education. For a fee, such a person could dictate a letter to my auntie, and she would write and mail the letter for him. She was also an active member and volunteer at the local Methodist church.

She was an excellent housewife, managing to keep Uncle's clothes pressed and fresh-looking so that he always appeared professional and well-kempt. Moreover, she was a skillful cook, preparing meals for her family and the numerous friends and extended family that came to visit.

Whenever someone came to visit, she would say, "Sit down, sit down," gesturing to a seat at the dining table. Then she would prepare a delicious stir-fried meal in her wok in almost no time. She cooked all different styles of chow mein and war mein, a deep-fried noodle with vegetable soup, along with wontons, soups, and Chinese pastries.

She helped raise funds for Chinese charities, including the Ming Quong Home for orphaned, abandoned, and homeless Chinese girls and the Chung Mei House for Chinese boys. The Presbyterian missionary Donaldina Cameron founded both as the only orphanages specifically for Chinese in the United States. Aunt Emily performed volunteer work at both homes from time to time.

Another of Aunt Emily's favorite charities was the Rice Bowl Fund, which supported the Chinese war effort against Japan. She even recruited Florinda and me to participate in the Rice Bowl Parade.

Together with other Chinatown youths, Florinda and I helped hold a massive Chinese flag, which was almost as wide as the street. We kept the flag parallel to the road so that it faced up. As we walked, the people of Chinatown cheered and clapped loudly, many with tears in their eyes, as the flag of their native country came into view. The crowds stood along the street and looked down from their businesses and apartments. Everyone threw money onto the flag in support of the Rice Bowl Fund.

In short, Aunt Emily was an active, cheerful, intelligent woman much beloved by her family and friends. She sewed and owned a sewing machine, which she was kind enough to let me use. I say "kind enough" because not everyone who owns a quality sewing machine will let a novice experiment. However, Aunt Emily encouraged me and even gave me a little money to buy fabric to make a dress.

"Oh, thank you, thank you," I said.

I was so excited at the prospect of crafting a dress for myself. I selected a pattern for a street dress with a knee-length A-line skirt,

Peter Pan collar, and long sleeves. Browsing among the bolts of fabrics at the store, I struggled to decide which of so many pretty materials I should buy to create my first dress. I draped the different fabrics over myself in front of the shop mirror, trying to imagine how each would look as a finished dress. Finally, after much excited indecision, I settled on a purple taffeta, thinking how festive and elegant it looked.

I proceeded with more enthusiasm than skill. I plunged into the cutting of the fabric, pinned the pieces together hurriedly and a little haphazardly, and then sewed almost as quickly as the foot pedal would allow. When I finally snipped the last threads and stepped into the dress to admire myself in the mirror, I was beaming with excitement.

Oh, I wore that dress whenever I had a place to go, even if it was just to the grocery store. Sometimes I wore it when I didn't have a place to go. It made me feel so pretty, and I was so proud that I had crafted it with my own two hands.

Of course, years later, I wondered what possessed me to pick such a bright shade of purple. I also wondered why I chose taffeta, which even then was not a fabric one tended to use for an everyday street dress. Examining the dress more closely, I also found it lacking in craftsmanship. I blush now to think how ridiculous I must have looked, but I chalk it up to youth and inexperience.

In 1939, the World's Fair came to San Francisco and took up residence for the year on Treasure Island in San Francisco Bay. The fair reopened in May 1940, a few months after my arrival, and continued through September. Aunt Emily took the opportunity to rent a stall, and she stocked it with knick-knacks typical in Chinatown: jade trinkets, silk fans, dragon figurines, paper lanterns, and the like. She left the care of the legal assistance business to her husband and their staff while she went to work selling souvenirs at the fair each day. When school let out for the summer, I had nowhere to go. So each morning, Aunt Emily brought me with her to the fair.

I had no money so that I couldn't partake in the attractions or carnival food. However, I walked around the fair area near my auntie's stall every day, looking at the billboards, watching the people, and listening to the carnie barkers.

"Step right up! Step right up," shouted the man in front of the building for Ripley's Believe It or Not! freak show, or Odditorium, as Mr. Ripley called it. "Come see the girl with four legs and three arms! See the only man living who can twist his body completely around while his feet remain in one place! Come see the human water fountain, who can spout a continuous stream of water from his mouth!"

There were a merry-go-round and other rides, and there was a great billboard with a large photograph of Sally Rand, the famous fan dancer. Miss Rand supposedly danced naked behind pink seven-foot, ostrich feather fans. She turned and spun them around her body, briefly exposing tantalizing glimpses of her beautiful flesh.

However, I could only imagine all these entertainments. I walked around the fair, looking at the crowds of families, couples, and groups of friends enjoying themselves, and tried to content myself in the role of observer rather than participant.

After I had lived with Aunt Emily and Uncle B. S. Fong for several months, it so happened that Aunt Emily ran into my father in Chinatown. He had returned to San Francisco some months earlier but had not contacted either Aunt Emily or me. During their conversation, it became clear to Aunt Emily that Ba had no intention of providing further for me or making any other arrangement on my behalf. He had brought me to America and left me in the care of my aunts. That was as much as he would, or perhaps could, do for me.

When Aunt Emily came home, she sat me down and communicated all of this quietly to me. Years later, I would feel sad recollecting this moment. I would have appreciated from Ba any personal greeting or expression of concern for my welfare.

Yet somewhere, somehow, I had come to accept Ba and his shortcomings. My culture encouraged me to respect my father above all others, be loyal to family, and draw strength from the clan to which I belonged. This clan encompassed not only my immediate family but also our extended family. Moreover, it was not in me to try to force change or resent the way things are.

Ba's own life had been painful. He had not been wholly good to me, but he had not been entirely awful either. He might easily have left me in China to be married off to an older man, but he had not. Instead, he had brought me to America and given me a seed of hope for a better life. After my years in China, just the chance to use a flush toilet and drink running tap water was a blessing. So the only thing was to go on living and surviving.

"It's all right," I said. "I'll manage."

I felt the need to relieve Aunt Emily of my care. Clan loyalties are strong, but I did not presume to have the same claims to her affection and material assistance as a son or daughter. I especially did not want to feel that I was a burden to her. She had four children of her own to look after. If Ba wasn't going to help her, then pride, respect, and affection compelled me to find means to support myself.

Aunt Emily also considered how to provide me with some means of independence. Scattered through Chinatown, some businesses tended to act as bulletin boards for the rest of the community. On the windows of these, people posted advertisements, including those for help wanted. Uncle B. S. Fong and Aunt Emily's legal assistance business was one such establishment. Many index cards and small sheets of paper were taped to their windows with postings for jobs.

"King Ying, why don't you apply for a mother's helper job?" Aunt Emily suggested.

One posting caught my eye. In exchange for caring for a two-year-old and helping with household chores, the successful applicant would receive a furnished room, meals, and a salary of twelve dollars per month.

Aunt Emily helped me contact this employer. I understood that I could study at school by day then perform babysitting and chores in the afternoon and evenings. This arrangement appeared ideal for continuing with school yet relieving my auntie of my expense. I applied for the job, and the family offered me the posted terms, which I accepted. A few days later, I packed my few possessions and moved out of Aunt Emily's home. I was seventeen years old and on my own.

22

ON MY OWN

My new employers were a Caucasian couple who lived in a modest home on Ortega Street in the Sunset District with their two-year-old daughter. The wife was brunette, slightly plump, and somewhat Italian-looking. She dressed casually, wearing little makeup and pants, though wearing pants was not the style for women at the time. When she wore a skirt, she paired it with a simple untucked blouse.

Her name was Alice, but her husband, Ralph, a traveling salesman, called her A.D., which stood for Alice Dear. Whenever he came home from one of his business trips, he would squeeze her around the waist, smack her on the lips, and say, "Hello, A.D." In appearance, he reminded me of the actor Fred MacMurray—strong-jawed, brunette, and attractive but with a receding hairline.

The house was a two-story stucco home with three bedrooms. The couple and the baby used the two bedrooms upstairs, and I was assigned the bedroom downstairs. I helped in the household by caring for the baby after school and in the evenings. I also helped cut the vegetables for dinner and cleaned the dishes afterward.

Ralph and Alice frequently had cocktail parties. Then the house filled with friends, mostly couples, dressed in smart cocktail attire, drinking, joking, and eating appetizers. On those evenings, it was my job to care for the little girl in the back of the house.

When Ralph was away on business, Alice invited two other friends, a man and a woman, over for drinks. She did not invite these friends when her husband was at home. Her girlfriend was married, but she never came with her husband. I did not know the marital status of her male friend.

The three would drink highballs in the living room through much of the night. By morning, when I tiptoed past the master bedroom on my way to the bathroom, I could see between the door and the jamb that all three slept in the same bed. I was so innocent that I only imagined that they had grown drunk and fallen asleep together.

Sometimes, the three took the baby and me with them to go barhopping. I was never clear why Alice felt it necessary to bring the baby and me with her to the bars when we could very well have stayed at home more comfortably. My impression was that she did so to assuage her conscience. She had told Ralph that she always oversaw the care of the baby.

So I would sit by myself with the baby in the restaurant while the three sat laughing and talking over drinks and cigarettes at the bar. Neither the baby nor I was happy. A smoky restaurant isn't a comfortable place for a baby to play and be relaxed. Sitting by myself while I watched my employer become increasingly drunk was unpleasant work.

It was not the only instance in which Alice demonstrated her lack of concern for my feelings or sense of dignity. Once, she accidentally walked in on me when I took a bath. Staring at me without the least reserve, she exclaimed, "Gosh, you don't have any hair."

Because of the malnutrition I had suffered, puberty had come to me only recently, and my body was not mature. As if this were not enough cause for embarrassment, Alice then called to her friend, "Hey, Edith, come see this. Helen doesn't have any hair!"

Edith came in to examine me, cringing and blushing crimson in the water. Still, neither felt the slightest need to apologize. I was only the Chinese servant girl, and these were two women who had long ago extinguished their modesty.

In short, it was a cultural shock to be transplanted from my usual home among working-class Chinese to a house of self-indulgent swingers and partiers. I didn't respect Alice, and home life was lonely. Still, I had to look at the fact that she provided me with room and board and twelve dollars per month when I didn't have a lot of other options. Despite my reservations, I stayed on.

Aside from providing me with a room and wages, Alice did me one other valuable favor. She noticed that I had rotting teeth since I had never had any dental care beyond brushing. In China, our whole family had only one toothbrush, which we shared among ourselves. She suggested that I go to the University of California, San Francisco (UCSF) Dental College for treatment because it charged on a sliding scale for work performed by its students.

When I went to inquire, the receptionist asked, "How much do you earn?"

"Twelve dollars per month, plus room and board," I replied.

After some consultation, she said, "All right, then, you can pay ten dollars per month until you've paid your bill."

"Oh," I said and hesitated because that was almost all my salary. But I knew that I needed this work performed for the sake of my health, so I said OK.

A student working with a professor cleaned, then examined my teeth and found several cavities. Carefully, and with the professor checking his every step, he then drilled and filled the holes. As it turned out, this was the best dental work I would ever have. In later years, more than one dentist commented that my UCSF fillings were topnotch. The work was carefully supervised and performed to textbook specifications.

I was fortunate to have dental work performed at this time. The cleaning and fillings preserved my teeth, whereas some of my sisters were not as fortunate. Some, for instance, had teeth that rotted past repair. Once the dentist pulled these teeth, the remaining teeth shifted so that the bite was no longer even.

Now I had only two dollars per month to spend, which wasn't a lot even then. However, my employer provided room, board, and toiletries, including soap and toothpaste, so I managed. I was allowed one Sunday off every two weeks. I usually used my two dollars to take the bus to Chinatown on my days off. I visited Aunt Emily and some of my mother's extended family who also visited, such as Samuel, my cousin through my mother's brother. Sometimes I would simply walk around the marketplaces to be among the familiar sights and sounds of my people.

I made a friend, Patricia, at school. Patricia was Caucasian, but I liked her for her pleasant face and because she cared to talk to me. She didn't mind that I was Chinese and didn't treat me like a second-class citizen. She said that she had heard of a temple in Chinatown with a fortuneteller and asked if I would take her to see him. So on one of my days off, Patricia and I took the bus to Chinatown, and I took her to see the fortuneteller. For a fee, the fortuneteller shook a container of joss sticks until one came out. He then noted the number on the stick, pulled out a corresponding piece of paper from a drawer, and read out our fortunes.

Patricia and I walked all over Chinatown, looking in windows and shops and observing the people. Then we rode home tired but contented on the bus, and Patricia thanked me for a lovely outing.

I stayed with Alice and Ralph in their home for about six months until one day, Alice noticed that some of her jewelry was missing. She immediately came to my room, white-faced with anger, to question me.

"Helen, did you touch my jewelry? I've lost my jewelry."

"I didn't touch nothing," I replied.

"Well, some of my jewelry is gone!"

I was so shocked that she should accuse me. As far as I could tell, I was the most honest and trustworthy person in the household. I wondered why she didn't question her drunken friends.

The more I thought about it, the more worried and angrier I became. It was one thing for Alice to sully her reputation with her indiscreet behavior. However, I didn't want her to cast doubt on me. I had nothing in the world of value except my honor and integrity. If I lost those, who would hire me then, and how would I live with myself?

I fretted for several days until I began to think that maybe my options weren't so limited. Aunt Emily had shown me how to find a job once before. Perhaps I could follow her example and find another.

So I walked once more to Aunt Emily's office window to see what jobs were available. Again, there was a posting for an au pair, this time in Berkeley, in the home of Mr. and Mrs. Frank and Rena Chung. In short order, I applied, was offered the position, and gave notice to Alice.

Alice was a little surprised at first, but she quickly recovered herself and coolly replied, "OK." I'm sure she could not help but notice that I acted differently toward her since she accused me.

Unfortunately, this was a case of moving out of the frying pan and into the fire. Mr. and Mrs. Chung both worked during the day, and they had five children whom I was to care for in the afternoons. I was barely more than a child myself, and two of the children were taller than me. All the children played rough together, running through the house, knocking things over, teasing, and yelling at each other. When they got out of hand, I tried to control them, but I couldn't. I would stamp my foot and yell at them, telling them to stop. The two oldest would stare at me, smirking and defying me.

When Frank and Rena came home, they restored some order. Rena could manage the children, and they behaved well enough upon her arrival that she and Frank were none the wiser about what terrors they were during the day. I never complained about or reported the children because I feared losing my position. But by the end of the day, when I was alone in my bed, I would be in tears, lonelier than ever, my faith in myself shaken. I began to wonder when I would ever find a happy situation for myself.

Still, Frank and Rena were kind and respectful to me, and the house was comfortable. It was a gray shingle home with three bedrooms and one bath. Rena treated me like one of the kids. Every morning, she prepared a bowl of cereal for me with a garnish of fruit, such as grapes or slices of orange.

Also, I earned more salary and paid off my dental bill. I bought myself a new pair of shoes and a few other incidentals with my wages, including a white starched bow from the five-and-dime store to decorate my hair. I took some pride in providing for myself. Across the street lived a doctor with his wife and their baby, and sometimes I earned extra money by babysitting for them as well. I enrolled in the tenth grade at University High School on Grove Street, signing up for English, math, science, and home economics.

Unfortunately, Frank lost his job less than a year later, and only Rena was working at her book-keeping position. She told me she couldn't afford to keep me anymore and could no longer pay my salary but that I could live with them until I had found a new job.

At the end of a week, it was evident that I hadn't yet applied for any jobs. So Rena and her friend, the doctor's wife, took me walking along the commercial district a few blocks from their home. We entered each of the stores and a restaurant along the street. In each, Rena inquired on my behalf whether there was employment suitable for a young woman. However, no one had any work.

Finally, we entered the Chinese Tea Garden restaurant on Shattuck Avenue near my school, where we sat down to eat lunch. At the end of the meal, Rena asked to speak to the owner.

When he came, she said, "This young lady is looking for employment. Would you have any work she could do for you?"

The owner looked me over a bit and replied, "How old are you?"

"Eighteen."

"What work have you done before?"

"I've taken care of children in two homes."

"Have you worked as a waitress before?"

"No, but I'd be willing to learn."

"Are you willing to work long hours?"

"Yes."

He looked at Rena and her friend, appearing to judge their character and mine by their appearance. Then he replied, "All right. When can you start?"

I had no experience waiting tables, and I was young. Yet the owner was willing to train me, so I saw it as an opportunity. I worked twelve hours per day on my feet at this new job with one Sunday off every other weekend. The restaurant was owned and operated by the Tom family, who worked there. They hired some of their cooks from outside the family, but I was the only non-family member working in the front. All of them worked hard to make the restaurant a success. Notwithstanding the long hours, they all treated me with friendliness and respect, as though I were a family member.

On one of my first days at work, one of the owner's sons, Peter, asked, "Have you ever been bowling?"

When I said that I hadn't, he said with a smile, "Well, one of these days, we'll take you bowling."

With great regret, I had to quit school, so tenth grade at University High School was the last of my formal education. On my last day, I went to each of my classrooms to give notice to my teachers.

"Oh," said my English teacher, her voice shaking, "I am so very sorry to see you go. You are the sort of student we don't like to lose."

I appreciated her words, but they made me feel all the sadder. I felt that my lack of education would forever stunt me because the more you know, the more the world unfolds and grows, whereas when you know little, the world remains small and limited.

I took the opportunity to learn what I could through my work. For one thing, I learned to translate Chinese to English and back again more accurately. For instance, one day, a customer ordered *siu mein*, which translates to "water noodles." So I went to the kitchen and asked for an order of water noodles.

The harried cook yelled at me, "What are you talking about? There's no such thing."

So I pointed to the item on the menu. "That's noodle soup," the cook said.

With my wages, I moved out of Rena's house and rented a room in a house with a shared bath a few blocks from the restaurant. I do not have a clear memory of this house as it was just another place where I was lonely. I remember in a vague and dreamlike way a lot of faceless fellow renters, mostly blue-collar men and women whom I did not know. There was a dark hallway with doors on either side, one of which was mine.

The room was furnished solely with a single bed, dresser, nightstand, and lamp, without any decoration. I had nothing to add but my few clothes in the narrow closet. When I came home after long hours, I jerked up the bed skirt to check under the bed, hurriedly brushed my teeth and washed my face, then locked the bedroom door behind me and collapsed into sleep. I took my meals at the restaurant. I lived this way for about six months.

On December 7, 1941, the Japanese attacked Pearl Harbor, and American involvement in World War II began. In Berkeley, the local branch of the federal government rounded up persons of Japanese ancestry for deportation to American concentration camps. Every night, we had to turn out the lights and use heavy drapes or shades to cover our windows. My employer's eldest son, Tommie, and his wife, Ruth, bought a three-bedroom home from an unfortunate Japanese family who had to sell it quickly before they left for a concentration camp. The price was $3,500, which was cheap even by the standards of the day.

The home was on Grant Street, a few blocks off Grove Street near the University High School. The eldest son and his wife didn't have children, so they allowed the two brothers to share the second bedroom and offered to rent the third bedroom to me. Though I had doubts about the origin of this good fortune, the opportunity to live again among a working-class Chinese family was appealing. I accepted the offer and was thankful to leave my lonely room in the house with the dark hallway.

It was a snug, painted clapboard home with small front and back yards and comfortable rooms with hardwood floors throughout.

The hallway was light and bright. As was typical of homes owned by the Japanese, the house was immaculate and in good repair. The eldest son and his wife and the two brothers took the rear and front bedrooms, respectively. I moved into the middle bedroom and shared the living room, kitchen, and bathroom.

They told me that downtown Oakland was not far. It was reputed to be a popular venue with thriving nightclubs and restaurants in beautiful deco-styled buildings. However, I didn't know how to get there, and since I worked so many hours, I never bothered to find it.

Still, the younger brothers, Peter and Eddie, who were close to me in age, made good on Peter's promise to take me bowling at an alley on Shattuck Avenue near Adeline. Their sisters, whom I only saw at the restaurant, were younger, so we didn't hang out together so much, but they chatted and laughed with me at work. I shared meals with all the family members at the restaurant and enjoyed their conversation. On my two days off per month, when I wasn't eating at the restaurant, I heated Campbell's soup for my suppers at the house. In all, it wasn't much, but for the first time in a long time, I felt as though I had a comfortable place to live and a place to eat as well as friendly companions who respected me. And that was enough for the time being.

23

THREE BACHELORS

There were three Chinese bachelors, Oliver, Rex, and Herman, who came to the Chinese Tea Garden every evening for their supper. Oliver also went by his Chinese name, Lai. They worked at a nearby machine shop, where they manufactured spray bottles. A little after five o'clock, they came in from work, sat at my table, ate their supper, and chitchatted. At the end of the meal, they would each leave a dime tip on the table and smile at me as though they thought that was doing me a favor.

This went on for several months until, one day, they decided that they wanted to take me out. They knew when I got off work but wouldn't approach me in the restaurant under the watchful eyes of the Tom family, so they waited outside in Herman's car. However, I usually timed my stepping out of the restaurant to the moment of the bus's arrival. That evening was no exception. As soon as the bus approached, I stepped out of the restaurant and dashed into the bus, so the fellows had no chance of intercepting me.

"Oh, she's getting on the bus," Oliver said. "Let's follow her."

When the bus stopped, Oliver jumped out of the car and hopped on. His friends continued to drive behind. I was so surprised.

"Lai," I said, addressing him by his Chinese name, "what are you doing here?"

"Herman, Rex, and me want you to get off the bus and join us for a bite to eat." The actual term he used for a bite to eat was *siu yea*, which literally translates to "midnight snack" but usually connotes a late-evening snack.

"Now?" I asked. "I just got off work. I ate already."

"Well," he replied, "we'd like you to join us anyway."

"Well," I said slowly, "OK." But I was kind of scared. I got off the bus and said to myself, *I hope I know what I'm doing.*

They took me to a restaurant in Oakland Chinatown, and we ate chow mein. Afterward, they took me home and dropped me off with a wave goodbye. It was the first time I had been to Oakland. Since they brought me back without incident, I figured they must be decent sorts of fellows.

After that, every so often, they would take me out for *siu yea* after work, but it was always a surprise. They never asked me out in advance. Suddenly, they would just show up and say, "We want to take you out." Because they seemed harmless, and because I was pleased to be asked, I usually went.

They were young men in their early twenties, the sorts who mostly talked about themselves in a boastful, self-congratulatory manner. In short, I didn't need to add to the conversation. They simply enjoyed me as feminine company and an appreciative audience for their humor. Often their stories centered around ex-girlfriends, whom they referred to in a boastful yet deprecating manner such as "the old battle-ax" or "the old battleship." For instance, one of them might say, "You remember that time when I took that old battleship, Debbie, out to the Valentine's ball? Geez, what a pain in the neck she was that night."

Finally, one evening, I said, "Gee, if you call all your ex-girlfriends 'old battleships,' what do you call me when I'm not here?"

"Why, Helen," said Oliver, "you're our little rowboat."

"That's right, Helen," said Rex, laughing. "You're our little buddy." They all laughed and grinned at me.

Then one day, when we were all in Herman's car on the way to a restaurant, Oliver said, "Helen, we would like to take you to the beach on your day off."

"Well, OK." I agreed because I had never been to the beach. On the appointed day, all three came to my house to pick me up. For the occasion, I clad myself in a casual dress with my oxford shoes and socks with a white starched bow in my hair.

As usual, Herman was driving because he was the only one of the three who owned a car. Rex and Oliver were sitting in the back, so I figured I should sit in the front. But as soon as I slid into my seat, Rex and Oliver started to jeer. "Hey, how come Herman has all the luck? Come sit back here with us." But I stayed in front, where there was plenty of room.

They took me to Playland in San Francisco, an amusement park by Ocean Beach. It was the middle of summer and a hot day for San Francisco. Playland was the old-fashioned sort of carnival park. There was a wooden rollercoaster called the Big Dipper, a funhouse with mirrors, a merry-go-round with wooden horses, and a giant slide that you rode down on a burlap sack.

Oliver didn't tighten his belt when we rode on the Big Dipper, so he kept sliding forward and back as the rollercoaster dipped and swooped. By the end, his knees were black and blue from slamming into the seat in front of him. We didn't go down the slide, but we rode on the merry-go-round and walked through the funhouse, where we saw our images distorted in the curved mirrors. There was also a large building with rows of mechanical horses. We each sat on a horse, put a coin in the attached box, and held on while the horse bucked jerkily.

We played carnival games such as skeeball and knocking down the milk bottles. Though the milk bottles often stayed standing even when we hit them, we won some prizes, such as animals made from colored chalk. One, for instance, was a silver-gray cat with an elongated neck. The chalk appeared to be ceramic from a distance, but if you knocked the animal against a surface, the chalk chipped. The guys gave their prizes to me.

When we grew tired of rides, games, and carnival food, we walked along the beach, occasionally pulling off our shoes to pour out the sand. At the edge of Playland, near the beach on a pedestal, was a giant red-cheeked mechanical lady called Laughing Sal, so named because she laughed continuously. We looked up, and we laughed with her.

After our day at Playland, the three continued to take me out for *siu yea* now and then, probably when they had some money and could afford it. These outings weren't dates, but they wanted female companionship, and I was agreeable.

When New Year's Eve came, Oliver asked me to go to a ball.

"I don't know how to dance," I said.

"Well," he said, "that's OK. We'll just go dancing."

I hesitated, worried I would have two left feet or not know how to behave. Still, it felt nice to be asked. "Well, OK."

Oliver borrowed a car and some money for the occasion and arrived beautifully dressed in a felt hat and an elegant suit. He brought me a gardenia corsage, as was the custom when a gentleman took a lady to a ball. I had freshly pin-curled and combed out my hair and wore a long light-blue dress with a fitted bodice and a gathered skirt according to the style of the day.

A Chinese social club sponsored the ball at the Scottish Rite Temple, today called the Regency Building, on Van Ness Avenue at Sutter Street in San Francisco. At the door of the hall, I received a dance card on which, I learned, gentlemen could sign their names if they wished to dance with me. However, I felt scared to dance with strangers, so I decided not to let anyone sign my card.

The ballroom had a soaring thirty-five-foot ceiling with an observation balcony, a large stage at one end, and bars along the floor's edge. Oliver ordered a straight shot of whiskey with a Coke chaser. He drank the whiskey and gave me the Coke.

There was a live orchestra that mainly played foxtrots and waltzes. Rex and Herman, who had also come with dates, informed me that Oliver was a good dancer. I had no basis for comparison, but looking back, I suppose that he was. Shortly after we arrived, he pulled me out to the dance floor. Though I had never danced before, I was able to follow somewhat.

At length, a Chinese fellow tapped Oliver on the shoulder and said, "May I have a dance with your lady?"

I vigorously shook my head no. I didn't want to dance with any stranger. The fellow appeared insulted. At the end of the dance, he brought over a friend and wanted to start a fight with Oliver because I wouldn't dance with him. During that era, this sort of behavior was not uncommon.

"Go stand with Henry," Oliver said, directing me to stand with an acquaintance of his. He then called his friend Vincent to accompany him, and together the four went outside to settle the dispute. Soon, Oliver returned. I do not know what transpired. Perhaps he told the fellow that I was new to dancing, that I hadn't meant to be insulting, and that he hadn't told me to respond in that way to other dancers. In any case, he was, fortunately, able to settle the issue without coming to blows.

For the next year, Oliver invited me to join him whenever there was a ball at the Scottish Rite Temple. In addition to the New Year's Eve ball, there was a Valentine's Day ball and a masquerade ball for Halloween.

In between, we went to nightclubs, popular entertainment in an era before television. We went to the Kubla Khan Chinese Theatre Restaurant on Bush and Grant Avenue, Lucca's at Francisco and Powell, or Andy Wong's Chinese Skyroom at Grant Avenue and Pine Street. There was always a central area, a cleared hardwood floor area, or an actual raised stage, surrounded by cocktail tables. If you came early, as we usually did, you could order supper, then stay for the show and cocktails. Dinner might cost one dollar or $1.50 per plate, but rather than pay this, many patrons came late just for drinks and the show.

The most popular club and by far our favorite was Charlie Low's Forbidden City All Chinese Supper Club at 363 Sutter Street. There were a large canopy and red carpet outside the entrance. From there, we walked upstairs to the club, left our coats at the coat check near the stairs, and Charlie Low himself greeted and seated us and all the other patrons. Once the show began, he became master of ceremonies and left the maître d' duties to his staff.

"Hello, boys," he would call out to the servicemen in the

audience. "Welcome to San Francisco!" The servicemen would smile and cheer.

He had the best performers of any of the Chinese club owners. A singer crooned so much like Bing Crosby that everyone called him Bing, and no one knew his real name. A couple performed beautiful ballroom dancing. Noel Toy Young, dubbed the Chinese Sally Rand, did fan dancing. She had beautiful, pale-pink ostrich-feather fans and riveted the audience. She swirled and twirled her fans, but somehow you never saw her body. There were chorus girls who performed the can-can and sang popular American tunes. The club claimed that all performers and waitstaff were Chinese, but some were of other Asian ancestries.

The Forbidden City was famous and a little scandalous in its time. During World War II, people were willing and able to spend money for the first time since the Great Depression. San Francisco became a liberty port for all the armed services. When the sailors, soldiers, marines, and air force men got liberty, they wanted entertainment, so there was good business for nightclubs in general.

But the Forbidden City was unique with its all-Asian entertainment. Military personnel, especially from parts of the Midwest, had often never seen a person of Chinese ancestry, let alone a Chinese singer or dancer. It was considered a bit daring to go there, and the club was an exotic curiosity. On any given night, there was a crowd around the bar at least four people deep all night long.

Charlie Low was gregarious and popular, socializing equally well with Chinese and Caucasians. During the time I went to his club, he had a series of wives. The fourth and youngest, named Ivy Tam, had a beautiful, flawless pearl-white complexion and shining black hair. She had a way of lighting up from within whenever she entered the room, so you couldn't help but smile back and admire her. After she married, she became a dancer in Mr. Low's chorus line. As his wife, she wished to immerse herself in his life and business.

As popular as the Forbidden City was, especially among Caucasians, many of the performers, particularly the women, were shunned by the respectable Chinese community. Performing in public and showing one's legs, as the chorus girls did, was considered burlesque and shameful. As a result, almost without exception, the performers were from out of town. Local Chinese families would not allow their son or daughter on such a stage.

Yet you could tell how much every one of them loved to perform. They had a passion for singing and dancing and put their hearts into each show. It was on this nightclub that Rodgers and Hammerstein loosely based their musical *Flower Drum Song*.

After the show, the chorus dancers came into the audience. As far as I could tell, their unstated purpose was to encourage a more extended stay and, consequently, more business for the bar. However, I honestly think that they enjoyed the post-show chitchat, joking, and visiting. They did not visit our table, for we were a table of men and women on dates. Instead, they usually visited tables occupied by groups of servicemen out for the evening. The fellows would treat the dancers to drinks to engage their conversation and buy more drinks for themselves.

Usually, Oliver and I went with friends, such as Ruth and Tommie Tom, my employer's son and wife, and one or two of Oliver's friends. Rex and Herman, who did not have steady girlfriends, usually did not go as they preferred to attend such events with a date.

Oliver and I were friends like this for two years before he started to take me out more often to movies and dinners or bowling without our friends in tow. He would catch a bus to my house in Berkeley. From there, we walked to the movie theater, restaurants, or bowling alley. At the end of the evening, we walked to the bus stop by my house and waited for the bus to take him home. One evening, while we waited, he kissed me goodnight. This is how I came to have a beau.

24

MOVING UP

After I had worked at the Chinese Tea Garden for about a year, I went to the Shattuck Hotel one day for a cup of coffee and a slice of apple pie. A Chinese waitress, Betty Chan, waited on me, and we struck up a conversation. I told her that I was a waitress too, and she informed me that the Shattuck Hotel had an opening.

"You should apply," she said. "I bet the wages and tips are better than what you get at the Chinese Tea Garden because our restaurant is more expensive. Chinese restaurants are always cheap, so everyone has to work extra hard to make ends meet."

"What about the hours?" I asked. "I work twelve hours per day, and I get every other Sunday off."

"I'm sure you could work just five days a week here, and I bet you would earn the same." She added again, "You should apply."

With Betty's encouragement, I applied for the job, was offered the position, and quit my job at the Chinese Tea Garden. The Tom family was understanding, and I continued to rent a room in Ruth and Tommie Tom's home. However, I found that the opening at the Shattuck Hotel was only a part-time position during the lunch shift. So I also procured a job at the Piedmont Hotel on Piedmont Avenue in Oakland for the dinner shift.

Unfortunately, I misunderstood the terms of my new employment. I quit my old job at the Chinese Tea Garden, believing I could start my new work right away. However, when I reported for duty, I was informed that the job didn't start for another week. Now I was in a quandary because I was living from hand to mouth. I had paid my rent for the month, but I didn't have money to buy food for a week. Usually, I ate meals for free at the restaurant, which was part of my compensation.

Later in the day, while I wandered through San Francisco's Chinatown, I happened to run into Ba. I never did know where in Chinatown he lived at that time. I suspected that he lived poorly in a rented room, but I was never sure. However, as Chinatown's commercial district was small, I commonly ran into relatives whenever I went there.

I had run into Ba once before. He had heard from Aunt Emily that I was a waitress. When he heard, he said that he was ashamed of me. To him, being a waitress was akin to being a chorus girl. It was a low, disreputable profession performed by women of questionable character.

Yet, later, he complained to Aunt Emily that I hadn't paid him one penny ever since I had been working. In China, it was customary for sons to tithe a portion of their income to their parents for their support through old age. Certainly, Ba had sent a part of his income to his mother ever since he began work at fourteen. If daughters also worked for wages, they, too, generally tithed their income for the support of their parents.

However, Aunt Emily knew how little my income was and sought to prevent Ba from considering me indebted indefinitely. "King Ying is earning so little," she said to Ba. "What do you think if she just repaid you her ship fare?"

Ba agreed that he could use this money to help bring the next family member to America. Aunt Emily conveyed this conversation to me and suggested that I repay my ship fare to Ba for the sake of smoothing our relationship. I agreed. So, month by month, I paid ten or twenty dollars or whatever I could afford until I had repaid the cost of my passage. These payments appeared to mollify Ba, for he afterward spoke to me less angrily.

Now I was desperate and in need of help. Pride prevented me from speaking to the Tom family or my other relatives, but I thought I could talk to Ba. When we spoke, I explained my situation. "I'm in between jobs. My new job doesn't start until next week. I don't have any more money." I stopped short of actually asking him for money.

"Heh, heh," Ba replied. He had a short, nervous laugh, often the precursor to anything he said, especially in social situations. However, without further reply, he pulled out two one-dollar bills from his wallet and handed them to me.

"Thank you, Ba," I said, but my heart sank. Two dollars was not enough money to buy food for a week. At best, I could last a few days.

With a young person's poor judgment, I bought a cup of coffee and a slice of apple pie as my first meal, thinking sugar and caffeine would give me energy. I poured as much free cream and sugar as possible into the coffee to fill my stomach. The effect, of course, was I felt jittery and a little nauseous afterward.

However, a few days later, I ran into my cousin Ngeo in Chinatown. He was the adopted son of my mother's brother, a young man in his twenties whom I had met at Fong family gatherings at Aunt Emily's house.

"Hello, King Ying," he said. "How are you doing?"

"All right," I said, and we exchanged pleasantries. But after a while, I added a little sheepishly, "Actually, I'm in between jobs. I found a new, better job. I thought I could start right away, but it turns out they don't want me until next week, and I already quit my old job. I've sort of . . . run out of money."

My cousin quietly looked at me for a moment, then opened his wallet and handed me a twenty-dollar bill.

I almost cried with gratitude. "Thank you! I've been hungry." Here was my guardian angel again.

"Well, get yourself something to eat," my cousin said with a kind smile. "I'm glad to hear you've got a new job. Try to save some money when you can . . . you know, for a rainy day."

"Right," I said. From then on, I learned to budget and to save more carefully.

Mostly working-class businesspeople and the University of California students frequented the Shattuck Hotel. You could distinguish the university students by their refined behavior. They were required to attend classes in etiquette and deportment as part of the university curriculum. They spoke intelligently with an excellent vocabulary. They sat up straight at the table, took small bites, didn't sit with their legs apart, didn't talk with their mouths full, and the fellows opened doors for their ladies. Something in the elegance of their manners reminded me of my mother. I wanted to be like that too.

The Piedmont Hotel had a small dining room. Just one other waitress, Jane, and I waited on tables. We were quite a pair. She was blond and tall at five foot ten, and I was black-haired and petite at five feet. She quickly perceived my innocence and inexperience in worldly matters, along with my limited English skills. She took this to mean that I wasn't too bright. She dubbed me "Beetle Brain."

Every morning, she would say, "Hello, Beetle Brain."

Finally, one day, I asked, "What do you mean by Beetle Brain?"

"It means your brain is small, like a beetle." She held up her thumb and forefinger about an inch apart to emphasize her meaning.

Notwithstanding her use of deprecating nicknames, Jane was a genial sort. We worked well together and were soon good work pals. Also, the clientele was friendly. Many single female teachers who worked at Technical High School in Oakland lived in the Piedmont Hotel and ate in its dining room. I preferred the Piedmont Hotel teachers to the Shattuck Hotel businesspeople. They were friendlier. They looked at me directly and spoke in a warm, respectful tone as a fellow human being, not dismissively like a servant.

I continued to work at the Piedmont and Shattuck Hotels until the war broke out. With so many men gone off to the war, there was soon a shortage of workers. Not long after, Tommy Tom's uncle, who owned the Paradise Café next to the Paramount Theater in Oakland, approached me about working at his restaurant part-time.

"But I'm not twenty-one years old yet," I said because I knew you were supposed to be at least that age to work at a restaurant with a bar.

"That's OK," Mr. Tom said. "If anyone asks, we'll say we didn't know. Come and work for us. We need the help."

I decided to accept. The Paradise Café was a huge restaurant with a bar and a large dance floor. Musicians on a stage played the popular tunes of the era. Music for dancing the jitterbug was especially popular. The business was brisk. Once the war started, jobs were plentiful, and everyone had money to spend.

The restaurant was especially popular with military men on leave. Sailors, soldiers, and military police all came in. Groups of sailors or soldiers would get rowdy—usually speaking loudly, flirting with each other's girlfriends, shoving, then coming to blows. The military police would haul them out to a wagon and take them back to their base or ship. They confined the truants for a few days. Afterward, the fellows came back to the Paradise Café, usually to start the cycle of rowdiness and arrest all over again.

The sailors often came in with their dates. After a few drinks, they would leave for a while, then come back. When they returned, their girlfriends would have grass on the back of their dresses.

"Say, why do you suppose that girl has grass on the back of her dress?" I asked a fellow waitress.

She replied with a knowing smile, "Those two have been over to Lake Merritt."

It was a testimony to my utter naiveté that I didn't understand the significance of this then or for many years afterward. I only thought to myself, *Doesn't that girl care that she has grass on her back?*

My employment was educational in other ways. One day, a lady came in and asked me, "Could you please tell me where the proprietor is?"

I didn't know what "proprietor" meant. I tried to guess at the meaning. It sounded like a fancy word for something private, so I directed her to the door leading to the ladies' room. The woman walked through the door, then immediately turned around with her face flushed and expression mad.

"That's the ladies' bathroom. I want to speak to your boss."

"Oh," I said, red-faced, and pointed her in the direction of the owner. That's how I learned the meaning of the word "proprietor."

I got off work from the Piedmont Hotel at 9:00 p.m. then worked at the Paradise Café from ninety-thirty to 2:00 a.m., plus I worked eight-hour shifts on both weekend days. Soon I was so tired at the end of each day that it was hard to sleep. I was exhausted, but at the same time, the adrenaline from pushing myself hard through long days kept me awake.

Far and away, I made the best money at the Paradise Café, so I approached the owner about working there full-time, and he readily agreed. I quit my jobs at the Shattuck and Piedmont Hotels and began working at the café six days a week, just eight hours a day instead of twelve. Now I was earning enough to save money, and I had a day off every week instead of every other week. Slowly, my lot was improving.

25

FINDING A NEST

On my days off, I sometimes visited Aunt Emily and her family. She always warmly welcomed me with her usual "sit down, sit down" as she set up her wok to cook me something to eat. Over our meals, we would chat about what was happening in our lives. I would tell her about the different people I observed during my restaurant work. She would report what was happening with her children, Uncle, and herself.

One day, she said to me, "King Ying, I think it is time for you to find a nest." It was her way of saying that she thought I ought to get married. As I had come to love Aunt Emily for taking a genuine and loving interest in my affairs, I absorbed this advice in my heart.

Oliver and I had been dating for about two years. All members of his peer group had married except him and Rex, so he also had decided that it was time to think of marriage. One day, seemingly out of the blue while we dined at a restaurant, he asked me quite matter-of-factly, "How would you like to get married?"

"How do you get married?" I asked, just as matter-of-factly, as though we were discussing a business concern. I had never been to an American wedding and had only heard Chinese weddings described.

"Well, first, we'd have to get a blood test." At that time, most states required blood tests for venereal diseases, such as syphilis, and genetic disorders, such as sickle-cell anemia, before marriage. The idea was to inform potential marriage partners of the risk of contracting an infectious disease and reduce the risk of congenital disabilities.

I did not consider whether I was in love. Culturally, I did not view marriage in that light. Marriage was for having companionship, raising children, and sharing the burdens of a household. I considered Oliver a friend. I had never dated anyone else, so I had no one with whom to compare him. I remembered that once when we were at a nightclub, a female acquaintance had said of Oliver, when he stepped away from our table, "Helen, that guy is no good for you." But she did not elaborate, and I did not inquire further. Instead, I shrugged this off as her opinion. Oliver paid attention to me, thought of me, and took me out on dates. He was not a bad-looking fellow. Aunt Emily, the adult whose opinion I most valued, had advised me to find a nest. With that in mind, I agreed.

Oliver took me to Dr. Jacob Yee on Franklin Street in Oakland's Chinatown for our blood test. Once we received the results, we went to the Oakland Hall of Records on 12th and Oak Streets to apply for a marriage license. We went up an elevator, and when we got off, we looked both ways, looking for a sign to direct us. A passing staff member pointed us to the proper window.

We stood in line, completed an application, and answered a few questions. Oliver paid a fee, and we had our license—it was as easy as that. Thoughts of choosing a wedding day next came to mind. Oliver suggested a weekday, and I agreed.

"But where do we get married?" I asked. I hadn't the slightest idea.

"We have to find a minister in a church," he replied.

On March 27, 1944, I met Oliver on the corner of Broadway and 13th Streets in downtown Oakland, wearing a two-piece dress I had bought for the occasion. It consisted of a knee-length skirt made of white rayon crepe, a matching long-sleeved jacket with rounded shoulders, and a Peter Pan collar with pleated trim. A profusion of tiny fuchsia bows covered the dress.

Oliver had not arranged our wedding, so we walked to Harrison from Broadway in search of a church where we could be married. We found one church, but only the church keeper was there, and he could not marry us. We found another, but the minister explained that he was busy and we needed two people to witness. Also, it was customary to make an appointment for marriage.

As though by providence, while we continued our search, we ran into Oliver's mother, Mrs. Chan, two of Oliver's brothers, Dean and Jack, and Jack's wife, Frieda. They were walking down the street.

"Hi," Mrs. Chan called out warmly to Oliver. "What are you doing here?" Mrs. Chan was a pleasant-looking, plumpish woman, less than five feet tall, with crinkles around her eyes from much smiling. She had a kind, jolly appearance. However, she dressed in a plain dark top with dark pants, with her hair pulled into a low bun. Oliver had sometimes spoken to me of his family, quoting his mother on particular subjects or indicating that he had taken her somewhere. However, I had never met her or any of his family.

In fact, I had never seen where Oliver lived. Once, when we were sitting around Lake Merritt in Oakland, and I asked where he lived, he pointed to a tall building in the distance and said that he lived there. But I never knew whether this was true or not. He had always taken the bus to where I lived in Berkeley. From there, we walked or took the bus to our dates. For special occasions, such as going to balls, he borrowed a car, and we drove straight to the event, then back to my house, where he walked me to my door and said goodnight.

"This is Helen," Oliver said. "We're trying to find a minister. We're going to get married."

"Oh!" his family said in unison. Apparently, he had never spoken of me or his engagement. But immediately, they collected themselves, said how pleased they were to meet me, and congratulated Oliver. Together, all of us went in search of a place to be married.

In the next church we entered, the minister happened to be available and said that he could marry us on the spot if we liked. "Who shall serve as witnesses?" he asked.

The family members glanced at each other, and as though by

mutual agreement, Dean and Frieda stepped forward. "We will," they said.

Oliver produced a platinum band with five round-cut, blue-white diamonds in a row. I had not bought him a ring in return as I didn't realize this was the custom. The ceremony was brief: a few statements, some repeated words, the putting on of my ring, a slightly awkward kiss in front of his family at the minister's direction, and some signatures on our license. Suddenly we were bound to each other "for life." It was the first wedding I had ever attended. In retrospect, I was grateful that at least some of Oliver's family members were present.

After the ceremony, we walked to Mrs. Chan's house on the outskirts of Oakland's Chinatown, where we visited and got to know one another. Oliver was the youngest of twelve children. Indeed, his Chinese name, Lai, meant "the last." Mrs. Chan had put her foot down upon Oliver's birth and said, "No more." Shortly after, Mr. Chan died, leaving her a single mother of twelve.

After a period of grief, Mrs. Chan took things in stride. It was not in her nature to fret or to try to manage things heavy-handedly. She was of the Hakka ethnicity. These are the boat people of China, living out their lives primarily as humble fishers. In China, they lived in the ports on their houseboats, wearing straw hats. She was uneducated but the sort of woman who was always happy to see people, hear the news, share good gossip, and laugh readily and heartily.

Her unmarried children, Dean, Emma, and Frances, still lived with her, and mostly she let them come and go as they pleased. Dean had tuberculosis in his youth and so had decided not to marry. Though he later recovered, he remained a bachelor. Emma worked as a grocery clerk in the evenings. Frances, in between jobs, cooked and took care of the household. Jack and his wife, Frieda, worked the early-morning shift at the post office and were off work by the time we met them on the street.

While we talked, Frances came home. To her great surprise, Mrs.

Chan introduced me as Oliver's wife. A little while later, Oliver's older, married sister, Dorothy, who came to visit her mother every day, also came by, and again I was introduced.

With my pin-curled hair, wearing red lipstick, and dressed in a white, knee-length rayon suit with fuchsia bows, I stood in contrast to Oliver's sisters. Both were profoundly modest and soft-spoken, dressed plainly in dark clothes with skirts that fell to the ankle, though knee-length skirts were the style, and they wore no makeup. I realized how Western I had become from working in American restaurants. Notwithstanding their surprise, however, both welcomed and greeted me with shy warmth.

Dorothy had to return to her family, but the rest of us went out for an impromptu wedding supper in Chinatown. In the Asian sense of the term, Frances was old-fashioned, or perhaps just terribly bashful. She insisted upon going to the sort of old-style Chinese restaurant where there were curtained dining booths to protect her modesty. Even at that time, such restaurants were increasingly scarce. But in the manner of an old-fashioned highborn lady, she did not wish to feel publicly displayed like some common woman. After the waiter had served the dishes, he closed the booth's curtain, and we dined in privacy. I later found that Dorothy had a similar character, and her mother had arranged her marriage.

Oliver had not secured living quarters for us. At the end of the evening, we each returned to our separate homes, I to my small rented room in the Tom family's house and he to the place that he rented. It was as though we had gone on a date, gotten married, had dinner, and gone home. I was twenty years old. Oliver was twenty-four.

Within the following month, my in-laws bought me jewelry as wedding presents. Though I was not surprised to receive such traditional gifts, their high quality touched me. There was a heavy twenty-four-karat gold, heart-shaped pendant and chain from Mrs. Chan, a bracelet of linked twenty-four-karat, diamond-shaped gold pieces from Dean, Frances, Emma, and Jack, and a gold ring with a rounded square top inscribed with traditional design from Frieda. I hid these in my bureau between some clothes and looked forward to wearing them on a special occasion.

Oliver and I soon rented a large room in a three-bedroom house on Lakeshore Avenue near McArthur Boulevard in Oakland. The room was furnished only with a dresser, a bed, and a nightstand. On our first day of living there, after setting our things in the house, we walked to the grocery store to pick up some wooden orange crates. I set one out as a nightstand for myself, on which I put my radio. I stuck thumbtacks into the upper corners of two others. On each, I attached a string across the thumbtacks and hung cloth over it to make a little curtain to cover the opening. In this way, we stored our possessions out of sight inside the crates. We set the remaining boxes out as chairs. Other people rented the additional bedrooms in the house, and we shared the bath and kitchen.

I would like to say that our first day of living together ended as pleasantly as it began. However, this was our belated wedding night. That evening, seeing a man's nakedness for the first time, I was so scared I couldn't speak. I had never imagined that a man's private parts were so strange. I did not know that a man penetrated a woman. I had no idea what was happening or why. I was frightened to the point of shrieking and tears, and I felt much pain.

In an era before television and sex education in school, when parents considered it a husband's responsibility to teach his bride about the birds and the bees, and when movie couples only kissed fully dressed, it was possible to be this innocent. In fact, up to that point, the only films I had seen were Shirley Temple movies, one Tarzan movie, and "Gone with the Wind," which Aunt Emily had taken me to see in 1940. At twenty, I had endured more pain, suffering, and hardships than most people experience in a lifetime. Still, I knew almost nothing of life's basic facts.

I ended the evening scared and unsure of myself. I had never learned to think about the long-term consequences of my actions.

My whole life had been about being happy to survive from day to day. I suddenly felt stupid and profoundly sad about not knowing how to get married or about intimacy between husbands and wives, or so many things. With little education and parents too bound up in their survival to guide me, I had learned everything through hard knocks.

But every situation in my life had been temporary, so whatever mistakes I made could be fixed. Now I had something permanent. In a sure sign of maturing into adulthood, I began to realize how much about life I still didn't know. I ended the evening wondering for the first time what life might hold for me in a year, five years, or ten. I saw that life holds many paths. For better or worse, I had chosen the first that opened to me.

26

EMPTY NEST

On our second day of living together, I went to work at the Paradise Café as usual. Sometime before we were married, Oliver had lost his job at the spray bottle factory. He now worked as a butcher at a 9th Street meat market on the outskirts of Oakland's Chinatown. I presumed that he also went to his job as usual.

That evening, however, he did not come home. We did not have a telephone, so I went to a payphone to call the police. I asked if there was a report of his being in an accident. The police said no. Late in the night, I hired a cab and rode to Mrs. Chan's house in my pajamas, loafers, and coat.

Mrs. Chan lived at 624 Jackson Street in a three-bedroom clapboard house all on one level. I arrived at 3:00 a.m. and rang the doorbell repeatedly. Because of the hour, it was Dean who came to the door.

"Oh, Dean, it's Lai," I said, for though Oliver called me Helen and spoke to me only in English, I always referred to him by his Chinese name. "He didn't come home tonight. Did he come here?"

Dean shook his head. "Well, what do you think happened to him? What am I going to do? What . . . what should I do?" I started to spill tears.

"Oh, oh, come in," Dean said. "Come in." He directed me into the house and guided me toward the kitchen. Hearing a familiar voice, the women of the house—Mrs. Chan, Emma, and Frances came in, dressed in their robes and with expressions full of concern.

"Helen, Helen, what's the matter?" they asked.

"Lai didn't come home tonight, and I don't know where he is."

Dean pulled out a chair for me at the kitchen table. He and Mrs. Chan, Frances, and Emma also pulled out chairs and joined me. I looked at them expectantly.

"Helen," Dean began and sighed. "When Lai has had money, he usually rents a furnished room. When in between jobs, he's come back here to live. And then sometimes he disappears for a week or a month. He's like that."

"But," Mrs. Chan added quietly, "he comes back. He comes back."

She spoke almost as though this were normal. I could see that Mrs. Chan cherished all her children in a grandmotherly sort of way. That was her gift to them. But as with so many matters, she let things flow as they would and did not try to manage or set boundaries. As a single mother of twelve, she had probably had to adopt this attitude as a survival mechanism. Indeed, she would later live to be a hundred years old, and I think her relaxed approach contributed much to her longevity.

"Where does he go?" I asked.

Dean exchanged a glance with his mother and sisters, who said nothing. He replied, "Well, we don't control his comings and goings. He is a grown man."

Before I could say more, he added, "Listen, why don't you stay here tonight? We'll set you up comfortably on the couch and drive you home in the morning." Mrs. Chan, Frances, and Emma nodded and murmured words in agreement.

I was profoundly tired. Despite my sense of something being terribly wrong, it was after 3:00 a.m., and my worry had exhausted me. I couldn't make any more effort. Dean and his family looked at me with expressions full of concern, so I nodded my head. Emma and Frances got sheets and blankets from a closet and put them on a couch. I lay down, numbly stared into the darkness for a few minutes, then fell asleep.

In the morning, we didn't speak anymore of Oliver. If his family did not wish to discuss the matter, I would not press them to talk of what pained them. Dean drove me home, where I went through the motions of getting ready for the day. I thought about how Oliver and I had gone out for two years, yet I didn't know him. There had been movies and dinners and carnivals and dances—all things I enjoyed after a childhood of deprivation. Still, I had learned little of his heart. I had only thought that if he cared to take me out and marry me, he must also care for me.

At last, Oliver came home.

"I didn't know where you were last night," I said. "I called the police and went to your mother's house to look for you."

"You didn't have to worry," he said as he removed his keys from his pocket and set them on the dresser. "I was all right."

He spoke as his mother had spoken, as though to say, "This is what I am. Accept it." From a set quality about his posture, I could see that he would not willingly continue this line of conversation. I was so angry and dumbstruck by this audacity that I couldn't speak. I turned and did not question him further.

As was to be expected, the mystery revealed itself. Oliver's acquaintances would approach him whenever we went out for coffee in Chinatown. "Hello, Oliver. Are you prospering?" they would say. Then they would look at me with great interest and curiosity.

"Those guys," Oliver said, chuckling and shaking his head. "Normally, they'd hardly give me the time of day. Now that I've got a wife, they want to see what you're like."

When we walked through San Francisco's Chinatown, chauffeurs standing on the sidewalk by cars held passenger doors open invitingly.

"Get inside," a chauffeur would say to us, smiling seductively. "You'll get rich."

By degrees, I came to understand from these exchanges that Oliver gambled. There were thriving houses of gambling both in the Oakland and San Francisco Chinatowns, and it was to these that Oliver went in the night. On the lookout for the sort of flashy patrons who would enjoy immersing themselves in the heady atmosphere of a plush gambling venue, these pandering chauffeurs stood ready to carry us to those houses if we wished. Possibly they recognized him from past visits.

But Oliver never went gaming when I was with him. He didn't wish to share this side of himself with me. Perhaps my mere presence would have had the unsettling effect of a guilty conscience, sapping all the pleasure from the games. Or maybe he simply wished to keep his two lives separate. Conversely, I never tried to seek him at any of these establishments. I never wanted anything to do with them. Maybe it was superstition, but I didn't want to be tainted.

There was the story of a young woman named Anne Chin, college-educated and assertive, who entered a gambling house one evening and dragged her husband out. The next day, the story was all over Chinatown. The fellow was a laughingstock. I would never have done such a thing. I had the strength of water, which flows through cracks and low places, carves through mountains, and remains unaltered. But I rarely bore the sword of the sudden cutting action. To do so would have blunted me.

If there was a silver lining, Oliver was not a gambler like my Uncle Ho Huang. He was not emotionally explosive, and he did not physically hurt or abuse me. He was simply addicted. And in his addiction, he cared more for his gambling than for me. So his abuse was one of neglect. I had married to find a home and companionship, as my Aunt Emily had advised. My nest, however, was empty.

After that night when I stayed at Mrs. Chan's, Oliver typically came home every night at about 3:00 a.m., and every night, I would lie in bed waiting for him and praying to God, "Please let him come home safely and soon."

I should have despaired past all bearing had it not been for the kindness of my in-laws. Mrs. Chan treated me like one of her daughters. When I came to visit, she always had a big smile and said she was glad to see me. She was eager to share and hear the daily news of friends, relatives, and current events. I was one of few who had the patience to explain such happenings to her. She was interested but had little education, and it was hard for her to read the newspaper or understand the vocabulary used on the radio. I spoke to her in simple terms so she could understand. Frances and Emma took me shopping and taught me how to cook, and Frances allowed me to use her sewing machine when I came to the house.

They took me to Swan's, a market with many stalls under one roof near Clay, Washington, and 10th Streets in Oakland. It occupied a city block with vendors selling meat, fruit, vegetables, cigarettes, and other household goods and knickknacks. Frances explained how to select a chicken.

"Feel the flesh around the pubic bone. If it is soft, it's a good young chicken. If it's hard, the chicken is old and tough."

I proceeded to squeeze the crotch of every chicken on the cart until the vendor loudly complained, "Hey, what are you doing touching all of my chickens?"

At the fruit stand, Frances explained how to select bananas. "Smaller bananas have a better flavor than larger bananas," she said. I experimented with both and found this to be true.

At home, Emma taught me how to stir-fry pork and string beans. "Put in the oil, wait until it has just started to sizzle, then toss in the sliced pork. Add the salt and pepper right away to get the flavor into the pork. After cooking the meat, set it aside, then toss in the string beans. Have ready a spoonful of cornstarch mixed with water in a small bowl. Add the meat in at the end again to reheat it. Toss in a few drops of soy sauce and a dash of sugar. Stir the cornstarch liquid rapidly as you pour it in to prevent lumps from forming. Shut off the heat when the liquid thickens. When cooked this way, the meat and vegetables are quickly seared and retain their flavor and crispness."

Dean was also considerate. In one of the apartments that Oliver and I later rented, our kitchen was so small that our table just fit between the stove and the counter. The kitchen cabinets hung so low that I kept banging my head on them when I leaned back. Observing this, Dean took it upon himself to raise them so I wouldn't hit my head.

In fact, of Mrs. Chan's twelve children, only two had problems: the eldest and the youngest. Mrs. Chan's first son, Bill, was an alcoholic and a womanizer. He'd come in then go out again with little conversation, and no one knew where he went. In this way, he and Oliver were alike. All of Mrs. Chan's remaining children worked at stable jobs. They had homes and families, or at least they contributed to Mrs. Chan's household in some manner. If Oliver had treated me as kindly as his family did, I should have considered myself blessed and happy.

But life with a gambler means your feelings, possessions, and entire being are in a state of flux. Once, he came home and proudly announced that he had won a car for us. A fellow gambler had gambled beyond his means and offered an automobile that he owned instead of cash.

I was excited about this until I went out to see the car, which was an ancient two-seater jalopy with a rumble seat in the back. It was nearly out of oil, so Oliver went to a gas station and asked for some used oil drained from another car as part of an oil change. He poured this into the car. On its strength, we drove across the bridge to San Francisco, with the oil leaking all the way. He got more used oil at a gas station in San Francisco, and we used that to drive back to Oakland. After that, the car sat parked on the street for some time until Oliver gambled it away to someone else.

On another occasion, he brought home a beautiful sewing machine that he had won for me. Again, I was excited because I was using Frances's old machine at Mrs. Chan's house. But a little while later, it was gone, for he had lost it again while gambling.

When he won big, he sometimes bought me extravagant gifts. Once when he had won big, I pleaded for a washing machine. Oliver suggested a fur coat instead.

"No, not a fur coat," I said. "Where would I wear it?"

As something like a compromise in his mind, he instead bought me a rich-looking wool coat with a thick beaver fur collar. On another occasion, he bought me a diamond watch. When he brought me these gifts, I wanted to cry because we didn't have a telephone or a washing machine. I washed our clothes on a washboard and walked up flights of stairs to the roof to dry them on a line. I also knew better than to believe that he bought me these gifts out of affection. He was concerned with appearances. He cared little for what he ate or for the state of his home, but when out, he dressed beautifully. He wanted to make an impression, and he wanted me to be an attractive accessory.

"Are you prospering?" his friends would ask, and he would smile, catlike, as though our appearance should answer their question.

"Show him your watch," he would whisper, nudging my elbow. Reluctantly, I would show off my diamond watch, but inwardly I was ashamed.

Are you prospering? The phrase had layers of meaning, depending on who asked. In the simplest sense, it could mean, "how are you?" However, a specific tone of voice and expression meant that the person inquiring wanted to be repaid for a gambling debt owed to him but demurred from making the vulgar demand in the presence of a wife.

About six or seven months after we married, Oliver lost his butcher job at the meat market. When we married, he had put twenty dollars as a down payment on my wedding ring then paid twenty dollars per month afterward. Once he was unemployed, I gave him the twenty dollars per month out of my paycheck to continue payments to the jeweler. But about three months later, we received notice that the jeweler planned to repossess the ring.

"But why?" I asked.

"Because we haven't received any payments for the last three months," said the exasperated jeweler.

I realized that Oliver had been keeping the money I had given him and was gambling it away. So I gave the jeweler three twenty-dollar bills on the spot and told him that from now on, I would personally come down to the shop each month and make the payments myself. In this way, I kept my ring.

About a year after we married, we moved out of our rented room to a studio apartment on 8th Street in Oakland. We had lived there no more than a month when I came home one day to find our apartment ransacked and robbed. Everything was in disarray with clothes pulled out of drawers and household items and furniture scattered and knocked down.

We had a great deal of cash hidden in the apartment, and all of it was gone. We had a savings account but no checking account, for we paid our bills in cash as our parents did. For instance, I paid our utility bills by bringing cash to the utility payment offices. That we even had a savings account was something of an advance over our parents' method of money management. My parents had never believed in or trusted banks, which were a foreign institution that had proven unreliable during the Great Depression. During the early years of their marriage, when my parents had money to save, they had invested in gold.

To pay everyday expenses such as groceries or the electric bill, I hid my tip money in various spots around the apartment, including under a radio. All this hidden cash was gone. Hurriedly, I searched for my gold wedding jewelry hidden in some clothes in my bureau. Oddly, though the clothes had been pulled out and rummaged through, none of the jewelry was missing. The robber had been strangely respectful of my wedding gifts.

I called the police, but when they met Oliver and me, they asked us to take a lie detector test. The detector drew a straight line when I answered the policeman's questions. When they interviewed Oliver, it scratched wildly back and forth. The police said nothing more, but that ended their investigation. With humiliation, I realized that Oliver had staged the robbing of our apartment to cover up stealing the money I had stashed.

Since he had lost his job at the butcher's, he worked intermittently at odd jobs. Without a regular income, he couldn't always gamble. But even without money, he had gone down to the halls just to be part of the atmosphere. His addiction drove him. Being unable to participate was a humiliation. Like my uncle before him, he resorted to stealing to feed his craving.

Eventually, his brother Dean sat me down. "Helen," he said, "I think you should take Oliver's name off your savings account so he doesn't keep depleting your money."

By following his advice, I took charge of our finances. I went to the banker to open an account in my name. Every other week, I pushed my paycheck across the teller's counter to deposit it. I had resolved to live only on my tips, which were the bulk of my income. Each time I went to the bank, I reviewed the gradually increasing sums typed into my passbook with grim satisfaction. Saving was the only way I could think of to hold on to my dreams and myself.

Oliver had a well-to-do brother named Hart, a successful restaurant owner skilled in personal finance. After I sought his advice, Hart sent to my home a financial services representative. The representative talked to me about mutual funds and whole life insurance, a type of insurance policy with a savings account built into it. I invested in these as well.

Slowly, gradually, I would become highly knowledgeable about managing my finances. This started for a dark reason—my husband was stealing from me. Within the darkness, I created some light.

27

SEED OF LIGHT

While living in the studio apartment on 8th Street, I found that I was expecting. When I first learned of this, I was filled with joy. *A baby*, I thought happily. But as the pregnancy progressed, I grew more and more concerned about the circumstances into which I would be bringing the child.

The studio had a wall bed, which I had to pull down each night to sleep. Late in my pregnancy, I found one night that I couldn't reach the top of the bed over my bulging tummy to pull it down. Oliver, as usual, was out for the night. I walked down to Chinatown to look for him and met a friend of his on the street.

"Do you know where Oliver is? I need him to come home. I can't get our wall bed down."

"OK, wait here a minute," he said. "I'll go find him and bring him back." Soon he returned with Oliver, who walked home with me, pulled the bed down, then promptly returned to Chinatown. He treated his nightlife as though it was a job.

He had not found any steady employment since he had lost his job at the butchers. We had no health insurance, so I called the hospital to determine how much a birth would cost and began saving money toward the bill. During this time, Oliver and I still had a joint account. I hid the passbook under the refrigerator, hoping that he wouldn't find it there. Unfortunately, he did find it there, withdrew all the money, and gambled it away. Then I had to scrimp and scrape in the final months of my pregnancy to pull the cash together.

Our landlord gave me her old bassinet and a blue enamel baby tub. As I was throwing garbage away in the dumpster, I noticed someone had thrown away a highchair, so I fished that out and cleaned it. I later bought a Taylor-Tot stroller. It was a toddler-sized wooden seat supported by a metal frame on wheels, with handles extending upward so the parent could push the seated child. Taylor-Tot manufactured the most popular brand of stroller at the time.

Oliver's brother Hart owned the Planter's Dock restaurant on Jack London Square in Oakland, overlooking the estuary. It was a bar and American-style dinner house, serving a few Chinese dishes. In desperation, days before the expected birth date, I begged Hart to give Oliver a job because soon I wouldn't be able to work anymore, and then we would have no income at all. Hart agreed, and to my tremendous relief, Oliver took employment there as a bar boy, washing glasses, wiping counters, mopping floors, and replenishing supplies for the bartender.

On the day that I went into labor, Oliver came home "early" at about 10:30 p.m. I called my doctor, who advised me to go to a hospital in East Oakland. Oliver then called a friend to borrow a car so that he could take me to the hospital at about 3:00 a.m. He waited through the birth at 6:30 a.m., long enough to find out that a daughter had been born to him. He then took off, leaving me in the care of the nurses and returning a couple of days later with a box of doughnuts to celebrate.

By then, I had named our daughter Stephanie Yuen Senn Chan. Yuen Senn means "like a star" or "the image of a star." Generally, the grandparents give a child their Chinese name. However, as I held my daughter in my arms with a heart swelling with pride and affection, the words "Yuen Senn" came to me, and I decided that was who she was.

Little Yuen Senn was born with a full head of black hair, which flopped to one side of her forehead, so almost my first thought was that she looked like a cherubic baby Hitler. When Oliver came by with a box of doughnuts, he offered one to me then took one for himself.

"The rest I'll bring down to the guys," he said, referring to his gambling buddies. "I figured on getting doughnuts since we've got a little girl."

I suppressed a rolling of my eyes. Doughnuts for a girl? Why? Because they have a hole in the middle? Perhaps that wasn't what he meant at all. Maybe it just came out wrong. Then again, it might well have been a crude joke, as I suspected. With his poker-faced expression, he was inscrutable.

My in-laws, as usual, were as good as gold to me. Mrs. Chan, Frances, and Emma took turns cooking our meals for the first thirty days after I got home. Unfortunately, when the doctor asked if I wanted to breastfeed or formula feed, I told her I wanted to formula feed. I thought I might have to return to work soon. I didn't realize that I could breastfeed for as short or as long as convenient for me. Also, I wasn't aware of the particular benefits of breast milk, particularly in the first weeks following birth. The doctor prescribed pills to take the milk away.

In the meantime, Mrs. Chan was cooking for me the traditional Chinese diet for new mothers: a great deal of soup, usually chicken soup with rice wine and pig's feet in a vinegar broth. All that soup caused me to swell painfully with milk despite the doctor's pills. With Mrs. Chan, Frances, and Emma vigilantly pushing me to eat and eat, I began to look plump in the mirror for the first time in my life. Finally, when I started to eat normally again at the end of the thirty days, my weight stabilized, and I began to return to my regular shape.

Conventional Chinese wisdom said that it was unhealthy to soak in cold water. The chill might cause rheumatism, especially for new mothers. As a result, Mrs. Chan insisted that I shouldn't be the one to wash Stephanie's diapers for a whole month after her birth. My brother-in-law Dean kindly volunteered to wash the diapers. Every afternoon after work, he came over to our apartment to perform this service.

I appreciated all this help during that first month after birth. I was tired from the labor and lack of sleep. I looked at Dean then and thought how sad it was that he had never married, for he would have made an excellent husband.

About six months after Stephanie's birth, Dean advised me that if I wanted to go back to work, Mrs. Chan would take care of Stephanie at her home. He knew how precarious our financial situation was. So just before the holidays of 1946, I took a part-time job at the Lemington Hotel, the only upscale hotel in Oakland.

Every morning, I would haul Stephanie and a large diaper bag to Grandma Chan's house about three blocks away. It was always hard for me to part with her, so I would find myself running to catch the bus for work at the last minute. My heart was a little damaged from my days of malnutrition in China, and it hurt my heart to run like that. But then it also saddened me to part from Stephanie. Still, I knew that she received a lot of loving care at her grandmother's. Grandma Chan doted on her, as did her Uncle Dean and Aunt Frances, who sometimes also looked after her.

Even so, during this time, I suffered from what today would be called post-partum depression. With Oliver out almost every night, I desperately missed having a companion in the evening. I wanted to share my concerns about Stephanie and the stories of her cute antics. I keenly felt my vulnerability in not having someone reliable on whom I could depend. So I spent a good deal of my free time in moping listlessness, which was uncharacteristic of me.

Ba had heard through my Aunt Emily that I was married. When he heard what sort of man I had married, he became so angry. Not only was I working as a waitress, a disreputable profession in his eyes, but he had expected me to marry a professional such as a doctor or a lawyer. He saw that as the great opportunity he had provided me in bringing me to America—the chance to marry well. Otherwise, I might as well have stayed in China to marry a peasant. He told Aunt Emily that he wouldn't have anything more to do with me.

Aunt Emily sadly conveyed this to me. I only thought I didn't know how I could have married a professional like a doctor or lawyer without education or connections or anyone to guide me. "What's done is done," I said. My heart felt clean. I knew I had always tried my best to do the right thing. I attempted to push the matter out of my mind.

However, a few months after Stephanie was born, Aunt Emily approached my father. She said to him, "You have a grandchild to consider now. You must put your anger aside and visit your eldest daughter. And you must bring a gift for the baby, a suit of clothes at least." My dear Aunt Emily took it upon herself to personally take him to the store to buy the gift and bring my father to see me.

"Hi, Ba," I said when I opened the door to greet him and Aunt Emily.

"Heh, heh," he replied with his characteristic laugh. He walked in with Aunt Emily, who greeted me warmly as usual. I served tea and pastries. Ba presented his gift, and then I pulled Stephanie out of her bassinet and put her in my father's arms.

She was four months old, that age when babies start to lose their skin discolorations and misshapenness and look like little cherubs. She was adorable, smiling and cooing up at Ba and reaching her little hands up to touch his face. My heart swelled.

Ba looked down at her for a long time, and as he looked, I saw something change in his expression. His face softened. Watching Ba gazing at Stephanie, I breathed deeply for what felt like the first time in a long time. He stared at her for so long, and then he began to speak soft baby words to her. Suddenly, he stood up and walked around the room with her, bouncing and cooing at her.

At length, he returned her to me. He said little else as he examined the meager furnishings of our apartment with his hands clasped behind his back. There was just a wall bed, a sofa, Stephanie's bassinet and highchair, a small bathroom, a tiny kitchenette with a table and chairs, and some orange crates for storage and sitting. Ba then left and went home.

After that, I did invite him over from time to time, and he

accepted my invitations. He traveled by the Key System train, which ran on the second deck of the Bay Bridge from San Francisco to Oakland. Whenever he came, he couldn't seem to get enough of holding and playing with Stephanie. He had lived in isolation and bitterness for many years. With his granddaughter, his sheltered heart opened a little.

28

FINDING MY SIBLINGS

In 1946, when Stephanie was less than a year old, Ba informed me that he and Seam were arranging for my sisters Katie and Jean to immigrate to San Francisco. I was ecstatic. It had been over six years since I had last seen any of my siblings.

Seam made inquiries among our family about who might host Katie and Jean when they arrived in Hong Kong to settle their immigration papers. As in the past, my mother's family was most helpful. Our Uncle Phillip's wife informed Seam that a Fong cousin was willing to put them up. So they boated down the Pearl River to Hong Kong and were greeted by this distant relation, whom they called Mun Kow Fu, meaning Uncle Mun, and his wife.

Mun was our cousin, but they called him Uncle and his wife Auntie because they were a generation older. Jean later told me that they were an elegant, professional couple who worked in banking. Mrs. Fong dressed beautifully in Western-style suits and *cheong soms*, the traditional Chinese dress with a high collar, fitted bodice, and slits along the sides of the skirt. She coiffed her hair in a lovely updo. Next to her, Jean and Katie felt like country bumpkins with their plaited hair and dressed in wooden clogs and baggy pants tied on with rope.

By letter, Seam had asked Auntie to help them buy Western-style dresses, socks, and shoes and take them to a salon for a permanent wave. She had heard this was the custom in America. Jean did not think that the tiny sum that Seam enclosed was sufficient for all these purchases, but Auntie nonetheless bought all these things for them. She helped them select flattering Western-style belted white dresses with puffed sleeves and flared skirts. Jean's had green flowers. Katie's had blue.

Unfortunately, Auntie left them to choose their shoes. Knowing nothing of Western fashion, they selected sturdy black oxfords and white socks to go with their dainty white dresses. These may have been shoes for boys. They were serviceable and comfortable, and Jean and Katie initially had no shame about their strange ensemble.

Seam had not thought or perhaps known to have them buy undergarments. They had never worn any with their village clothes. They only wore the cloth bandages that Seam bound across their chests to keep their appearance modest according to Chinese custom. They simply rolled up their baggy pants and wore them underneath their full skirts in place of underwear.

Uncle and Auntie were a couple without children who loved city and cultural life. At night, they sought entertainment, and they were kind enough to take my sisters with them. Again, Jean and Katie felt like villagers because they were overwhelmed by the dazzling, bright streetlights at night. It was the first time they got to see Chinese opera and American movies. Jean liked the actor Van Johnson. He was a blue-eyed, carrot-topped, freckle-faced fellow who always played a sailor or soldier in all the films that she saw. His appearance was so foreign and exotic. She didn't understand English, but she could follow the story's outline by watching the images, and the romantic scenes were an eye-opener. She said she could never imagine our parents behaving that way.

In short, she and Katie had the loveliest time, but after a month, their immigration papers were still not ready, so they returned to the village. Jean said that the villagers were impressed by their appearance.

"How modern you look," they said, not knowing any better than they that black oxford shoes do not go with white floral dresses. So they were proud and felt that they had status.

Not long after their return to the village, they heard their papers were ready. Returning to Hong Kong, they stayed a few days before departing as passengers on a U.S. warship, a troop carrier, returning to the United States.

Aboard ship, they slept in army bunkbeds in a large room with other women. They noticed that several of their fellow passengers dressed in silk or satin pajamas and bathrobes in their sleeping quarters at night. Jean thought these were so lovely that she asked, "Oh, where are you going?"

"I am going to bed to sleep," replied the bemused passenger.

"People go to bed in such beautiful clothes?" she asked. She couldn't get over that. In the village, all of us had slept in the same clothes that we wore during the day.

When they arrived in San Francisco, the city looked so big, overwhelming, and foreign that Jean grew frightened. Katie and Jean no longer remembered any words of English. Jean knew nothing of American customs or procedures, and she realized that she couldn't quite remember how I looked. It had been so long, and she knew that I was a grown lady now, Westernized and married. When they docked, all the other passengers debarked. Katie and Jean stayed aboard, scared to leave the ship's safety and unsure what to do.

Finally, some crew members shooed them off. "Go! Go," they said. "You can't stay on board."

As they walked down the plank, Jean said her heart was pounding in her ears. She was so scared. She thought, *What if King Ying is not there, or we have missed her? What if we don't recognize each other? What will we do then?* Fortunately, I spotted them right away.

"King Shu! Tuey Jean!" I called out. Jean said that relief flooded her.

I was thrilled to see Katie and Jean at the pier. How lonely I had been in America without my sisters! It had been six years since I last saw them. We were all so reserved by habit that we did not hug or kiss, but our hearts were nonetheless full, and our eyes were shining with happiness.

I had sought Aunt Emily's advice on how to house Katie and Jean when they arrived. I could not possibly keep them in my studio apartment. Aunt Emily volunteered at one of the Ming Quong Homes for orphaned, abandoned, and homeless Chinese girls. There were several such charitable homes in the Bay Area. She spoke to the officials at the home in Oakland and recommended my sisters to their care. When my sisters arrived, I had only to tell the director that my sisters were the ones my Aunt had spoken of, and they were directed to a room to share.

Their room at the Ming Quong Home cost fifteen dollars per month. Ba paid for the first two months, but after that, he left for China to see Seam and to retrieve James. I then paid for their room and told them to come to my apartment to have their meals.

But soon, they stopped coming for breakfast and lunch. Oliver slept during the day while I was at work. He pulled the covers over his head when they entered the studio apartment. He had been raised in America and spoke little Chinese; they spoke little English. The situation was awkward, and they decided not to bother him during his sleeping time. They bought boxes of cheap saltine crackers to fill their stomachs for breakfast and lunch. Only in the evening did they come to my apartment for supper.

Soon, however, someone reported them, and the staff of the Ming Quong asked why they ate only crackers for breakfast and lunch. When they explained their situation, they allowed my sisters to eat three meals per day. In exchange, they helped in the kitchen by peeling and slicing potatoes and vegetables and washing dishes. When they had been there a year, Aunt Emily appealed further on their behalf. She explained that both their parents were in China, and they were supported solely by me, who was also struggling to support and raise an infant. The home then allowed them to room there for free.

I bought them underwear and bras, and I sewed skirts and blouses for them, so they began to look American in their shape and clothing. In the meantime, the Ming Quong instructors taught them Western habits and customs. They learned to eat with knives, forks, and spoons and to set the table properly. Staff instructed them in table manners and other etiquette. They also gave them a daily routine, including English classes for immigrants at the local elementary school.

I had so much fun with them. I often took Katie and Jean to the corner drug store for sodas or a milkshake or to a coffee shop by the Paramount Theater. Sharing our stories of hard knocks, survival, and naiveté in China and America, we often laughed so long and hard that we were hardly aware of our surroundings. Once, we started to cross the street at a red light. Then the beat cop shouted at us to get back on the curb.

Jean told how their teacher, Mrs. Linn, told them to pull the shade in their room each morning and lower it in the evening. Neither Katie nor Jean had ever used a roller shade before and hadn't any idea how it worked. Jean studied it for some time. At last, she climbed up to the window, removed the shade from its holder, rolled up the shade by hand, then replaced it. When Mrs. Linn caught her doing this one morning, she burst out laughing. She then showed Jean how to use a shade properly with the spring action. Jean was surprised and embarrassed, but she had to laugh too.

The Ming Quong Home was not only a place to live while attending school. It was also a place for people like my sisters, who had been living in a primitive way, to learn the necessary skills of modern life. Everything was new and strange to them. Their caretakers were Caucasian, except Mrs. Linn, who was Chinese. She was the only staff member who could speak to them in their native tongue. Katie related that while living at the home, they were instructed to dust their room and mop the floor as part of their daily routine. After Katie's first time cleaning, she asked Mrs. Linn in Chinese what she should do with the dust mop.

In English, she replied, "Take it to the backyard and shake it out." Katie didn't understand the meaning of "shake it out," but she went to the backyard and saw a faucet; she decided to wash the dust mop as she had seen other girls rinse their wet mops after cleaning the bathrooms. She then attempted to throw the mop head over the branch of a tree to dry. Instead, she threw the entire mop over the limb and into the neighbor's backyard, which so upset her that she ran to Mrs. Linn to tell her what happened. Mrs. Linn told her to just walk into the neighbor's yard to retrieve it. She also instructed her not to wash the dust mop with water anymore.

Katie and Jean were a strange couple to be paired together as roommates. Jean was a social, go-getter sort of girl who cared little for appearances and decorum as long as she could get things done quickly and move on to the next project. Katie was always concerned with being proper and refined in her behavior and appearance. They sometimes grated on each other's nerves as two sisters who love each other but who are of different temperaments will do.

Katie was meticulous in her dress, making sure to iron each piece of clothing before putting it in their shared closet, and she kept space between each outfit to prevent further wrinkling. She felt mortified when meeting someone uncouth. She might comment with distress, for instance, on the ill manners of an acquaintance blowing loudly on his soup.

All of this grated on Jean so that she was sometimes intentionally mean to Katie. She was blessed with a good sense of direction and could usually tell which way to go at a crossroads. Katie had little perception of direction and was always getting lost and asking how to get to places. So when they walked down the street together, Jean sometimes purposely strolled, pretending to window shop or observe the houses. Katie would walk on ahead, get to the street corner, look about bewildered, and have to wait for Jean to catch up to tell her which way to go. Of course, she was annoyed with Jean's intentional slowness.

Yet in high school, Katie gave Jean such good advice, for which Jean was ever afterward grateful. Ba had sent money for Seam to buy them ship tickets to America, but Seam had heard of an American program to loan expatriate Chinese American citizens passage money to return to the States. As Seam felt that Ba had not been sending enough money for their support during the war, she decided to keep the money and instructed Katie and Jean to apply for a loan at the American consulate. "Once you are in America," she reasoned, "you will be able to earn money to repay the loan." Jean dreamed only of attending college. She was excellent in math and had ambitions to be an engineer, teacher, or other professional. Initially, she enrolled only in academic, college preparatory classes until Katie sat her down one day.

"Be realistic," she said. "College is expensive, and who will support you while you attend? We each have a loan to repay when we get out of school. You must take classes in a trade so you can support yourself when you get out of school." At Katie's advice, Jean enrolled in typing and business English courses so that she might have a chance to work as a secretary or an office assistant when she got out of school and could no longer live at the Ming Quong Home.

Indeed, when Jean graduated high school, she took a comptometer course at Merritt Junior College in Oakland. A comptometer was a calculator machine typically used to do billing and payroll work. She did so well that when a recruiter came to the school, the teacher recommended her, and she soon had a job in the billing department of America News, a magazine and newspaper distributor. Jean and Katie were nineteen and twenty-one years old, respectively, when they returned to America. They were twenty-two and twenty-four when they graduated high school.

* * *

Ba returned to China in March 1947 then began his return journey to America with James in November. James related to me that the day that they walked from Tai Ting Pong village to the city of Dick Hoy to catch the boat to Hong Kong, Margaret and May skipped school to walk with them and say goodbye. May was silent and sober until they boarded the motorboat that would take them downriver. Then, at last, she bid them a sad goodbye. But Margaret cried, saying that she hoped to see James in the United States as Seam had promised and hoped she would not change her mind.

Seeing her tears, James began to cry too. They would not see each other for a long time, and it was just she, May, and Wanna left behind in the village with Seam. By then, Margaret and May were 19 and 16 years old and James was 14. They had survived in the village for eleven years. Wanna was 10.

James worried about Margaret especially. He had once overheard a conversation between a strange man who came to visit their home and Seam, which led him to believe that Seam might marry her off and leave her in China. However, James had never repeated the conversation to Margaret as he didn't want to worry her.

They parted at last, and James and Ba were soon boating their way down the Pearl River to Hong Kong. Ba had planned to stay in a hotel before departing. However, they learned that their ship was delayed by five days, so our father decided to return to the village. He could save the hotel expense and see if Seam, who was expecting a baby any day, had given birth and if so, find out if the child was a girl or a boy.

Our Uncle Lum, Seam's younger brother, who had a small apartment in the Repulse Bay District of Hong Kong, cared for James. He had also looked after me during my stay, but now he was married with a four-year-old daughter. When Ba returned, he was happy to announce that Seam had given birth to a baby boy whom he had named Shew Hang, or Ronald.

The following evening, Uncle Lum borrowed a car from work to drive Ba and James to the pier, and they boarded the *General Gordon*, a ship used as a troop carrier during World War II. Aboard ship, they took their meals cafeteria-style on steel trays in a mess hall. After the first supper, which they ate shortly after boarding,

James went on deck to view the city lights as they departed the harbor at dusk. James recalled a beautiful panorama, and the air was fresh and bracing.

When he went to the restroom, he found that toilet paper came in rolls, which fascinated him.

Even in Hong Kong, toilet paper came in sheets. In the village, we had used any kind of paper available. But this paper on a tube rolled out endlessly. James unfurled a large wad, stashed it in his pocket, and then quietly showed it to Ba.

"This is hard to find. I am going to keep it. Is it all right, Ba?" he asked. Ba smiled and told him to throw it away, for soon, he would see lots of this kind of toilet paper in San Francisco.

They arrived in San Francisco on December 17, 1947. Or, rather, they arrived at the outskirts of San Francisco Bay, where they waited to be cleared by the Health Department. When they were approved, they entered the harbor and docked at a pier.

Immigration personnel boarded and began their final check before they could disembark. James and Ba knew that the process should go smoothly for them, for they were citizens. However, immigration staff called names in alphabetical order. Since their surname was Yee, they would be last or nearly last to leave. They waited for a long time, but the officials never called their names. When it was quitting time for the personnel, they left, and James and Ba had to stay overnight aboard the ship.

In the meantime, Oliver and I were down at the pier, waiting to pick them up. We also had to go home after a long wait and return the following day. At last, the next day, they were released. While the customs agent was checking his suitcase, James kept looking about to see if he could spot me. He wasn't sure if he would recognize me. It had been eight years since we had last seen each other. As he and Ba walked out of the customs area, I called "Ba!"

Father turned and, spotting me in the crowd, smiled. "King Ying," he replied. Addressing James by his Chinese name, he added, "Min, do you recognize your big sister? And this is your brother-in-law, Oliver." Oliver shook hands with James, and James greeted him. Still, James kept looking at me. I think he did not recognize me as the gawky sixteen-year-old who had left the village so many years ago. I was now twenty-four. I wore a Western-style ladies' suit with lipstick and my hair curled.

Oliver and I had Stephanie with us when we went to pick up James and Ba at the pier. James quickly took a liking to Stephanie, appearing fascinated by her. He talked to her, tried to make her laugh, and then asked if he could carry her, and I let him. She was nineteen months old and small for her age. But though James was a teenager, he was so thin and slight of build that I thought he looked like a kid carrying a kid as I walked behind him.

Oliver and I took James and Ba out to dinner in Chinatown, and then we brought them to Trenton Street, where Ba lived. In all the time that Ba lived there, he never invited me to see his apartment. Trenton Street was a narrow alley and not in the best part of town. I sensed that he did not want me to see how he lived, so we dropped him and James off at his door, and there we said our goodbyes.

Ba shared his flat with two other men who also kept wives in China. James said he was amazed by the gas stove and the metal pots and pans. In the village, Seam had to burn wood or hay to fuel the stove and used only clay cookware. He also was amazed by the hot and cold running water. There would be no more going to the well to haul heavy buckets. Everything in this new world was unimaginably modern.

A few days later, Ba found a job as an out-of-town house cook. His employer required him to live and work in their home six days a week with Sundays off. Ba gave James an allowance of five dollars a week to buy groceries. He explained how to prepare rice on the gas stove and enrolled him in a Chinese school for three dollars per month, which he was to attend in the evenings after public school. Ba then left James to care for himself while he was gone. Ba had started working and looking after himself when he was a teenager, so he thought James should be capable, too.

In public school, James began to learn his ABCs and some phrases of English. He started in a sixth-grade class, where he found the math easy because he had gone far beyond that level in China. Still, his inability to speak fluent English held him back in every other respect. After a month, he started an English class for immigrants, where he felt comfortable because they were all in the same boat, struggling to learn a second language.

Soon, he got a newspaper route when a schoolmate gave his up, and he earned a promotion to district manager's assistant. He received twenty-five dollars per month. When Ba learned that he was making money, he stopped paying for James's groceries and his Chinese school tuition. James began to shine shoes on Saturdays after his newspaper job to increase his income.

James lived with Ba until he was seventeen, at which point Ba abruptly informed him that he should now be supporting himself as he had done at that age. James was shocked. When he told me, I was shocked too, but we both knew that Ba meant what he said. I helped him get a job at my brother-in-law Hart's grocery store in Oakland, and he quit his shoeshine work and newspaper route in San Francisco. I also helped him find a room to rent from my sister-in-law in Oakland so he could go to high school there while working weekday evenings and Saturdays.

* * *

During the summer of 1949, Ba sent money for Margaret and May to return to the United States. They had waited thirteen and a half years to come back to the country of their birth and were now 21 and 18 years old. They were especially anxious to return as China was now engaged in a civil struggle between the Nationalist and Communist parties.

The journey could not happen too soon, for the Sino-Japanese War had taken an enormous toll on them. They had been slowly starving to death with never quite enough to eat, and they had suffered through much ill health, but they were still alive.

I sent a piece of fabric to Seam to make a dress for each. The material was yellow rayon with a gray butterfly and flower pattern, and there was enough to make two dresses. However, also wanting to make an outfit for Wanna, Seam cut their skirts to knee-length, though calf-length was the style. May recalled that the fabric was wrinkled, and they had no iron, so she tried rolling a rock over her dress to flatten it, but that had no effect. They simply wore their dresses wrinkled and too short.

May had a little more luck in her wardrobe. Living two doors down from her in the village was a relatively well-to-do woman. Her family had fled Canton with the Communists' coming, for they feared torture because of their wealth. When she married, she came with her procession through the village in a beautiful wedding dress made of blue silk with a pattern of hearts and flowers. May had always told her how much she admired her dress, and seeing how poor May was, the woman altered it to fit her and gave it to her as a going-away present before her leaving.

For the journey, Margaret's friend suggested that she ought to have a set of undergarments to wear beneath her clothes. She had never had the luxury of underwear in the village, and May didn't have any either. However, Margaret's friend kindly offered to sew some for her if she could provide her with fabric. The only money she had was her *lai see* (lucky money) from the Lunar New Year's celebration. This was just enough to buy a small quantity of burgundy muslin. With this, her friend sewed undergarments resembling a blouse and a pair of shorts.

The fabric was coarse, but Margaret nonetheless wore her new underwear throughout the trip.

In addition to making Margaret and May Chinese dresses for their journey, Seam had somehow provided them with stockings but without either garters or garter belts. She did not know that some device for holding up their hosiery was necessary. Margaret recalled that, consequently, in addition to the discomfort of her coarse underwear, she had the trial of frequently pulling up her stockings lest they slide down around her knees. Uncle Lum took them to buy Western-style shoes. Seam had always taught them to buy clothes a size too large, so they would have room to grow. They each selected white heels that were too large for them and went clomping and tottering in those for the rest of their journey.

In Canton, they had their hair set with a permanent wave at a beauty shop as Seam had directed. They thought they couldn't comb or wash their hair or the curls would disappear, so they just picked at it a bit in a futile attempt to shape it, and their hair became quickly matted and dusty. With their matching, wrinkled, short dresses, saggy stockings, oversized shoes, and dirty, tangled hair, they walked the streets of Canton and listened to derisive whispers all around them. "Here come girls from the village . . . ha, ha!" They felt so ashamed.

Margaret and May traveled with an acquaintance, Sam Lim, who posed as their brother. Only Sam was not related to them in any way. When Ba had returned to the United States after bringing us to China, he declared to immigration officials that a son had been born to him while he was in China. Our half-sister, Wanna, had not been born yet, but knowing that a child was on the way, Ba declared a son to obtain a citizenship document for his offspring. If the child was a boy, then Ba could bring him over as a citizen. If the child was a girl, he could sell the citizenship paper for a high price and bring the child over by other means, such as through marriage. It was Sam's family who bought the citizenship paper from my father. So Sam posed as their baby brother, Sam Yee, for purposes of immigration.

Sam, May, and Margaret traveled to Canton city from the village, where they stayed with Sam's relatives. The apartment was small, so they slept in the hallway. Margaret and May walked to the American consulate nearly every day, trying to procure permission to return to the United States. At other times, May liked to wear her beautiful blue dress. However, when she and Margaret walked to the immigration office, they wore their matching yellow dresses to make it clear that they were sisters. Repeatedly, the officials there looked at their immigration documents, looked at them, then said that they couldn't help them and to "try back another day." They waited for weeks.

Sam's extended family, although unrelated to them, allowed them to stay with them because Sam posed as their brother. But they felt no obligation to feed them as well. As Margaret and May had no experience eating away from home, they continually bought bread from street vendors for their meals.

At last, they decided to be brave and eat at a restaurant. Though the restaurant was owned and operated by Chinese, they served an American menu. Margaret and May ordered chicken, and they each received a big piece on their plates, which they were to eat with knives and forks—only they had never eaten with such utensils before. The waitress stood nearby, looking at them so loftily and snootily, as though they were riffraff, that they felt uncomfortable. Margaret said they felt their cheeks burning as they looked at their meal helplessly, not knowing how to eat it. Unwilling to look any more like village fools than they already felt, they finally got up, paid, and left their precious food untouched. They did not tip, for they did not know that was the custom.

By chance, one day, they ran into our cousin Sam Fong, a relation through our birth mother, on the street. When they told him of their plight, he kindly offered to speak for them at the consulate, and they readily agreed. He flagged down a one-man rickshaw. They all squeezed into the carriage until they were stopped by a police officer and told to get off, for it was a violation for one man to pull so many people. They walked the remaining distance to the consulate, where Sam spoke in English to the officials. He soon procured permission for Margaret and May to leave without getting any of the runaround that they reserved for inexperienced villagers.

They were extremely fortunate, for one month later, the

Communists took power in China. Anyone left behind experienced far more difficulties in going if they could leave at all. They now traveled from Canton to Hong Kong, where they booked passage on the *General Gordon*. This former World War II troop and cargo carrier was the same ship by which James and Ba had previously traveled.

In Hong Kong, they stayed with our Uncle Lum, Seam's younger brother, who had hosted James and me before them. Uncle's apartment was small. He, his wife, and their children usually slept in one little room together. But during their stay, Uncle kindly slept outside on the balcony so they could sleep inside. Fortunately, Hong Kong's weather was warm and balmy, so he was not too uncomfortable.

Margaret said that when it was time to board the ship, she felt scared to walk up the gangway when she saw the vast water beneath her. As soon as they were aboard, they were separated from Sam, for men and women were assigned segregated sleeping and living quarters. Margaret and May went to a large, open, dormitory-style room, which they shared with many other women.

Once the ship set sail, nearly all the women were seasick and vomiting in their quarters. Margaret and May were quartered many floors below deck and felt dizzy. However, it so happened that there was a distant relation aboard the ship who lived in a nearby village. He knew Ba from Detroit, where he had also had a business. Knowing that Margaret and May were aboard, he searched for them to see how they fared. They called him Gok Way Suk, meaning Uncle Gok Way, in deference to his being a generation older than them. He asked how they were feeling. When they told him they were lightheaded, he told them to walk up on deck to get fresh air immediately. Afterward, they felt much better and were never sick after that.

They became acquainted with some Chinese boys about their age and began the habit of remaining in the dining hall after dinner was over to join them in playing cards. The boys were always polite, addressing each of them as Miss Yee in Chinese, as in "Miss Yee, it's your turn." But one evening, a crewman approached their table and addressed Margaret as Miss Yee in Chinese. She didn't know whether he understood what he was saying. She believed he only repeated what he heard the Chinese boys call her. He held a pillow over his waist, and when she turned to look, he removed it and exposed his private parts to her. She was so frightened and upset that she immediately rose, ran to her quarters, and never stayed again to play cards.

When their ship arrived in the Port of San Francisco in July 1949, Margaret said that the city lights amazed her. She kept repeating, "All those lights! All those lights!" In the village, it was always dark at night. There were no electric lamps in the homes, streets, or alleys. They did housework and schoolwork at night by the light of an oil-wick flame.

Due to new procedures, I could not meet them at the pier. Instead, upon debarking, Margaret and May were transported by bus to immigration barracks on Sansome Street in San Francisco. Their roommates told them to "count on being stuck there for at least thirty days." Hearing this, they were depressed and anxious. However, they were American citizens, though they didn't look like it, and the very next morning, an official called out their names, beckoning them to follow her.

They jumped up to leave, but a detainee admonished that they couldn't go without cleaning their area. They scrambled to strip their beds and fold the sheets and blankets. Then they walked out with the official, carrying their belongings in small bamboo suitcases.

There I was in the waiting room with my brother-in-law Dean. Dean helped me pick up Margaret and May because I didn't know how to get to the immigration office in San Francisco, and I couldn't find Oliver to take me.

Margaret afterward said that she thought we looked like American movie stars in our smart suits. She said she was particularly impressed by my appearance with my red lipstick and curled hair. We ushered them to Dean's car, and Margaret said it was a fantastic experience to ride across the beautiful Bay Bridge.

I took them out to dinner, and when we got to my apartment, I gave each of them a set of underwear consisting of a bra and panties. I knew that coming from China, they would not have Western-style undergarments, so I had those prepared for them. Afterward, Dean and I drove them to the Ming Quong Home, where they were to live.

In the meantime, Sam Lim's parents picked him up from the immigration office and brought him to their home and laundry in Oakland. Though he was not related to us, a friendship developed between him and our family. He later often visited my home for tea and conversation, and he came to regard me as a sort of big sister. Many years later, he took advantage of an American amnesty program, which allowed him to confess his true identity and retain his citizenship.

I had tried to get Margaret and May into the Ming Quong Home under the same sort of work agreement that Jean and Katie had enjoyed, but I was refused and told that it would cost thirty dollars each per month for their room and board.

Initially, Ba paid for room and board for Margaret and May. During this period, they attended classes at Lincoln Elementary School in Oakland to learn English as rapidly as possible. Margaret said that her head sometimes ached from concentrating so hard on trying to think and speak in another language.

May said she was struck by how softly everyone spoke. People talked loudly, laughed raucously, and expressed their anger bluntly in the village. It was an adjustment to speak in a low voice in the manner of the American ladies she observed. However, none of us siblings ever got over laughing loudly. That is not a bad thing, I think.

When Ba unexpectedly stopped paying Margaret and May's room and board, the Ming Quong Home evicted them. May recalls that they burst into tears and cried and cried, for they didn't know what would become of them. They had waited so long to come to America, and it was still so new and foreign that they hadn't any idea how to manage. However, the staff soon secured live-in house jobs for them both so they would have a place to go.

Margaret began by working for a Mr. and Mrs. Berman, who lived on Trestle Glen Road, a well-to-do area of Oakland. She spent part of her mornings, afternoons, and evenings vacuuming, dusting, making breakfast, preparing food for dinner, and doing all the family's ironing. She received twenty-five dollars per month plus room and board.

Mrs. Berman taught her to prepare American-style breakfasts, including fried eggs, pancakes, and bacon. As soon as she heard running faucets, flushing toilets, or other indications that the family was getting up for the day, she went to the kitchen to begin cooking. By the time the family was dressed and ready, breakfast was on the table.

With a deft movement of the wrist, Mrs. Berman demonstrated how easy it was to flip eggs in the pan without a spatula. How many eggs Margaret wasted trying to learn that movement! She would flip the eggs, they landed on the stove, and she would throw them away to start over. Eventually, she would have a successful flip, but it was nerve-wracking to go through that process every morning. She said she ought to have asked Mrs. Berman to buy her a spatula, but she was too shy to approach her.

After chopping the meat and vegetables in the evening, Mrs. Berman cooked dinner herself. Margaret had to eat her share in the kitchen while the family ate in the dining room. Margaret tried hard to iron correctly, but the little boy was particular about his clothes. If he didn't think she had ironed them perfectly, he handed them back for her to redo.

All too soon, Margaret was desperately lonely and sorely missed her days in the Ming Quong Home when she had pleasant companions who treated her as an equal. One month after starting work for the Bermans, she fibbed to the Ming Quong staff and said that she couldn't live with them because she didn't like to eat meat, and the Bermans made her eat meat. It was a silly, made-up story, but she so hoped that the staff would allow her to return to the home.

Instead, they found her another house job in worse circumstances. She began working for a widow and her spoiled, bratty daughter who lived in Piedmont, a well-to-do enclave across the bay from San Francisco. Now she earned only twenty dollars a month, and she had to endure a teasing little girl who frequently locked her in her room as a practical joke. She attended Technical High School in Oakland, and it was a long walk to get there from Piedmont.

Margaret immersed herself in her studies whenever she could. She attended Technical High School in Oakland full-time for one and a half years, then part-time for one year, graduating in January 1953 at 25 years old. As was her custom, she worked hard, and as she had in China, she earned a place on the honor roll.

In the meantime, May's first job was for a Caucasian couple, Mr. and Mrs. Olstrum, who had a seven-year-old daughter and a baby son. Mr. Olstrum worked as a salesman, and Mrs. Olstrum was a housewife. May's job was to clean the house, care for the children on weekends when Mr. and Mrs. Olstrum went out, and wash and cut up meat and vegetables for dinner. Mrs. Olstrum cooked the food May prepared. Every night, she served May and the seven-year-old one hot dog, peas, and a potato. May ate this every night for the two years that she lived there. Later in the evening, Mr. and Mrs. Olstrum ate their dinner alone, and May observed that they ate different kinds of foods, including steak and other meats.

The couple had a huge dog, which they kept in the kitchen at night, and it was usually still there in the morning when May was getting ready for school. She was frightened of the dog, so she never ventured into the kitchen for breakfast and always went to school on an empty stomach.

Her bedroom was diagonal from the parents' bedroom, and they kept a television in their room, which they watched late into the evening. The little girl kept coming into May's bedroom, hoping she would play with her or talk to her. As her parents neither engaged her attention nor told her to leave May alone, May found it hard to study.

May was supposed to earn twenty-five dollars per month. Instead, Mrs. Olstrum would ask if she felt like eating Chinese food for a change.

"Of course," May would reply.

Mrs. Olstrum would then use May's salary to buy enough takeout food to feed her family and May and, in this way, keep much of the money that she was supposed to pay. May was not the only one from whom she stole. May sometimes observed that she pulled money out of her daughter's piggy bank, which she used to catch the train to San Francisco to eat lunch in her mink coat.

There were some months in which May did receive her salary. Out of these earnings, May recalled buying seven pairs of bobby socks, one pair of oxford shoes, two sweaters, three skirts, and three blouses. The rest of her salary was for public transit and incidentals.

One day when she returned to the Ming Quong Home to visit, one of the staff members asked how things were going. When she explained her situation, the staff member was upset and immediately reported the case to the local labor office. Officials there helped May get back all of her missing wages.

In the meantime, the Ming Quong staff found another job for her working in a large, beautiful home for Mr. and Mrs. Banks of Piedmont, California, across the bay from San Francisco.

Unfortunately, this situation did not work out any better.

Though the house had six bedrooms, Mrs. Banks would not allow May to use any of them and instead put her in a storage room off the kitchen, where there was an old couch with a large hole in it on which she was to sleep. May used wadded magazine pages to fill the gap, but the sofa was still so uncomfortable that she soon had a chronic backache from sleeping on it.

Here, at least, she earned forty dollars per month and received her salary. During the school year, she worked after school and into the evenings, and during the summer, she worked all day, six days a week, doing housework. Her work included washing laundry, ironing clothes, sheets, pillowcases, and tablecloths, washing Mrs. Banks's underwear by hand, preparing the breakfast, and then serving it to Mrs. Banks in bed. She cleaned all the windows, vacuumed and dusted, polished a considerable quantity of silverware, cleaned out the attic and closets, and helped prepare, serve, and clean up after dinner.

Every Friday, an Uncle Charlie came for supper, and May helped Mrs. Banks prepare a large meal with many courses. After making the meal together, it was May's job to serve. Mrs. Banks taught her to serve each person from the right and remove the dish from the left. After serving a course, she was to wait in the kitchen until Mrs. Banks rang a handbell, which was her signal to bring out the next dish.

After the meal, Mr. Banks and Uncle Charlie adjourned into the living room for conversation and drinks. Mrs. Banks then came into the kitchen to tell May which dishes she was allowed to eat for her supper, and then she also went into the living room. May felt bitter about being told which foods to eat when so much was available. She would eat in the kitchen with a lump in her throat and tears rolling down her face from loneliness. Afterward, she washed and dried all the dishes and put them away.

One day, Mrs. Banks asked May to clean and organize her closet. May counted that she had thirty-six pairs of shoes, and she exclaimed, "Oh, Mrs. Banks, you have so many shoes. I have only one pair." Someday, she hoped to have more than one pair of shoes.

May said she was always polite to Mrs. Banks, though she felt bitterness inside.

Sometimes Mrs. Banks would pour a small amount of Coca-Cola into a glass for her and say, "Here, you may have some Coke," as though she intended this as a treat. Although May found the gesture humiliating, she would say thank you and drink it.

During the school year, May went to Oakland Technical High School. There, she made a friend, Bob, who became her boyfriend. Whenever he called her at the Banks' residence, she began to cry. To hear the voice of someone who cared for her was a relief from her loneliness. However, seeing that she cried whenever Bob called, Mrs. Banks asked whether they quarreled. *If only you knew what is in my heart*, she thought, but she said nothing.

Sundays were her day off, though she still had to make breakfast and serve Mrs. Banks in bed.

Afterward, she would catch the train from Piedmont to 21st and Broadway Streets in Oakland and then take the bus to the Ming Quong Home. Sometimes she went just to be in its comforting environment and sometimes to meet Bob.

She worked for Mrs. Banks for about six months when a Ming Quong staff member asked her how things were going. When she explained all that she did and her living and working conditions, the staff member was appalled.

"Mrs. Banks is taking advantage of you," she said. "My goodness, nobody irons their sheets by hand anymore when it's so cheap to send them to the laundry. The laundries have big machines for pressing sheets nowadays."

So May quit her job with Mrs. Banks, and the Ming Quong staff set about finding a third job for her. This third job was to be different. Her employer would be a nurse who rented a one-bedroom cottage with one bed.

As she worked a night shift, she proposed that May sleep in her bed at night, and then she would sleep there during the day while May was at school. Furthermore, the nurse had a boyfriend who had a key to the house and might come in as he pleased.

May did not like the idea that this boyfriend could come into the house whenever he wanted, nor did she like the idea of sharing a bed that the nurse shared with her boyfriend. She approached me to ask whether I might have a spare twin bed that she could borrow to create some small private space for herself within the house.

But when I heard what her living conditions were to be, I also disapproved. After speaking to Oliver, I offered to let her stay in our duplex with a twenty-dollar monthly allowance, and she readily agreed. The duplex had a separate bedroom for Stephanie. May shared Stephanie's room and said she expected to help me with housework as she had done in her previous jobs. However, as I was already in the habit of keeping my home immaculate and preferred to do my housekeeping, I didn't leave much for her to do except to help me prepare dinner.

May lived with me for about a year and afterward said that, by far, it was her best year since coming to America. For the first time since leaving the Ming Quong Home, she had a sense of family. I treated her with respect and as an equal.

* * *

Donaldina Cameron was a staunch Presbyterian who founded the Ming Quong Home in 1915. Though she had long since retired, the home still required all teachers and girls to attend the Chinese Presbyterian Church in Oakland's Chinatown. Katie and Jean soon adopted the Presbyterian faith, having experienced firsthand the kindness and generosity of its practitioners.

At church, Jean met a young man named John, who admired her. After they had dated for a while, he asked her to marry him, but Jean declined, saying that she had a dream of going to college, and for that, she was willing to put off even marriage.

"Well," he replied, "we can get married, and you can still go to college." She was touched that he understood and respected her ambitions. She felt herself relenting, but, still, she said no. "You don't know how to drive," she said. "How can I marry someone in America who doesn't know how to drive?" She thought that if she had children, she would have to transport them everywhere by bus, and she didn't want to do that.

So John enlisted his best friend, Gordon, to teach him to drive, and he obtained his license from the Department of Motor Vehicles. Then he showed her his license and asked her to marry him again. Seeing how earnest he was and remembering his promise that she might go to college even after marriage, she accepted.

Because she got engaged before Katie, she might have married before her. However, since Katie was older, they decided that she should be married first. That was considered proper in China. If a younger sister married before an older sister, the younger sister had to give the older one a pair of Chinese pants as a wedding gift. This gift symbolized the older sister "skipping back over" the younger sister to restore the proper order of family life.

However, fortunately, they did not have to wait long before Katie also met a fellow, got engaged, and married. While attending school, she worked on Saturdays and Christmas and summer vacations as a saleslady in the stockings department of the National Dollar Store in Oakland. There, she spotted a Chinese manager, Harry Lew, who oversaw the housewares department in the basement. During her break time, instead of going out to drink coffee or smoke as others did, she walked around the lower floors, hoping to be seen by Harry while he made his rounds.

Her strolls about the store had the desired effect, for one day, toward the end of May 1950, he asked if he could take her out for a date on Memorial Day when the store was closed. Of course, she accepted his invitation.

He drove her to San Francisco, where they visited the Legion of Honor Park with its beautiful columned temple and the pond with ducks and swans. Katie said they had a wonderful time, so they continued dating and going to church together. A few months later, he proposed to her at Lake Merritt in Oakland, where they had stopped at Lover's Lane to admire the view. He placed a platinum band with diamonds on her ring finger as he proposed. Katie said that she was so surprised and touched to see such a beautiful ring on her hand that she couldn't speak, but somehow she knew that they were engaged.

When she went home that evening, she proudly told Mrs. Linn of her engagement and showed her ring. Mrs. Linn said how happy she was for her and suggested that she buy candy and pass it around to all the girls in the home. In this pleasant manner, Katie announced her engagement to her friends and acquaintances.

Harry and Katie married in October 1950 at the Oakland Chinese Presbyterian Church and had a reception at the Ming Quong Home. I made all her bridesmaids' dresses, the flower girl's dress, and the ring bearer's suit. I served as matron of honor, Stephanie served as the flower girl, and my sisters were bridesmaids.

Now it was Jean's turn to get married. She saw a beautiful lace wedding dress in a bridal shop window and fell in love with it, but it cost two hundred dollars, an exorbitant sum, and she knew that she couldn't have it. But John said, "No. Get it. I'll buy it for you." Her heart leaped. John worked at a National Dollar Store, one of a chain of department stores, as a sort of all-around employee, opening and closing the store, counting and depositing money, sweeping the floor, working in the stockroom, and so on. However, he had been living with his parents and saved a good deal of money.

John and Jean married in 1951 at the Chinese Presbyterian Church with a catered reception at the Ming Quong Home. Again, I was the matron of honor, and Stephanie was a flower girl. Margaret and May were also in the wedding party. Katie declined because she was pregnant at this time, and there was a superstition against being photographed while pregnant.

After the embarrassment of my wedding, I was proud to see my sisters marry well. I was glad to help them have a proper church wedding with our family and friends in attendance, with flowers, bridesmaids, groomsmen, cake, and food. I was honored to serve as their matron of honor and glad to sew the bridesmaids' dresses so they could each have a beautiful wedding party.

Many years later, when Jean and John's third daughter began

elementary school, Jean reminded John of his promise to let her go to college since she now had a little free time. He agreed, and she enrolled in classes at Merritt Junior College. She earned her associate degree in computer science in midlife by attending classes part-time over nine years. Although she did not obtain a bachelor's degree, her courses at Merritt satisfied her desire for advanced education. She was able to find a job as a computer programmer, thus realizing her dream of working as a professional.

* * *

James graduated high school in 1954 at age twenty and then joined the army to get the last GI benefits. The Korean War ended in 1953, but the draft was still active. After a tour of duty in Europe, the army discharged him to Monterey, California. He hitchhiked to my house in Oakland, where he lived until he could get back on his feet as a civilian.

He enrolled in a sheet metal class at Oakland Junior College and worked at the Acme Meat Market. His friend George told him that his sister Anna and her friend Florence shopped at Acme and that he would ask them to look for James. Over the weekend, Anna and Florence came in, and James spotted them in the pork shoulder area. They fit George's description, so he asked if one of them was Anna.

"I am Anna," replied the shorter one. "This is my friend Florence." Anna had her freshly washed hair in curlers wrapped in a scarf and wore eyeglasses. Florence was so bashful, she spoke not a word, but Anna chatted while James weighed and wrapped her pork roast.

When James saw George in school the following Monday, he asked if George thought Anna would join him for the spring semi-formal dance. James had taken ballroom dancing lessons with me at the YWCA, so he felt confident in asking. George replied that he thought his sister would be pleased to go and that he would ask her. The next day, he told James that she had agreed.

I advised James that it was customary for a gentleman to buy his date a corsage when he took her to the ball, so he bought one. He dressed in his high school graduation suit and his army dress shoes, which were the only dress-up clothes he had.

James said that when he went to pick up Anna, she looked completely different from when he saw her in the meat market's pork shoulder area. Her hair wasn't in curlers, and she wore a white dress with a bow on the back. He thought she looked beautiful, but he said nothing. After the date, he said he wished he had complimented her, but he lacked experience with things like that. They continued dating.

One evening, they returned home so late that Anna suggested that James sleep on the couch in the living room. From her house, they could leave for another place that they planned to go to the following day. He slept poorly on the couch and questioned his wisdom in staying there. However, at about 6:00 a.m., he overheard Anna's parents talking to each other. Anna's mother said that she thought James would be a member of the family someday.

"So by rights," she said, "he should help us clean up a bit around here, especially since Lunar New Year is around the corner. All the light fixture covers need cleaning." The next day, James asked Anna for a stepladder. He spent two hours taking down the light fixture covers, washing them, drying them, and putting them back up.

Suffice it to say that Anna soon knew the reason for his washing the light fixtures. After completing a semester and a summer term of sheet metal classes, James began an apprenticeship at the Melrose Sheet Metal Shop in Oakland. In his second year, I helped James pick out an engagement ring. On Valentine's Day, February 14, 1960, James and Anna married at the Oakland Chinese Presbyterian Church. Their wedding was not fancy, but they had two hundred guests. The entire wedding and reception cost them six hundred dollars, including a beautiful cake from Neldam's Bakery in Oakland and a formal wedding photographer.

* * *

After graduating high school, Margaret enrolled in a course on operating business machines, such as the comptometer and the Marchant mechanical calculator, at Merritt Junior College in Oakland. She earned a business machines certificate. Combined with her education in accounting that she had received in high school, she was able to secure employment at Grandma's Baking Company in West Oakland.

Being fully employed, she returned to the Ming Quong Home, where she now rented a room. She attended the Chinese Presbyterian Church and taught children in Sunday school. In 1954, a friend arranged for a young man named Bill Wong to take her to a party and bring her home.

Bill was a postal clerk in Oakland. She thought that he was kind, good-looking, and respectful, though both were shy. At the end of the evening, he asked if he could call on her again.

They dated for two years and soon found that they enjoyed kidding each other on the spur of the moment whenever a situation struck them as funny. They could take things seriously too, but they enjoyed seeing the humor in a given event and laughing about it whenever possible. They became the best of friends.

Two years was a long time to be courting in those days—so long that her friends became concerned. Miss Musgrave, the director of the Ming Quong Home, said to her one day, "Bill seems to be a nice guy. You have been going together for a long time. When is he going to ask you to marry him?" Of course, she could not answer. Bill was concerned about being able to support a family. As a postal clerk, he earned less than Margaret made as an accounting clerk.

At length, the Ming Quong Home directors announced that they would be shutting the doors for good. Margaret searched for an apartment but had no luck, for there was much discrimination.

Most people who owned decent places to live were white, and they would not rent to Chinese or other minorities.

Several people went so far as to slam the door in her face, yelling, "We don't rent to Chinese!"

One was an elderly man who acted like he had seen a ghost when he saw her. After this had happened several times, Margaret blurted out as soon as a door opened to her, "Do you rent to Chinese?" The answer was always no.

Bill was concerned. Aside from her difficulty finding any place to rent, he did not like to see a young woman living alone. He appealed to our sister Jean and her husband, John, whether they would be willing to take her in, and they said yes. Jean and John had two daughters and only two bedrooms in the unit they owned. However, when Bill inquired on her behalf, all four willingly squeezed into one bedroom without complaint and gave her the remaining bedroom. Margaret paid them a stipend to help with expenses. She thanked them repeatedly for their sacrifice in giving her a place to live.

However, in 1956, Jean found that she was expecting her third child, and in this way, she found means to help Bill see his way to marriage. "Oh, Bill, we are expecting our third child," she said, "and we do need the room. So John and I were wondering if you were going to marry Margaret. Otherwise, she won't have a place to stay."

I do not think that Jean would have kicked Margaret out without a place to go, but it got Bill to think more seriously about the matter. In this way, he came around to asking her to marry him, though he was still concerned about his finances.

In 1956, Bill and Margaret married at the High Street Presbyterian Church in Oakland. I served as matron of honor, and Jean's daughter, Janis, was her flower girl. Again, I made all the bridesmaids' dresses, including my own.

* * *

After graduating from high school, May enrolled in Merritt Business School. When she got her keypunch certificate, she found work at the Remington Rand Company in San Francisco.

Her boyfriend, Bob, asked her to marry him. He worked as an aircraft radio repair technician for Oakland Airport. Bob proposed to borrow a car that he was planning to buy from a friend, drive her to Reno on a Wednesday to be married, and return the following day. She agreed to this arrangement, and Bob borrowed $350 from me to buy her a ring.

May let me know that she would be leaving to get married on a particular date and return the following day. "Oh, OK then," I said pleasantly. "I'll get a cake and refreshments, and we'll have a little celebration here in the apartment when you get back."

I invited my sisters and brother over to greet Bob and her upon their return, and we ate cake in the kitchen. May also invited a Japanese girlfriend she met through the Merritt Business School. She was the only guest besides our family.

Bob and May went to live with his parents for one year. His mother, who May called On-Geen, meaning "mother-in-law," was old-fashioned and difficult. She was unhappy that her son had not gotten a wife from China. She thought that American-born Chinese were empty-headed and ill acquainted with the customs and etiquettes of a proper Chinese wife.

On-Geen was in her forties, yet in 1955, just twenty days before May gave birth to her eldest daughter, Melissa, On-Geen herself gave birth to a daughter. Afterward, she returned to work in her laundry and made May responsible for caring for her daughter and May's.

When she came home, she was critical of May's care and accused her of not adequately feeding her daughter. She directed May to prepare the evening meals, which May said she might not have minded except that On-Geen would lie on a couch, shouting directions about what and how she should cook.

As a result, though they paid no rent, May soon hated her living situation. She had worked at Remington until she was seven months pregnant and managed to save about one thousand dollars.

At last, she and Bob combined their savings and bought a house in Hayward. While living there, their second daughter, Ginger, whom they called Gigi, was born.

Even after they stopped living with May's in-laws, they went to eat with them every week. Over meals, On-Geen would speak in an approving tone of acquaintances who beat their wives. She advised Bob to be sure to keep his wife "in line." Bob listened, and his mother influenced him.

Suffice it to say that May's marriage was unhappy. Years afterward, she said that although she no longer even remembered the exact date of her wedding, she remembered that she had been married for eighteen years, nine months, and two days. There were some memories that she blocked and some that she never forgot.

Bob had not been abusive when they dated. Sometimes they argued, but that was all. After their marriage, however, May found him wildly possessive and controlling. Once when she didn't come to bed on time because she wanted to finish some sewing, he came out from the bedroom and snipped the cord of her sewing machine. Another time, when they argued bitterly, and he threatened her, she said that she would call the police, and he yanked the telephone cord out of the wall.

If she cooked something he didn't like, he might throw the dish against the wall. Soon, she said, she felt as though her body was in the marriage to care for their children, but her spirit was far away. She wondered what terrible things she had done in a previous life to deserve this treatment.

She thought of divorce for years. But she worried about her reputation and especially whether she could make it on her own and care for her children. Still, she remembered our Uncle Ho Huang, how he had treated his wife and how he never got better. When her daughters were nearly grown, she decided to go forward. It was the 1970s, and attitudes were changing.

When they divorced, May had little money, but she felt as though a weight had lifted from her heart, and she enjoyed her newfound freedom. She took part-time work as a waitress and studied English and library studies at Chabot Junior College in Livermore.

At the restaurant where she worked, three bachelors who worked for Lawrence Livermore National Laboratory began to sit at one of her tables whenever they came in. They were Burt, Ron, and Jerry. One day, they asked if she would join them on a ski trip to Lake Tahoe. She hesitated, and one of the fellows said he was also bringing a lady friend so that she wouldn't be the only woman.

She declined. She didn't know how to ski, was not athletic, and didn't want to date or get married again after her marriage. She knew these men as customers with whom she exchanged pleasantries but nothing more. She thought she would feel uncomfortable vacationing with three bachelors and a strange woman.

However, when she got home and told her daughter, Ginger said, "Oh, Mom, you should have said yes. Skiing is so much fun, and Tahoe is beautiful." She looked disappointed that May had lost the opportunity, and May thought she would have liked to go.

The next time the fellows planned to go skiing, they asked May again, and for Ginger's sake, she said she would go if she could bring Ginger along. Melissa, by this time, was already in college. The guys readily agreed.

They had rented a beautiful cabin in Tahoe with a fireplace, so the setting was idyllic with white snow and pine trees all around, but May did not have a good time. She had her period and so was tired and uncomfortable. She knew nothing about skiing and kept missing the lift so that the operator had to stop it for her to get on. One day, she skied off the track and into a telephone worker about to climb a pole, causing his tools to scatter. She twisted her ankle.

Ron drove her home, and Jerry stayed to ski with Ginger. She, at least, was having a good time, and May was glad about that. As the fellows had rented the cabin and paid most of the expenses, May said she would like to contribute some food. Not wanting her to spend too much, they said she could make breakfast.

Jerry helped her cook, and she appreciated that. At night, she slept by the fireplace. Jerry helped her light the fire and set the alarm so that she could get up at the right time. They were small kindnesses, but they meant a lot to May. She began to like him. Ron, who had driven her home when she twisted her ankle, said that he thought that Jerry liked her too, and she was glad to hear that, but she said nothing of her feelings.

Two weeks after the trip, Jerry called her on the phone, and they chatted for two hours. She said she found it so easy and comfortable to talk with him. He asked where she had been, and she said to San Francisco and a few other places in California, adding that before she died, she would like to see Hawaii. He said that he would like to take her and, in fact, that he would like to show her the world. He asked her to dinner on a particular evening, but she said no because she had to work.

He asked her about other evenings, and she kept saying no, for it is not customary in Chinese culture for a woman to appear eager. Finally, he asked her out for breakfast, and she couldn't pretend that she worked at breakfast, so she agreed but was quick to add that she had to work at lunch.

The morning of their breakfast, she laid her uniform out on her bed so she could slip into it as soon as she got home. Jerry ended up driving her to work with her buttoning her dress and tying her shoes on the way. The pleasant morning had passed so quickly that she hardly had time to dress if she was to get to work on time. After dating for a couple of months, Jerry asked her to marry him.

"I don't want you to get married unless you are one hundred percent sure," she said.

Jerry said he was sure. Still, she demurred. "I can't get married while I have Ginger living with me. If you two fight, whose side will I be on?"

So he waited two years for her, and when Gigi went to college, they married at last in a beautiful seaside setting in Carmel, California.

A year or so after Margaret and May had returned to the United States, Ba returned to China to get Seam and Ronald. When I went to the pier to pick them up, I watched as they walked down the plank from the ship. Ba proudly bore three-year-old Ronald in front of him like a trophy, and Seam walked several paces behind, weighed down with all their luggage. They had left Wanna behind in China with a relative since Ba had sold her citizenship document to another family. About five years later, in 1955, Seam would declare that Wanna was her niece whose parents had both died and that she wished to sponsor her as a refugee. In this way, she brought her daughter to America at last. Wanna was then 18 years old.

Our second half-sister, Lily, was born in the United States after Ba and Seam settled in San Francisco. Ba had nine children in all, two of them, Ronald and Lily, younger than my daughter, Stephanie.

It took ten years to reunite with my sisters and brother, but it was a blessing to be together again. To this day, I consider them among my best friends. While Margaret and May were still in China, I sent a photograph of myself to them. Much later, Margaret told me that she had found the photo inspirational.

I laughed, thinking of my early years after returning to America. I wore stockings with my dresses, but I didn't know how they were supposed to be held up, so I kept tugging at them to keep them from falling to my knees. One day, an acquaintance asked why I kept yanking at my stockings, and I told her that I didn't know how to keep them from falling.

"Don't you wear a garter belt?" she asked.

"What's that?"

As we happened to be alone, she hitched up her skirt and showed me the undergarment with clip attachments used to hold up her stockings. So that was the secret! Of course, I immediately bought one, thinking with an inward chuckle that you could take the girl out of the village, but you couldn't take the village out of the girl.

But when I laughed, Margaret only said, "It might be funny to you, Helen, but it wasn't funny to me. We were desperate to get out of China, where we were starving to death. Your photo was the hope of what I could be if I could get to America."

By sharing our stories, my siblings and I would laugh until we cried and cried until we laughed. Though we separated in our childhood, we had many experiences in common. We spoke the same language and understood one another. A friend once said that we were made from the same mold, and it was true. We were family.

29

ON BEING A WAITRESSS

A round the time when May was taking her class in business machines, I wished to enroll in a similar course. I wanted to advance my station in life by continuing my education. However, Oliver would not stay home to care for Stephanie even on the two nights per week required for me to attend one class.

Being a waitress was to be my lot in life, so I decided to make the best of it. My reward was sometimes helping a grumpy customer be more cheerful or helping a coworker or customer overcome their prejudice against Chinese. Sometimes, a long-time customer would bring in his or her son or daughter or grandchild to meet me. In the end, I came to enjoy the challenge of rendering exceptional service to customers of differing temperaments. Remembering the orders, anticipating the needs of each table, providing service efficiently, knowing when to be sociable or not all kept my mind sharp. To be a waitress was to have a view into the lives and habits of a great many people, which was an interesting study. I found that you can tell so much about people by how they eat, behave with family, friends, and acquaintances while dining, and treat the waiter or waitress.

In 1947, I quit my part-time job at the Lemington Hotel and went to work at Pland's Restaurant in Oakland across from Kaiser Permanente Hospital, where I stayed for the next seventeen years. Pland's was part of the Macarthur-Broadway shopping center, an upscale outdoor mall featuring restaurants representing different countries, which was a new concept at the time. There were no chain restaurants or stores in the mall. Each restaurant and store was independently owned and operated.

Pland's was a gourmet English-style dinner house decorated with coats of arms and miniature suits of armor set into dark frames with red and gold matting. It was a large establishment, including a coffee shop, a dining room, a cocktail lounge, private rooms for parties and banquets, and parking for up to five hundred cars. It was the sort of restaurant where an organist or pianist was playing every night, and the waitstaff provided "silver service." We served with sterling silverware, including silver flatware, sugar bowls, creamers, and covers for each plate. Commensurate with the fineness of the serving ware, our service was of the highest quality.

We kept a close watch over our customers to ensure that we showed up promptly when they appeared ready to order or had any need or when they seemed prepared to leave and wanted the check. After the customers dined for a short while, we would ask if everything was all right to handle complaints promptly. We also strove not to show up when not wanted, as when customers engaged in a lively conversation.

We set the table to exacting standards. The silverware had to be one inch from the edge of the table and placed in the correct order with the cocktail fork, salad fork, and dinner fork on the left and the knife, teaspoon, and soup spoon on the right. We set the butter dish to the left and the water glass to the right.

The maître d' or manager personally checked every place setting to ensure that it was correct before bringing customers to the table. We served and poured from the customers' right to not reach across for the water glass. Also, assuming we were right-handed, it was the most natural and graceful way to serve. After customers left, we cleaned the crumbs from each chair, and again the maître d' inspected our work. If a single crumb was left, the maître d' crooked his index finger at the responsible waitress and brought her over to see the offending morsel and clean it up. Finally, we were to present ourselves professionally and cheerfully to contribute to a pleasant atmosphere.

Caucasian waitresses, dressed in crisp white calf-length dresses with aprons, were assigned to work in the coffee shop and dining room. Chinese waitresses, dressed in satin Chinese-style pantsuits, were assigned to work in the cocktail lounge. The cocktail lounge soon became so popular that management decided to have food served there too. We provided excellent service, and customers considered it a novelty to have a Chinese serving person in a cute satin outfit. Hence, customers packed the cocktail lounge while the dining room took the overflow. I observed that wives out with their husbands especially preferred a Chinese waitress. There was no dating or marriage between the races at that time, so we weren't a threat. The wives would gush over us, saying how adorable we were in our uniforms.

Society ladies, car and truck dealers from the auto row on Broadway, International Harvester salespeople, Kaiser Permanente hospital staff, and Granny Goose potato chip manufacturing plant employees came to Pland's. The worst customers were society ladies, the wives of judges, wealthy businessmen, and local politicians, including the mayor. The ringleader was the wife of Judge Murphy. It was she who usually brought in the others. The ladies came dressed to the high heavens in their fur stoles, I. Magnin clothes and fancy hats. Then they left the smallest tips while expecting the waitstaff to cater to their every whim.

Mrs. Murphy would begin by saying, "Well, ladies, shall we start with a martini?" Each would ask for a gin martini or Gibson, a dry martini with a cocktail onion instead of an olive. Purportedly, this was to be followed by a sandwich. And then, repeatedly, each would wait until I brought the food to say, "Oh, you know, I think I'll have one more martini before the sandwich." So I would bring the sandwich back to the kitchen and order a fresh drink from the bar. I knew that having at least two or three martinis or Gibsons was their habit before eating. Still, I had to go through this ritual of bringing the sandwiches back and forth. It was as though they wanted to pretend that they came to eat when really they came to drink.

When I was finally allowed to serve the food, each would take her sandwich, which the cook had already cut in half, and cut it further into eighths. Then they took mincing little bites as though this were a more refined manner of eating. When I brought out the coffee, they would say, "Oh, can you please put that into a demitasse cup?" A demitasse cup is quite small, so they would drink their coffee in the same mincing, pinky-extended manner in which they ate the sandwiches. They had so much time on their hands; they sat for hours chatting and drinking with their friends, occupying valuable table space, and then tipped poorly. I dreaded their coming.

Employees from Granny Goose, the potato chip company, were more gracious. They spoke to me as a fellow human being. They would ask how I am, tell me about their children, and inquire about my daughter. I once asked if I could buy some chips for a dance party that Stephanie wanted to host when she was in high school. They brought me a whole case, refused to accept payment, and said it was their pleasure.

But the best customers were the Kaiser Permanente Hospital staff. There was no fuss or muss in serving them. They would order, eat, depart in a timely fashion, and leave generous tips. They were warm and happy by nature, demonstrating concern for each other as well as for the waitstaff. Often they chitchatted confidingly about their lives and asked me about mine. Dr. Gavce, for instance, told me about his trips to Russia, where he was learning to speak the language. He would bring in his girlfriend, and when she stepped away, he wryly confided, "Oh, I don't want to get married. I don't want to get married." But then she left him for a month, and he missed her so badly that he asked her to marry him. They wed almost immediately and soon brought in their children.

Ivy Tam, formerly of the Forbidden City Nightclub, came to work at Pland's in about 1962. She had divorced Charlie Low and was no longer a dancer, but she was still beautiful and elegant. There were always Japanese big-spenders, businessmen by appearance, hanging about to take her out after work. They would come in to dine shortly before closing, wearing elegant clothes and big rings, and leave excellent tips. When the restaurant closed, she went with them in one of their grand, flashy cars. I looked at her a little wistfully then, thinking of my difficult marriage and the old jalopy that Oliver and I drove.

It was at Pland's that I met Walter and Frances Edmonds. They were friends and regular customers of my coworkers Luella and Ruby. For a long time, we said hello but did not know each other. When they later heard through Luella and Ruby of my difficulties and sadness, they sat at my table one evening to befriend me. They invited Stephanie and me to dinner at an upscale Japanese restaurant on Fisherman's Wharf in San Francisco.

They were a Caucasian couple of English descent and were English in their habits. They took afternoon tea and ate formal dinners, seated across the dining table from each other. They were Episcopalian, a religion descended from the Church of England. Yet they had a passion for all things Asian and had their home and garden constructed in the Japanese style with paper sliding doors and a koi pond and bonsai plants everywhere. I liked them because they treated me as an equal. They weren't like those Caucasian wives who spoke to me condescendingly about how cute or adorable I was. They were interested in my stories, opinions, and view of the world. They didn't mind my limited English and didn't correct my pronunciation. They listened and behaved as good friends, and we stayed friends for life.

I had my regular customers too. For instance, there were Mr. and Mrs. Graham, an eccentric, wealthy couple who had no other occupation but to live off their dividends. To save a trip to the bank, Mr. Graham would sign a dividend check over to Pland's to pay for his meal, and we would give him the change. He carried a stack of dividend checks about him and appeared to enjoy sifting through them periodically. Mr. Graham dropped Mrs. Graham off at the restaurant one day before parking his car. She was drunk, and when she came in, she slipped and landed with her legs straight up. Another customer commented to me afterward, "That was the most awful sight you ever saw. She didn't wear any underwear!" Mrs. Graham was in her sixties at the time.

If management felt they could differentiate between Chinese and Caucasian staff in terms of assignments and uniforms, some of the Caucasian waitresses also treated us differently. Most were friendly toward us, and we got along fine, but a few were unkind. Every morning, a waitress named Phyllis, for instance, would say, "Helloo, Helen," in a la-de-da nasty manner and then pinch me hard. At first, I was surprised and said nothing, but when she didn't stop, I finally got so mad that I slapped her hard across the back one morning, shoving her away from me, and said, "Stop pinching me!"

Phyllis reported me to the hostess, who was her supervisor. But the hostess said, "I would like you two to sit down and talk about this." Phyllis explained her side of the story, and I told mine. The hostess listened and then said, "Well, I would like you two to leave each other alone." After that, Phyllis never pinched me again.

Other Caucasian waitresses would sometimes pick up my orders from the chef before I had a chance to pick them up myself or would pick them up in front of me. For instance, if their customer had ordered the same dish as my customer, and my order was ready before theirs, they would take my order from the pickup area. It then appeared that their service was fast. I would tell the chef that so-and-so took my order, and he would prepare the second order for me, but then my service appeared slow. I never did report those waitresses to management but simply tried to make lemonade out of lemons. Customers were less in a hurry in the cocktail lounge, so I let them know of the delay and asked if they would like another cocktail while they waited. Usually, they did, and this ran up the bill a bit.

Still, Mr. Lynn, the manager, did like the Chinese waitresses and spoke to us gently and with respect. If he segregated us from the Caucasian waitresses, it was a sign of the times, and I doubt he thought twice about it. A 1950 advertisement for the restaurant shows a photograph of the Chinese waitresses and busboys in our satin uniforms with the caption "Lounge waitresses and assistants to assure you of good service with that Oriental atmosphere."

The caption for the photograph of Caucasian waitresses and staff reads, "Well-trained waitresses schooled especially for Pland's and office personnel to see that everything served is of the best quality." African American and other minority staff members were limited to working as dishwashers or in the pantry, where they chopped and shredded produce to prepare salads, or in the bakery, where they made desserts.

At the Lunar New Year, Mr. Lynn gave each Chinese staff a small bonus in a lucky red envelope out of his own pocket. I was grateful to him for hiring me and giving me a chance to learn from his expertise. It wasn't easy as a minority to find work at a high-quality establishment. I belonged to a union that was supposed to help me find work, but they never did. They would send me out to restaurants where the positions had just been filled, or the manager would see that I was Chinese and shrimpy and wouldn't promise anything. It wasn't until the late 1940s that the Chinese were even allowed to join some of the unions. Then if a manager or owner hired a Chinese man as a bartender, he called him a bar boy, no matter how old he was.

Pland's closed in 1963 when new owners tore down the shopping mall, yet many still have fond memories of that restaurant. To this day, some old customers who I run into now and then will say, "Oh, that was the place to go. We just loved Pland's." It was a grand, old-style restaurant. The customers were so regular that they not only addressed the waitstaff by name, but they greeted each other as they arrived and sat at the same tables every night. During the holiday season, many of my regular customers gave me an extra tip inside a Christmas card.

The new owners transformed the shopping center into an indoor mall. From that point on, it went downhill. When it was an open mall, there were high-quality, independent businesses, such as fine restaurants, a beautiful floral shop, and an elegant men's clothing store. Once the shopping center became an indoor mall, the new owners got rid of the restaurants and installed a food court. Without waiters, waitresses, and independent owners overseeing the clientele, a different class of people came. These were people who just sat in the food court without spending much money because no one would kick them out. Gangs began to gather. From then on, the mall declined.

In 1962, while still working at Pland's, I took a second job at the Tonga Room in the Fairmont Hotel in San Francisco. Established in 1947, the Tonga Room was a classic tiki restaurant, a Polynesian fantasy restaurant prevalent in the 1950s, '60s, and '70s. Other such restaurants included Trader Vic's and Kona Kai.

In common with other tiki restaurants, the Tonga Room featured Pacific island décor, including tiki statues, outrigger canoes, carved wooden masks, bamboo wall panels, thatch-covered tables, potted palms, and a ship's deck, used as a dancefloor. A small garden at the entrance featured fake exotic plants and tiki statues lit by colored lights. The high ceiling was black, and the restaurant was dimly lit with bamboo torches and candles on the tables to add to the jungle-like atmosphere. We served cocktails in tiki-shaped cups with colorful little umbrellas and pineapple slices. The Tonga Room advertised its cuisine as Pacific Rim. However, much of it was basic Cantonese fare, including Cantonese-style pork ribs enlivened with slices of pineapple, wok-fried chow mein, and spiced duck.

Its indoor lagoon set the Tonga Room apart from other tiki restaurants. The site had formerly been the location of the Fairmont's indoor swimming pool. When the owners converted the space into an exotic restaurant, they kept the pool as a centerpiece, surrounding it with potted plants and adding a thatch-covered boat on which a band played Hawaiian pop music. "Storms" occurred periodically, complete with strobe lights, a thundering soundtrack, and "rain" falling from a sprinkler system over the pool. The Tonga Room was perennially popular as a tourist and special-occasion destination.

All the waitstaff was Asian. Waitresses wore Chinese-style satin pantsuits, and waiters wore satin Chinese jackets with slacks. I worked in the cocktail lounge, called the Hurricane Bar, and was the only waitress assigned there. It was a large lounge, so I had to hustle to keep up with all the orders. I asked customers to pay as soon as I served the drinks. If I didn't collect the money immediately, they might get up to dance then move on to the dinner table, and I would lose the payment and tip entirely. The Tonga Room was famous for its Mai Tais, so that was the most popular drink, especially the Mai Tai for two, served in a bowl with two straws. Other popular cocktails were scorpion punch, piña coladas, and zombies.

I made good money at the Tonga Room. The usual customers were men on their best behavior bringing well-dressed, attractive women for a date or special occasion. They were usually in a mood to impress, and they left generous tips. This lounge was not the sort of establishment where single men and women came to meet each other. Almost all my customers were couples on a romantic outing, so I did not get to know them as well as I got to know customers at Pland's. Single people preferred to sit at the bar. Ella Fitzgerald was one. She would come in on her breaks from performing in the Venetian Room and sit at the bar, mopping the sweat from her neck and brow with a hankie.

In 1971, I went to work at Francesco's restaurant in Oakland, which was closer to my home. Francesco's was an upscale lunch and dinner house near the Oakland Airport, the Oakland Coliseum, and some business parks. Customers included businesspeople, air traffic controllers, sports fans, sports players and coaches, and local politicians. It was an Italian restaurant in the 1970s, so my uniform consisted of a flared green miniskirt trimmed with red rickrack and a white form-fitting blouse. Cocktail waitresses wore hot pants and white go-go boots, and most of us sported bouffant hairdos. For our heavier waitresses, the hot pants uniform was a particular challenge in terms of trying to keep cheeks from sagging below the hemline, but such were the times. When the A's were repeatedly in the World Series in the early 1970s, we were all made to wear baseball caps jauntily perched atop our bouffant hairdos.

If society ladies were challenging at Pland's, sports celebrities posed unique problems at Francesco's—or, rather, their groupies caused the problems. By groupies, I refer to those women who would do almost anything to hang out and be seen with and bed their favorite sports celebrities. The women would swarm into the entry area after a game dressed in miniskirts and tight tops. In the brief time when the players passed through the entry area before being seated, they hoped to connect, usually by gushing over how wonderful they thought the players were. If a groupie was "lucky," a player would ask her to meet him somewhere after he dined. Sometimes, a groupie would continue talking to a player even after he had gotten to his table. However, they did leave when the waiter or waitress arrived to take the order, and it was clear that the player did not intend to invite her to dine with him.

We were in the awkward position of having to keep a straight face when a player one night brought in his wife and another night brought in his mistress. They trusted us to behave as though nothing were amiss. A well-known place kicker for the Raiders, for instance, would ask to be seated at a good table in the front of the restaurant when he brought in his wife. He would ask to be seated behind our workstation, where we cut bread and butter and stored the cream and butter when he came with his mistress. The casual viewer looking in at the door could not see this table behind the workstation.

We also served players from the opposing teams. In general, they traveled with their wives until they bore children, and then the wives stayed home. It was then that some players fell prey to the groupies. It was not my place to say anything, but I always felt sad for the wives when I saw this happen.

Sports players were not the only men to engage in this behavior. Some businessmen alternated bringing in their wives and mistresses. When these men brought in their wives, they ordered, ate, and left. They didn't appear connected, and their whole attitude conveyed, "I've done my job. You've been fed and taken out." By contrast, when such a man brought his mistress, he was protective and concerned, ensuring she dined on the best food and wine.

A particular businessman lunched with his secretary daily in a corner table behind the organ. They thought they were safe from view, but from where I sat folding napkins, it was not difficult to see the groping that went on beneath the table. I could see this because I am short. Both were married, and this went on for years until she bore him a baby boy. She brought in the pictures to show him. However, she discontinued the relationship and continued her life with her husband after that.

This behavior was not limited to men. Some women whose husbands traveled for work kept boyfriends who appeared to be on call when the spouses were out of town. These were well-to-do women, and they footed the bill when they came with their boyfriends. One was the wife of a shipping company magnate. Her husband was out of town for a good part of the year, and she and her boyfriend came to dine regularly. They were always gracious to me. They enjoyed chatting with each other and appeared compatible and happy together. When her husband died in Hawaii in a helicopter crash, she and her boyfriend abruptly stopped coming to the restaurant.

Politicians came in, but they usually talked only with their colleagues, so there was no chance of getting to know them. There was, for instance, a prominent California state senator who would come with his entourage, and there was Secretary of State March Fong Eu, who would come with her bodyguard.

As always, the most enjoyable customers were working-class folks. I especially enjoyed the sports fans. They would come in happy and enthused, behave considerately, order, eat, go, and leave generous tips. They didn't linger long, so the space was quickly available for another customer, and the fast turnover resulted in more tips for me. Air traffic controllers were also gracious customers. A couple who owned an airplane parts company always gave me an extra gratuity in a card at Christmas.

Hockey players were among the nicest of the sports players. Oakland used to have a hockey team called the Seals. The players were mean at play but gentlemen when they dined. Most were Canadian. They were easy to wait on and tipped well. Occasionally, one would give me a spare pair of tickets to a game, though I never asked for any. In the evening, they would eat steak or chicken, but they would eat pasta before a game for quick energy and better vision. Meat, they said, took too long to digest, made them sluggish, and blurred their vision.

With long-time customers, I often knew their children and grandchildren from babyhood to adulthood. The jockey Mr. Holtz, and his wife, for instance, began by bringing in their baby grandson and putting him in a booster seat. As their grandson got older, I saw him less and less. Still, I always asked about him, and they enjoyed telling me of his accomplishments until one day, they brought him in as a grown man. He was six foot three inches, and his grandfather was only five foot two inches. He was a young gentleman, and it was a pleasure to meet him.

While working at Francesco's, I began to see the old patterns of discrimination and favoritism change. Two of my regular customers worked for Nike and were friends of my employer's son, Frankie, who managed the restaurant. They were good tippers, and they brought in free pairs of Nike shoes for Frankie. One day, they jokingly asked him, "So how come you keep this one on for so long? She's been here for years."

Frankie replied, "She's my minority."

He referred to the Affirmative Action program in place at the time, which required employers to hire a certain number of minorities in their establishment proactively. However, Frankie's statement was misleading. Although my presence helped fulfill Francesco's minority requirements, Frankie's father, Dewey, had hired me before Affirmative Action existed. I had known both Dewey and Bob, the maître d', through previous employment, and they had both recommended hiring me. Moreover, other minorities were working there. Frankie's reply, spoken as a not very gracious joke, reflected the conflicted sentiments surrounding Affirmative Action.

When I first came to Francesco's, it was my impression and understanding that Frankie had never associated with Chinese before, and he took a wait-and-see approach toward me. It didn't take long, however, before he came to like and respect me, so much so that he would cup my ears with his hands before saying a swear word as he knew that I didn't want to hear that kind of language. I was told that he said of me, "There's no one who can work the counter and front station like Helen."

The irony was that it wasn't a prime station. When Bob, the waitstaff manager, hired someone new, he ought to have promoted me to a better location, but he never did. He was an old-school manager who liked to pat and fondle the waitresses and call us "girls." He had been like that at Pland's, too, and I observed that the waitresses who responded positively to his overtures with flirtatious remarks and smiles were most likely to be advanced.

I wouldn't play that game. I chose instead to make lemonade from lemons and build up my station as well as I could by providing the best service. As a result, I developed a following of regular customers who chose to sit at the counter and tipped well.

When Frankie's younger sister, Theresa, took over management of the dining area in the mid-1970s, she and her father hired a female maître d', whom we called Billy. With Billy, there was no favoritism. She reviewed our performance, and on that basis, she promoted me to a better station. Also, Theresa took it upon herself to get rid of the old miniskirt and hot pants uniforms, which her father had established. Our new outfit consisted of white tuxedo shirts with black cummerbunds, slacks, and bow ties.

It was a favorite pastime of mine in all my employment to observe how my customers dined. There were sophisticated diners, average diners, and chow diners. There were gracious and generous customers and stingy and poorly behaved customers. With all, I tried to act well and not take bad behavior personally. I would walk up with a smile and greet my customers with a "good afternoon" or "good evening" and say something cheerful. Usually, they greeted me cheerfully back. I would judge whether they were there to talk business or on a date or out for a special occasion and wait on them accordingly. I tried to keep up on current events and fit my conversation to their interests, such as the stock market, real estate, cars, current affairs, sports, and so on. Some, however, I could tell wanted to eat quietly.

I had not always been so savvy. In my early days at Pland's, the owner spoke to the maître d' about me, saying that he observed that I was a good worker but hardly talked to the customers. He asked the maître d' to encourage me to be friendlier and more conversational. So I listened to what a fellow waitress said to one of her customers. When she served a slice of cheesecake, she joked, "Be careful now—you'll get fat," and she and the customer laughed. So when my customer ordered some strawberry shortcake, I tried the same line. But instead of laughing, my customer became upset.

"Are you insinuating that I'm fat?" she asked heatedly. I guess the other waitress knew her customer better. Still, after that, I kept listening to what the other waitresses talked about with their customers. After a time, I did get the knack of making small talk and pleasantries.

I observed that sports players were often less sophisticated diners than one might imagine, given their wealth and status. Basketball players were notorious for confusedly scanning the menu as though they didn't understand the terms and then looking up upon my arrival to ask, "So what's good today?" When I would name a suggestion, usually the special of the day, they would reply, "OK, I'll take that."

Once when I was working at Pland's, a husband rushed his wife to a booth, pulled the table out, seated her, and pushed the table back in. He then tossed the menus down on the table in front of her and shouted loud enough for everyone to hear, "You wanted me to take you out? We're here. Now order." She ordered but couldn't eat. They were well dressed and appeared well to do, but obviously, they weren't getting along.

One customer complained about the slice of lemon that I put in his iced tea. He said it took up space in the glass that could be filled with more tea. He felt cheated. I just apologized and filled his glass and offered more tea after that. Another customer at Francesco's complained that the spaghetti was so long that it was too hard to eat. The correct way to eat spaghetti is to begin by cutting it crossways and then twirling the spaghetti on a fork with the tines supported by the tablespoon. Cutting makes each bite manageable. However, rather than lecture my customer on spaghetti etiquette, I simply offered to exchange his meal for another and asked the cook to accommodate him. Finally, periodically, customers wanted the chef to alter a dish so much that the name on the menu would hardly apply.

I became an expert at spotting potential walkouts. One customer kept playing around with the bill, folding it and unfolding it. Then he stealthily deposited it in his shirt pocket. He got up, stopped by the cash register to get a toothpick, paused to say a few words to the cashier, and then walked out. I quickly reported him to the owner's son-in-law, Michael, who worked as a chef and was also a bodybuilder. He took off his chef's jacket, exited the side door, caught the customer in the parking lot, flexed his muscles, and asked the guy if he had paid the check.

In the meantime, I had followed the customer out the front door, and as he turned to talk to Michael, I saw him wrinkle the bill in the palm of his hand and toss it to the ground. "There it is," I said and pointed to the crumpled bill. Michael took the man by the arm and walked him back to the restaurant, saying, "Now let's go take care of this, OK?"

One couple sat at their table long after they had finished eating. The man got up to go to the restroom and was in there for a long time. I alerted the manager to watch the table and bathroom, thinking that the couple was staging a walkout. Sure enough, the woman got up and headed for the front door. At the same time, we heard the rear door buzzer ring. The manager immediately stopped the woman and had her wait while he went to the back and caught the man, at which point he walked him back to the front of the restaurant and made him pay.

When my father first learned of me being a waitress, he was ashamed of me. The Chinese considered waitressing a low, disreputable profession. Combined with my marrying a man he disapproved of, Ba refused to speak to me for a time. Essentially, he disowned me.

However, it is not only the Chinese who look down on waitresses. Even among Americans, many view waitresses as easy. The only time in my career that I refused to serve a customer was when one asked me how much I charged. And how many times have I heard the expressions "cheap waitress," "bubblegum-chewing waitress," or "She's just a waitress"? All of this hurt, especially as I took pride in my work. Most waitresses work hard. We've got families to care for and mortgages or rent and bills to pay like everyone else.

Unfortunately, during my long career, I did meet a few bad apples, the sorts who give all of us a bad name. The worst was a coworker who liked to brag about her sexual exploits in the employee lunchroom. She did get one fellow to marry her. He was a recent divorcee who enjoyed her performances, but he quickly divorced her. His family then sent him to Hawaii to help stabilize him. This coworker then thankfully left our place of employment.

Another unprofessional coworker bragged that if there was a guy she liked, she could get him to marry her. She did manage to get one man to do so, after which she quit work and got him to move with her to Texas to be near her family. The marriage didn't last long. After he divorced and returned to California, he came in to eat. He told me that the members of her family were like vultures.

Two of my regular customers at Francesco's were retired firemen. They had developed a business setting up performances with lights, sound systems, props, and the like. Sometimes they gave me spare pairs of tickets to shows that they set up, such as the Ice Follies ice-skating show or the circus. Their business was successful, and they drew a good pension from their fire career. They could live well, driving beautiful cars and going on expensive vacations. One of the fellows was married, and his wife wore fashionable clothes and looked professionally groomed. The other was recently divorced.

One of my gold-digging coworkers got the divorcee to ask her out for a date. The next day, his friend came in, shaking his head about it. "Jeez," he said, "they went back to her house, and he decided to stay over. By the time she removed her wig, her makeup, and her false teeth, which she tossed into a drawer, he lost his appetite, so to speak."

Again, most of my coworkers were not like this. There are some from Pland's with whom I am still friends. My friend Luella successfully raised three children and cared for her husband through his bout with cancer until his death before her retirement. My friend Lily stayed married to her husband for over sixty years until he died. And my friend Elsie continues to work to put her grandchildren through college. Now and then, we get together for lunch and fondly reminisce about the old days. I worked as a waitress for fifty-five years and only quit because of declining health and strength.

Whenever I go into a restaurant where the service is outstanding, I become nostalgic. I miss those days when I served people from all walks of life, from everyday working folks to wealthy businesspeople to politicians and celebrities, with my back straight and sturdy as I carried many dishes balanced on my arms or a tray above my head.

The day I picked up my last paycheck at Francesco's, my boss presented me with a sterling silver tip tray. Engraved words read, "To Helen. In appreciation for years of silver service."

30

RAISING STEPHANIE

My daughter was the great treasure to come from my marriage. Because of Oliver's neglect, she was for a long time my whole life, my pride, and my joy. Before I was married and had a child, I sometimes went to picnics or other social gatherings, but I didn't know the traditional songs people sang or how to participate in the sports or games that people played. I felt like an idiot. I told myself that if I ever had a child, I would make sure that she had many lessons so she would never have to feel left out or awkward as I did.

So as she was growing up, I gave her lessons in piano, violin, swimming, tennis, and ballet. I wanted her to have exposure to music and dancing, as well as athletics. At her pediatrician's recommendation, I bought her corrective shoes to straighten her legs, and later I bought her braces to straighten her teeth. I also took her to Sunday school at the Chinese Presbyterian Church. I wanted her to learn something about Christianity and God and have a place to learn right from wrong aside from home and school. I was particularly concerned that she should have some guidance in this respect since her father was not around much, and I was at work for most of the day.

I did the best that I could, but it wasn't easy on either of us. My limited English often restricted me. Once, when Stephanie was a baby and suffering from colic, I sought her pediatrician's advice. I didn't quite understand what he said but thought he recommended a teaspoon of oil. So I force-fed Stephanie a teaspoon of vegetable oil, and when this didn't work, I called the pediatrician again.

"You fed her a teaspoon of oil?" he asked, shocked. "I wanted you to rub it onto her belly."

I was so inexperienced and had few people around me with whom I could consult to know what was normal and what was not or what was a good practice, and what might be harmful. One night in our studio apartment, Stephanie was crying and fussing, so I pulled down the wall bed and lay her next to me, thinking this would comfort her. Her little hands were so cold, so I pulled a space heater next to her side of the bed to warm her. She continued to cry, but I thought nothing more of it until I noticed that she had developed a heat rash on her skin. Then I shoved the space heater away, feeling horrified.

When she was older, I could not afford childcare, so I brought her to a free preschool near the low-income housing projects in Oakland. Every morning, she was crying when I left her, and so I would cry on the bus all the way to work. When I went to pick her up, her nose might be clogged, or her pants might be wet, but she was so happy to see me, and my eyes filled with tears again.

Sadly, she bore the brunt, directly or indirectly, of my frustration and anger with Oliver. Like any toddler, she would dawdle over breakfast, and I would get so frustrated because I was in a rush to go to work, and Oliver didn't help me.

"Open up! Open up," I would say. If she didn't comply, I slapped her on the head so she would open her mouth, then I shoveled spoonsful of food into her. Then I dragged her behind me as I rushed down the street to get her to preschool on time. I am not proud of those episodes, but at length, I forced myself to stop slapping her because I knew it was wrong, and I didn't want to repeat my father's mistakes.

I never explicitly said anything unfavorable about Oliver to Stephanie. Whatever my feelings were about him, he was still her father, and she could and did form her judgment. Once when we were in the pediatrician's waiting room, there was a Newsweek magazine with a cover story about brainwashing. She could read a little and asked, "What is brainwashing?"

I explained that the article described a theory of how North Koreans controlled American prisoners. The idea was that by applying coercive mind-control techniques and repetition of propaganda, they sought to change the prisoners' fundamental beliefs and habits. Stephanie quietly considered this. That night, as Oliver prepared to leave for his gambling, she ran to stand on the threshold of our apartment, her arms and legs spread open to block the doorway.

"You can't leave," she said. "I am going to brainwash you!"

Oliver chuckled and tried to move past her. Stephanie moved to block him, so Oliver dodged to the other side of the doorway, and again she barred him. Finally, he pushed her aside and walked past her, much to her disappointment.

Another time, she called her father in our apartment. "Dad?" Oliver didn't answer, though he was certainly within earshot. "Dad?" she asked again. Still, Oliver did not reply. "Dad!" she called more urgently, and Oliver said nothing. "Oh, look," she said. "It's Marilyn Monroe!" Oliver's head spun around to look. I wanted to laugh and cry at the same time.

Still, there were bright spots. As a little girl, she had a vivid imagination and a set of imaginary friends. Superman was a favorite. She would tie a blanket around her neck to make a cape then jump from her dresser onto the bed. Stephanie did this so many times that the bed began to sag, and eventually, I bought her a new one. Once when I asked her to stop playing so I could send her to the grocery store for milk, she said, "Wait a minute . . . wait a minute," and she scribbled a note on a scrap of paper before leaving. After she left, I read her letter.

"Dear Superman," it read, "I am going to the store to buy milk for Mom. I will be right back."

Another time, I came home to find a note that read, "Mom, I went to . . . ," and there was a brown crayon smudge. I had no idea what this meant, and she wasn't supposed to go out of the house by herself once she got home from school. Nearly an hour later, she returned home, by which time I was frantic.

"Where have you been?" I demanded.

"Didn't you get my note?" she asked. "I went to the Brownie meeting with the Fong girls." She didn't know how to spell the word "Brownie," but she thought I would guess the meaning of her brown smudge. The Fong girls lived next door. These were the nieces of March Fong Eu, who later became California's secretary of state.

I loved to dress and groom her beautifully. Most people who remember her as a little girl recall her Shirley Temple curls, for I set her hair in curlers after each washing. Because her hair would usually have been straight, I took her to the salon from a young age for a permanent wave. When the beautician told her that there was a minute left for the chemicals to finish their work, she would loudly count backward from sixty to the amusement of the other customers. I splurged on beautiful clothes for her, which I starched every week to keep them fresh and crisp. When she slept, I polished her white leather shoes, so they were shiny and clean.

For fun, I took her to the movies and to stage shows. *Peter Pan*, both the stage show and Disney movie, was a favorite. When we first went to see it, she was thoroughly engrossed in the story and genuinely concerned for Peter Pan's wellbeing. Would Captain Hook capture him? Would he rescue Tiger Lily? Eventually, we saw it so often that she knew the script by heart and mouthed the words. "Do you believe in fairies?" Peter would ask, and Stephanie would clap her hands to say that, yes, she believed. She was thrilled to see him fly over the audience in the theater. I think she loved his sense of freedom as she was so much cooped up in the house while I was at work.

She loved comic books, and I bought her lots out of guilt for all the time she had to spend alone waiting for me to come home. Superman, Buck Rogers, Archie, and Little Lulu were favorites. In those days, funny books, as we called them, weren't graphically violent the way they are now. They were wholesome entertainment for children, and I had no apprehension about buying them. This era was the golden age of comics, and Stephanie treasured her collection. No matter where we were, she read her new comic books as soon as she received them.

In 1954, shortly before Stephanie entered the third grade, I bought a house on 236 Frisbie Street in Oakland. At the beginning of my marriage, I had saved money, which Oliver then gambled away. But once I followed Dean's advice to open a savings account in my name only, I was able to save three thousand dollars for a down payment. The house cost ten thousand. Oliver's brother Hart found it for us, and it was also Hart who found a broker to loan us the remaining balance.

Stephanie was to start third grade in a new school, and when some of the neighborhood children heard that she was going to have a Mr. Axelrod as a teacher, they all made faces, saying, "Eww, we don't like him. He's so strict." But as it turned out, Stephanie enjoyed the discipline. She flourished in his class, gaining confidence to participate more fully in class discussions. She appreciated the high expectations that Mr. Axelrod set for his students and strove to live up to them.

Similarly, she flourished under the tutelage of her violin instructor, Mr. Lee Cardo, who was quite strict and severe with her. He came to our house and gave the lessons in our living room with the door closed. From outside, I could hear him hollering at her and slapping his violin bow on my hassock. "No, no! The rhythm is duh-*duhn*-dun-dun, duh-*duhn*-dun-dun. Play it again." She would emerge from her lessons with tears in her eyes and her mouth shaking, and I felt so bad for her.

"Do you want to quit and try something else?" I asked one day. She shook her head and whispered no, almost too choked up to speak. I think that at some level, she knew that Mr. Cardo cared about her playing well and saw her potential, and that meant a lot to her, given that her father was so little involved in her life. In addition to her pride and love of music, I suspected that she also played to please me.

She worked hard, and by junior high, she earned a place as first violinist and concert mistress in the Oakland Junior Symphony Orchestra. She was responsible for helping tune the instruments of all the other players. Mr. Cardo was the conductor of the Richmond Symphony Orchestra, and he later invited her to play for that orchestra as well. I went to every one of her concerts, usually in my waitress uniform, because I didn't have time to change between shifts.

When Stephanie was about eleven years old, she and her girlfriend Cora asked to walk from our home on Frisbie Street to Piedmont Avenue, where there were shops and cafés. After confirming this was all right with Cora's mother, I gave Stephanie three dollars in spending money and told her to be back in a couple of hours. When she returned, I asked what they had done, and she replied that they had browsed through shops then stopped at the Key System Coffee Shop on 41st Street and Piedmont Avenue to split a milkshake. At the time, Oakland had a Key System Train, which took passengers across the Bay Bridge to San Francisco. The milkshake cost $1.75 plus 4 percent sales tax, and Stephanie put down an extra ten cents.

Cora asked, "What're the extra ten cents for?"

Stephanie explained, "It's the tip for the waitress. When a waitress serves you, you must tip her. That's how she earns a living." I was proud of her for saying that.

If we had continued to live on Frisbie Street, Stephanie would eventually have gone to Oakland Technical High School, which was not a well-rated school. So shortly before she was to enter high school, I began to look for a home in a better-quality neighborhood. Because Frisbie Street was in a poor area, we had no problem buying there. Now that we wanted to move up, we encountered many difficulties.

Our first real estate agent took us around to a few homes, but we never got to see the insides. He would leave us outside each house while he went to ask the owners if they were willing to sell to Chinese people, and the answer was always no. When he gave us this news, Stephanie and I would look at each other with disappointment. "Gee, they don't want to sell to us," I said. "Well, I guess we'll have to look elsewhere." We would walk away with our heads hung down, feeling discouraged. In my heart, I thought, *Those people are not any better than me.*

It was the same story with a second real estate agent. A third agent said he couldn't get anyone to loan me money, so he didn't bother showing us around. When I went to see lenders on my own, no one would talk to me even though I had a 20 percent down payment.

Finally, I went to a small, unknown real estate office and met a soft-spoken realtor there. After considering my story, he said he knew of a house that might work for me. A minister, whom he believed would sympathize with my case, owned a house at 2003 Hoover Avenue. It was a three-story home in excellent condition with a vast, sloped backyard. It was quite a bit more space than we needed, and it cost twenty-five thousand dollars. Still, it was a quality home in a good neighborhood where Stephanie could attend the newly opened Skyline High School, a much better school than Technical High. I told the realtor that I was interested.

The minister said that he would sell to me. However, there was still the problem of financing. The realtor found a bank that would loan to me if I put 28 percent down, a payment of seven thousand dollars, and I had only five thousand. The realtor again appealed to the minister, and he agreed to loan me two thousand dollars.

Now that I had two loans, one with the bank and one with the minister, I took a second job at the Tonga Room in San Francisco. I wanted to pay off the minister's loan as quickly as possible. I was so grateful to him for what he had done for Stephanie and me. I usually paid double the amount required each month and managed to pay off my loan with him in just two years.

I tried to help Stephanie with the homework at her new school the best that I could. She asked me to help her with algebra, for instance.

"Well, let's start with the first sentence," I would say. After reading each sentence, we would talk about it and decide what we thought it meant. Fortunately, Stephanie was bright, and she usually caught on quickly. I also helped her by quizzing her in memorization exercises such as for Greek mythology, spelling, or recognition of composers for her music class.

Once when I was quizzing her about compound words, she gave the example of "double-delicious."

"No, that's not right," I said.

"Yes, it is," she insisted. "I heard it on TV. There's double-delicious double-mint gum."

"No, no." I laughed. "That's a made-up word." When I really could not help her, such as with the writing of essays, I sometimes hired a tutor.

She didn't have any siblings, but she had several boy cousins about the same age, the sons of her Aunt Emma, and from them, she learned to be a tomboy. I would have preferred that she had not played with them so much, for they played rough, and she was as likely as any of them to come home with a bruise or black eye. But I could hardly keep her apart from them when they lived across the street, and they were family.

Perhaps because of her friendship with them, she learned to be athletic and mechanically inclined. Her counselor in high school said that she worked well with her hands. She was virtuosic with the violin, but she also had a knack for figuring out how things worked. She even performed minor maintenance on her car, such as draining and refilling the radiator.

She had always played a variety of sports. In elementary school, she had loved her corrective shoes because they were rigid, which enabled her to kick the ball the farthest in the kickball games. She won a broad-jumping competition in junior high, even beating a girl reputed to be particularly good at it.

In short, she was all that a mother could hope for, being thoughtful and intelligent as well as musically and athletically gifted. Out of all my sad and disappointed feelings concerning Oliver, perhaps my greatest was that he never realized his daughter's talent. He never once attended any of her concerts or sporting events to see her perform as the first violinist and win competitions. He never helped with her homework to see how smart she was. He threw away a real life, real love, and a real family for the artificial glitter of gambling and didn't even realize what he had lost.

Once I begged him to join us on a family day, and he agreed to attend a movie with us. On the way to the theater, Stephanie asked from the backseat whether we could see a film in which she was interested.

"Who's paying for this? You or me?" he replied. "We'll go see . . . ," and he named a movie that he wanted to see. So that was our family outing.

Another time, we went on a trip to Lake Tahoe. On the way there, we stopped to fish. For a fee, a man cleaned and cooked our fish for us, and we ate it at a picnic table outdoors. For a brief time, it felt like being happy together. But once we arrived in Tahoe, Oliver kept bugging me for cash to go gambling. When I objected that this was supposed to be a family vacation, he angrily replied, "We may as well go home. What's the point of staying?" So I relented as there would be no pleasure in attempting to keep his company. Oliver hit the casinos while Stephanie and I swam and walked around the beaches.

Oliver took Stephanie and me to the family gatherings at Grandma Chan's home on holidays. He would stay for half an hour and then leave. I didn't ask where he went, and I didn't know when he would return. We had become two people living in the same house but leading separate lives.

In the end, everyone but Oliver could see the value of what was right in front of him. Once when I was recounting Stephanie's accomplishments to a customer, a man I did not know sat listening nearby. My words and pride so moved him that at the end of his meal, he gave me the cash left in his wallet, which was twenty-eight dollars, and said, "You buy something nice for that daughter of yours." I never saw him before or afterward.

Under trying circumstances, I did my best to bring up my little girl. I made mistakes, but I did understand that there aren't any shortcuts to raising a child. A child knows when she is cheated of the love and care that she deserves. So I also know that there was a hole in Stephanie's heart where her father ought to have been. The apple does not fall far from the tree. I also had a painful relationship with my father. Yet Stephanie had my blessings as well. She understood how to grasp what opportunities I could provide and make the most of them. I could not ask for more.

31

THE DARKEST TIME

Not long after starting to work at Pland's, I suffered from chronic illness. Often, I had a headache and sinus pain that felt like something was jerking inside my head. I thought my busboy's strong cologne might be the cause. There was an I. Magnin department store buyer who dined at Pland's. She would arrive drenched in expensive perfume, and the busboy complimented her fragrance so much that she offered to select a cologne for him. Soon after, he came in reeking of the stuff. I have always been sensitive to scent, and if his was not the cause of my headache, it certainly did nothing to relieve it.

So I went to the doctor, who prescribed a pain reliever. But a few months later, I was again in his office complaining of a constriction or lumpy feeling in my chest, which made it difficult to breathe. On another occasion, I complained of pain in my liver area. These visits, during which I complained of various aches and pains, occurred every few months for a period of some eighteen months. One day, the doctor, noticing my perpetually downcast expression, asked, "Helen, are you happy?"

At these words, tears rolled down my face.

"Tell me everything that is happening in your life," he said. Weeping, I told him everything. I explained how my husband gambled, how he was frequently unemployed, how he didn't come home at night, how painful it was to see my daughter without a real father. I told him so many things that I had never discussed with anyone. Ba disapproved of Oliver so intensely that I donned a brave face in front of family as though to prove him wrong.

When I had finished my story, the doctor told me that my symptoms were real but that disease was not the principal cause. My great unhappiness was the cause of most of my physical pain.

"Would you like me to talk to Oliver?" the doctor asked.

I said, "Yes, I would like that."

I told Oliver that the doctor wished to meet with him to discuss my health, and he agreed. I was not sure what to expect. The doctor always spoke to me gently, so I was taken aback at his tone of righteous anger in speaking to Oliver.

"Now listen," he began, "this girl is ill. It's like a cancer. Her great unhappiness, the result of your poor treatment and neglect, is causing her to have a real physical illness. I think you should let her go and let her get a better life, or else you take care of her like she's your real wife. She's a young woman, only in her thirties. She deserves to be cherished, to be loved, to be respected, to have a real shot at life before it's too late."

The doctor went on and on in this manner so that Oliver's face turned red, and I stood with my mouth half-open. In all my life, no one had ever stood up for me like that.

After this talk, I thought things might get better between Oliver and me. Instead, he was furious that I had brought him in to be chastised as the cause of my illness. He took me home from the doctor's appointment and immediately went out again without a word. Soon, he was staying out even later at night. When I related this to the doctor, he advised me to divorce him.

"If you don't divorce him, you will continue to be ill of a broken heart." I thought of my mother and how unhappiness had also contributed to her poor health. Still, within the constraints of my culture, I did not imagine my life would improve through a divorce.

I quietly replied, "There is no divorce in my culture. It is a disgrace." The only Chinese person I had ever known to get a divorce was Charlie Low, the Forbidden City nightclub owner. In general, among the Chinese, divorce was considered such a moral failure as to be unthinkable. Over a decade later, May would divorce in the early 1970s, but the culture had shifted by then, allowing it to be somewhat acceptable.

Just as quietly, the doctor replied, "Then you are going to have to accept him. You will have to accept him the way he is, and you are going to have to get on with your life the best you can. You must let him go in your mind and focus on living the best life that you can."

I did try. Oliver was now sometimes gone for days, and I didn't ask where he went. My sister-in-law mentioned once that he had gone to Nevada. She said it in a way that assumed that I knew his whereabouts. When I expressed surprise at her comment, she was embarrassed, for she had thought that I knew.

Yet I was happier to a degree. I made Stephanie my life, focusing on her progress and accomplishments. Most importantly, I stopped waiting for Oliver to make a life with me. I stopped waiting for him to join us for movies and vacations. When I wanted to see a show or get away, I invited Oliver to join us, and when he declined, we went on our own. I took Stephanie on a trip to Detroit to visit my cousin Kerwin. Another time, we went to Hawaii with my friend Lily Gee. In short, I stopped waiting for my life to happen.

Some ten years passed in this way. If it wasn't a complete life, it was part of a life, and I hoped for something better for my child. I had bought the house on Frisbie Street, traveled a bit, played mahjong with friends now and then, and treasured Stephanie's successes in my heart.

Then, one day, my marriage collapsed with surprising abruptness. On an afternoon in 1960, I came home to find condoms on Oliver's nightstand. Condoms were not our form of birth control. I was shocked.

I have to do something, I thought, feeling faint. In hindsight, I suppose I should have expected this, given our estranged relationship. But for me, marriage was so sacred an institution that I had trusted. When you are married, that is it, I thought. There is no one else.

I had considered Oliver's gambling as a disease or addiction, something not wholly under his control. But infidelity was a deliberate breaking of the last thread of covenant between us, and he had done it in my own home that I had earned with my hard work. That was the straw that broke the camel's back. Suddenly, I wasn't confused or scared anymore.

I went to work on the dinner shift at Pland's. In a daze, I told a fellow waitress what happened and that I was thinking of divorce. I had never believed in it before, but now I thought of it. The bartender overheard our conversation and said, "If you want a divorce, you can use my lawyer." On the spot, I got the phone number from him.

When I had completed the filing, I calmly handed Oliver the papers prepared by my lawyer and explained what they were. "Stephanie and I will stay in the house," I said, "and I want you to move out. I've found you a room for rent not far from her, and I've paid the first month's rent, so you should leave immediately."

He said little and appeared resigned. He packed his beautiful suits, but he left without signing the papers. Later, I learned that my breaking of our marriage had a more significant effect on him than I had imagined. Not long after our separation, Stephanie came home one day to find him passed out on my bed with a trickle of blood coming from his mouth, and she was unable to wake him.

I had long complained about how bad his mouth smelled, for he neglected the care of his teeth entirely, and they were rotting. After I filed for divorce, he decided to have all his teeth removed and replaced with false teeth. He had come to the house to tell me or show me what he had done for me. But the dentist had administered so much anesthesia that he passed out.

Stephanie, in her panic, called for an ambulance, which took Oliver to the hospital. My in-laws contacted me, and Dean brought me to the hospital to see him. I asked him if he was OK, and he mumbled something. We exchanged some polite words, and then I left. The gesture did nothing to change my mind.

My lawyer said I could take everything and encouraged me to

do so, for he considered that Oliver had abandoned his wife and daughter. There was the house, some stock, a whole life insurance policy, and our two cars. I could have taken it all and left Oliver destitute. But I would not. I kept the house, my car, and half the insurance, leaving him his car, the stock, and the remaining insurance. Vengeance is one of those dark emotions that scar the soul, and I wanted to quit the marriage with a clean heart.

If I was initially confident that I was making the right decision, I doubted myself in the following weeks. In China, divorce was an almost unheard-of disgrace. If the situation wasn't quite so extreme in the United States, Americans still viewed it askance. In either culture, marriage gave a woman status. However, the American divorcee was the subject of crude jokes and regarded as a moral failure by many.

However, an event soon happened that solidified my determination. I was walking across Piedmont Avenue in Oakland when a car came fast around the corner of a side street and struck me, knocking me the length of several storefronts down the street. The impact knocked out my two front teeth and twisted my eye teeth. I remember the moments before the car struck as though they were in slow motion. I remember seeing the speeding car and wanting to get out of the way and the sickening panic of knowing there wasn't time.

I do not remember what happened immediately afterward, but I know that I went into shock in the ambulance. I felt so cold that I shook uncontrollably, no matter how many blankets the paramedics piled on me. In the emergency room, the physician gave me a drug to treat shock, which caused me to break out in hives. He then administered another drug to counteract the allergic reaction. The rash and shaking began to subside. Amazingly, the impact had not broken my bones.

At the hospital, I contacted Jeannie to pick up Stephanie, so she could stay with her. After a night, the hospital released me, but I suffered from severe whiplash for a week and a half. I took a pain reliever, but this only dulled the sensation. Pain, drugs, and confinement brought depression. I couldn't stop crying.

Oliver's family came to visit, and my good friend Lily Gee also came to see me. Stephanie did the best that she could to care for herself while I was laid up. She was about thirteen years old. I appreciated that she supported my decision to divorce. Before filing, I had sat down with her to discuss my plans and ask how she felt. She told me she was on my side, that she could see the unhappiness in my face, my voice, and my whole body. She hoped divorce would turn the tide of our lives.

The shred of silver lining from the accident was that I regained resolve. I considered that I had nearly died, and my life to that point had amounted to so little. Was this all that I wanted to look back upon at the end of my life? I decided that I still wanted my slice of happiness on this earth before I left.

On the appointed date, I went to court for the divorce hearing. However, Oliver didn't show up. When the clerk called my name, my lawyer spoke with the judge for a short time, and then the judge granted me a no-contest divorce. I was free at last.

Or so I thought. Almost as soon as my divorce was final, everything I feared came to pass. Entering the dining room at Pland's, I could sense the whispered gossiping around me.

"Now there's one who's hot to trot I'll bet," cracked a bartender. I hated that expression. I had wanted to be a lady and respected all my life, and here was my colleague speaking of me as though I were cheap.

As for my Chinese friends, they all wanted to get me married off again as soon as possible. Nature abhors a vacuum, and the Chinese abhor an unmarried woman in her thirties.

"Hey, Helen, I have a friend who's looking for a wife," one said.

"I'm not interested," I replied.

Another invited me to her house for a party. "Don't bring any food. Just come and enjoy yourself. You don't have to do anything. We'll have fun," she said. So I agreed, but she introduced me to a single man there almost as soon as I arrived. I really had no interest, so I spent most of the evening avoiding him, and then I left early.

Another friend, Betty, said a fellow at her son's office wanted to take someone to the office Christmas party. "It'll be a nice time for you," she insisted. Reluctantly, I agreed. But when we got to the party, I found that everyone was drinking like mad, and they wanted to load me up as well. I had barely started one drink when the hostess put another in front of me. This crowd was not for me.

My date and I had come in separate cars. I asked him to take me to mine, and as soon as we got there, I jumped in and drove off. I didn't want to see him again, and I didn't want him to know where I lived. But the next day, he parked in front of the restaurant, apparently waiting for me to leave work. So I left out the back door. The following day, he again parked in front of the restaurant, so I exited out the back once more. To my relief, he did not appear on the third day.

In the mornings, it was my habit to arrive early at the restaurant and sit at a table to eat muffins and coffee while preparing my checks for the day. Soon, a bartender named Lindy began to join me. He breakfasted, too, and engaged me in conversation so that I began to like and trust him. After a time, he asked me out for a date, and I accepted. He flirted, showered me with compliments, and made me feel special. I felt like I was falling in love.

But when I happily related this to another bartender named Bonnie, she told me that Lindy was married and that he had made me the subject of a boast. Bonnie had said of me, "Now that one is untouchable," and Lindy had replied, "Wanna bet?"

At these words, I felt sick to my stomach. Suddenly, I felt utterly disgraced, stripped of what little status and dignity I had ever had. I had been unhappy in marriage, and it appeared that there was to be even less happiness out of wedlock. In blinding tears, I drove home from Pland's. I drove so erratically. It is a wonder that I did not crash the car.

All my life, I had thought that a guardian angel looked out

for me—my dear mother in heaven perhaps, someone who kept me alive and hopeful even when I fell into the worst straits. But now, I couldn't see or believe in my angel anymore. Not since my stepmother had laid me out on the death board in our village in China had I felt so hopeless. I couldn't see any silver lining, and all I knew was that I didn't want to think or to feel. Blindly, I swallowed sleeping pills and aspirin and fell into a deep, dreamless sleep from which I might not have awakened.

However, my guardian angel had not abandoned me after all. Stephanie came home after school to find me passed out in bed, still breathing but beyond her ability to rouse me. She telephoned James, who was thankfully at home and called for an ambulance, which took me to the Highland Hospital Emergency Room in Oakland. I remember as though in a dream that a nurse undressed me and said to her assistant, "She's a very pretty girl."

They let me sleep off the drugs, and after a one-night stay, James and Anna brought me home. They stayed a little while and then left. We never spoke of this incident afterward, nor did we speak of it to our family.

I still did not see happiness for me, but if it was Stephanie who saved me, then it was for her that I must go on living. She was in junior high and needed a mother. For her sake, most of all, I was ashamed of what I had done. Finding me had been a shock and fright for her. So, gritting my teeth, I resolved to get on with my life.

32

TOM

My divorce was final at the end of 1961. Oliver's mother had passed away years ago. A cousin, Lily, remained friendly, but for the most part, the family quietly withdrew contact. I was no longer part of their clan. Only Emma was so angry that she insulted me to Stephanie and poured sugar down my gas tank so I couldn't drive my car. It was a parting blow. I didn't retaliate as that is not my nature. However, we lived on the same block; I knew it was time for a fresh start. Stephanie and I went house-shopping, and that was when I bought the minister's house.

In the following year, I worked hard. I dated here and there when my friends insisted on matching me with someone. However, I soon concluded that if I was to date, it must be with a man of my choosing. He must be Westernized, the sort of fellow who would open doors and offer to carry things for me. Mostly, however, I wasn't looking for anyone. Dating and marriage had been nothing but trouble.

At the end of 1962, a man named Tom came into Pland's. He was a high school teacher who was there to meet a fellow teacher for a first date; however, the woman never showed. I happened to be the waitress attending him. Our first meeting was an ordinary interaction between a customer and waitress, as far as I recall. Nonetheless, I must have made some impression, for the next night, he came again to dinner and asked for me. My coworker Daisy informed him that I had just left since I wasn't working that evening's shift.

He returned the next evening and, seeing me, asked the maître d' to seat him at my table. We chitchatted, but I still did not suspect anything and only thought that he was conversational. However, he returned the following evening for supper, and we chatted again. He told me that he was a math teacher and had recently moved to California from Oklahoma. I noticed that he ordered the same entrée each time—the cheapest on the menu, beef stew. I supposed that Pland's was upscale for a teacher's salary.

I also noticed that he never had any money on him. Instead, he would ask to write a check for five dollars to cover his bill as well as the fifty-cent tip. Usually, when someone presented a check, I was supposed to get the manager to approve it, but I thought he had an honest face and manner, so I OK'd it myself. That meant that if he bounced a check, I would be responsible for it. But none bounced.

The following week, Tom came again on the first night shift that I worked. This time, he invited me to join him at a concert of the San Francisco Symphony for which he had tickets.

"Well, I'll think about it. Maybe we could meet for coffee tomorrow," I said, and he agreed. Then I told my good friend Elsie that Tom had asked me out and asked her opinion.

"Don't go with him," she replied emphatically. "Look at the company he keeps."

There was a woman recently separated from her husband. She came to the restaurant with her girlfriend as she knew that her estranged husband ate there, and she was trying to win him back. Her husband ate there every evening after closing his business. She would come with her girlfriend and sit at the table next to him to drink cocktails. Both women dressed in form-fitting, low-cut dresses.

The ex-wife was loudly witty, occasionally throwing out a seductive conversational lure to her ex-husband, who would grunt noncommittal replies from his table. He had no interest in returning to his former situation. Still, the woman didn't tire of trying to win back his affections in this manner. Tom began sitting at a table next to both parties. He appeared to enjoy the view of the ladies as well as the drama and humor, occasionally chuckling to himself. Elsie did not think much of him because of this.

I told Stephanie that this guy wanted to take me to a concert, but I was going to coffee with him first to check him out and make sure he was all right. We went to the city of Orinda to an ice-cream parlor that I liked. I had just three hours for the date between work shifts. We each had a scoop of ice cream and a coffee. He talked about the upcoming concert in San Francisco and other inconsequential matters. I liked that he was not pushy or overly familiar. He wasn't the kind of guy who tried to put his arm around me on a first date. We just talked, and he said that he thought my accent was cute. When I got home, I told Stephanie that he seemed decent.

The following Sunday, he suggested going on a tour of the three Bay Area bridges: the Bay Bridge, the Golden Gate Bridge, and the Richmond-San Rafael Bridge. We stopped for refreshments at a restaurant with a cocktail lounge on Van Ness Avenue on our way through San Francisco. Tom ordered a Manhattan, and I said I'd have the same. I had never had a Manhattan, and after a few sips, I realized that I wasn't a bourbon drinker. I've never had a Manhattan since.

I figured that a guy who would take me on a tour of three bridges for an outing was probably trustworthy. When he brought up the topic of the concert again, I agreed to go. Toward the end of the date, I said that I needed to go to work because I worked a Sunday evening shift in the cocktail lounge of Father Hine's restaurant on Jack London Square. Father Hines was a famous blues singer who had opened a restaurant in his retirement.

The following week, we went to the San Francisco Symphony. I didn't fully appreciate the music. Mostly I knew about classical music because it was what Stephanie played on her violin. I proudly said in a loud whisper, "My daughter is the first violinist in her orchestra. I go to see all of her concerts." But Tom, enchanted with the music, was a little annoyed that I talked during the performance.

Over the next few weeks, we went to a movie here and there, but we often didn't have enough time or money to go anywhere. At night when I got off work, he would pick me up to bring me home, and at first, we would sit and talk in his car with the windows rolled down because I didn't feel that I knew him well enough to invite him into the house. Tom's car was an ancient Plymouth station wagon that he had affectionately dubbed Old Jessica. It had a door that didn't close too well, and its top speed was thirty-five miles per hour, so everyone gave us a dirty look on the freeway, not that I ever cared or even really noticed. Stephanie was bothered by it when she joined us for a ride. She was so embarrassed going that slow on the freeway that she slumped down in the backseat so as not to be seen through the window.

My good friends, the Edmonds, who dined regularly at Pland's, soon took notice of Tom's attention toward me at the restaurant. "Now, what's going on between you two?" Frances asked me with a sly smile. So I introduced them to Tom, and they kindly invited the two of us to dinner in their beautiful Japanese-style home. They served a formal, English-style dinner on their lovely collection of porcelain. In the end, they smiled and nodded goodnight to the two of us as though to say that they approved.

A little over a month after our first date, the subject of marriage came up, which was a complex topic for me. Even at thirty-nine years old, I could not say that I understood how to give or receive romantic love. My parents' marriage had been about working and surviving. My father taught me to believe that physical affection was "dirty" or unwholesome. I still remembered when I watched a couple kissing on the street, and my father slapped me for my curiosity. My first marriage had been disastrous from the beginning. Still, I had stayed for sixteen years because, as the saying goes about that era, "Divorce? No. Murder? Yes."

But as for Tom, when he said he would do a thing, he did it. And when he said he would be at a place at a particular time, he was there on time and usually early. I liked that he wasn't pushy, that he behaved like a gentleman, and, most of all, that he appeared to have integrity.

We had our share of differences. When I visited friends, I would call ahead and then bring food to share. In my culture, one must bring something to share—oranges, teacakes, cookies, or something similar. It is bad manners to show up empty-handed. But Tom, being Caucasian, couldn't understand it and would get a little impatient when we had to stop at a grocery store to pick up goodies on the way to someone's house. He'd say, "Where I come from in Oklahoma, if we've got a friend, we can just show up when we feel like it, and they're glad to see us, and they serve iced tea. We don't have to bring anything."

He had a master's degree, and he was fond of books, especially about military history, having served in the navy during World War II. He could hold long conversations with educated people, citing historical references, dates, and quotes by famous personalities. Yet when it came to everyday matters of household management, he was impractical. I asked him once to hang a set of pictures for me in a configuration, and he looked dubious and said he wasn't sure how to do it. I was surprised, wondering how a mathematician could not figure out the proper spacing between objects to create a pattern. At any rate, I went ahead and got out the hammer and nails myself, made some measurements, and got the pictures up in little time.

Still, in my line of work, I had observed all types of people from all walks of life. I saw many people who cheated on their relationships or were ill-mannered or selfish. I had seen more good customers than bad, and I had observed and experienced enough in my life to know that integrity meant all the world to me. I did not know much about romance, and there were these cultural, educational, and financial differences between us. Still, I knew what was fundamentally important to me if I entered a marriage again, and that was integrity.

I believe that Tom appreciated my consideration. One evening, he had a bad cold and wasn't feeling well. When we parted, I said,

"I'll say a prayer for you to feel better." Afterward, he said that he felt touched by that.

So we discussed marriage for several evenings at some length. Tom also had been married before and had three high-school-age children. They mostly lived with their mother but stayed with Tom at certain times of the year. So we discussed what each of our children was like and how our living arrangements might work. Finally, when it appeared clear to me that we had decided to get married, I said, "But we can't just get married. We have to get engaged first."

He apologized that he couldn't afford a ring yet because he didn't have enough money. His divorce had left him in debt, and he owed monthly alimony and child support. I replied, "Well, I know of a place where we can look."

Oliver's brother Hart had told me of a wholesale jeweler with whom he was on friendly terms. We went to the jeweler's office on 15th Street in Oakland between San Pablo and Telegraph, where the jeweler buzzed us in. We went up a flight of stairs to an office, where the jeweler brought out trays of rings and loose gems. I selected a platinum set with a half-carat diamond. It cost $250, and I paid for it myself since Tom was so broke. Someday, he said, he would buy me a ring that was just from him. Then we selected a plain platinum band for him.

He suggested that we celebrate by going out to dinner on Valentine's Day. "Where do you want to go?" he asked, and I suggested the Tonga Room at the Fairmont Hotel in San Francisco. We brought the engagement ring with us to dinner and made a little ceremony of his putting it on my finger. The restaurant's photographer came to our table and snapped a photograph. We look a little tentative and awkward in it, almost like a couple on a first date. After all, in just over a month after meeting, we were now engaged to be married.

Tom was still new to California. He later told me that he thought I was beautiful as soon as he met me, but I looked so different from the sort of girls with peaches-and-cream complexions that he saw in Oklahoma that he wasn't sure he could get used to me. However, he thought I was kind and thoughtful, and he was lonely and getting older. Neither of us believed in sex before marriage. Tom said with a smile, "Well, when I made up my mind to like you, naturally I was eager to get married."

We had planned to marry in April 1963. However, my friend Elsie, a follower of Chinese astrology, determined that April would be an unlucky time. She insisted that we move our date to March 16, just a month after our engagement. The Chinese frown on divorce and second marriages, so I didn't feel it was my place to have a big wedding or celebration. We decided to get married quietly on our own. Through the National Automobile Club, I made a reservation for a chapel in Reno, Nevada.

At the time, Tom was renting a room from a widow named Mrs. Cling. When he gave notice and informed her of his plans to marry a Chinese, she initially expressed her disapproval, for she did not think much of Chinese. But when Tom talked about the things he liked about me, she, at last, gave her blessing. She sewed two dog-bone-shaped pillows that she stuffed with her old stockings as a wedding present. I was happy to receive them as a token of her friendship. I still have one, which I use as a comfortable neck pillow now and then. I gave the other to Stephanie when she said her neck was hurting her.

Stephanie was cautiously happy for me. She perceived that Tom was honest and that he genuinely cared for me. However, after a lifetime in which she could only depend on me, she worried what it would be like to have a new father figure in the house.

After leaving Stephanie with her Auntie Jeannie, we drove up to Reno on a Friday after I got off work and checked into separate rooms at the Mapes Hotel, as we were not yet married. The following afternoon, we went to the Park Wedding Chapel across the street from the Washoe County Court in downtown Reno. The chapel held wedding ceremonies all day by appointment. When we arrived, the previous couple had a moment ago finished their service and were preparing to leave. We noticed that they were dressed in crumpled, casual clothes as though they had just driven up and stepped out of the car to get married.

But Tom wore a suit, and I dressed in a pink, knee-length wool dress with silk flowers in my hair. I carried a white leather Bible that Tom's mother had sent me and a flower tied with ribbons for a bouquet. The chapel was small but cheerful, with a few rows of seats decorated with pink bows. Candles and sprays of flowers decorated the altar and recorded church music played. The minister explained what to expect and then proceeded with the ceremony. An older couple came in to act as witnesses, a photographer snapped a photo, and, in short, we were married.

After our ceremony, we walked back to the Mapes, where we attended the free entertainment offered in the lounges. On Sunday, we drove back home in time to go to work on Monday.

I had taken Tom to meet my parents at their apartment house in Chinatown shortly before our marriage. They had purchased a small triplex; they lived in one unit and rented out the others. My stepmother served tea and Chinese sweet and savory pastries. My father was polite, but privately he counseled me, "Be careful of these Caucasians. They use you up in your youth and dump you when you get older."

"I don't think Tom is like that," I replied, and I thought it ironic that he should say this to me when it was a Chinese man who had used up my youth. Ba was, however, a little pleased that Tom was a teacher, for he had always wanted me to marry a professional.

James also was wary of the match, saying, "Well, I hope you have not jumped out of the frying pan and into the fire." However, all my sisters were warmly welcoming toward Tom and told me that they liked him.

A little before our wedding, I had written a letter to Tom's parents, Tom and Ruth Cochran, introducing myself. Tom also had written to let them know of his impending marriage. I had already got to meet his youngest brother and sister-in-law, Bob and Pat when they came to visit from Oklahoma.

In reply to Tom's letter, his mother, whom we called Moms, wrote back as follows (spelling and punctuation not corrected from the original):

Dear Tommy and Helen,

Well, my thoughts are all with you all today. I don't seem to be able to get my mind on my work, for thinking about you and if you have had your wedding yet. I just pray for your happiness for you both seem like such nice people.

I do wish we had have gotten to talk a little more the other night, but maby we will before to long. Helen, we were so glad to talk to you even tho it was just a little while.

About you coming to see us, we want you to, just as soon as you all can. About you being accepted back here, you will be by all of our friends, and the others don't count as far as I am concerned.

One of the best friends I have is a Mexican, and she is accepted in all the social affairs in Sentinel the same as we are. Of course, this is just a small place, but we do have nice friends. Now I don't want you to think another thing about what people might say about your nationally as far as I am concerned you are my daughter in law and your being Chinese is no different than my being a mixture of Scotch, English, and a few other things such as some Irish and I don't know what else.

I do believe the people have changed back here in the last few years about such things. For we have had a Japanese family or two living in Sentinel, and they were sure well-liked.

I do hope your father is pleased about your marriage by now. I can understand him being concerned about what kind of a person Tommy is, but when he get to know him, I'm sure he will like and respect him. The important thing in a person as far as I am concerned is their character, and I know Tom has a good one and that you do to so that is what counts. Helen, Bob and Pat wrote us such nice things about you. They really did love you from the very first time they saw you I think. Pops and I was talking last night about going out to see you all some time this summer, and we both want to if we can at all. We have never been to San Francisco, so would love to see the country up there.

Pops said if he couldent get off that I could go any way. But I would enjoy it so much more if we can come out together.

Tommy, we were so happy to hear about your progress in your teaching. The coaching job sounds like it would be kinda fun for you as well as you like ball games. We are just so proud of you, but of course you know. O, say Tommy, Ruby [a family friend] said to tell you that they were so happy that you had found some one you could love and that loved you and that they were looking forward to seeing you all when you came home.

Why don't you all take some pictures of your home and of all four of the children and you all and send us. Dosen't Mari or Sherri have a Kodak?

When Jack and Faye [Tom's younger brother and his wife] come up we will take some pictures and send you all.

Lots and lots of love to both of you, Mother

P.S. Pops said to give you all his love and say that he was looking forward to seeing all of you. Tommy you know he just dosent write unless he is forced to. Moms.

And so, with expressions both of concern and welcome from both of our families, my new life began.

33

KIMMIE

About a year after our marriage, I found that I was expecting. I had mixed feelings about this. On the one hand, I had anticipated that I might begin a family with my new husband. On the other hand, being forty, I worried about how my age might affect the baby's health. With Stephanie about to graduate from high school, it felt hard to be starting over. I remember being a little angry to find that I was pregnant and Tom replying something like, "Well, it took two to tango." However, there was no turning back, so I reconciled myself and began to look forward to the child.

Over nine months, I gained just thirteen pounds because I felt pain around my sternum every time I tried to eat. In the mornings, I could eat only one slice of toast. I never needed to buy or make maternity clothes as the style in women's clothing was already high-waisted. We agreed that if the child were a boy, Tom would name him and if a girl, I would name her.

On December 26, 1964, sometime after Tom had gone to sleep, I felt myself going into labor. So I rose, dressed, put on a little makeup, and fixed my hair. When I was completely ready, I woke Tom and said it was time to go. I didn't want to wake him earlier because I thought he would have time to panic and get us excited. If he only had to dress and get in the car, we would both be calmer.

We had expected the baby around the time of the winter solstice, so we had already packed our bags. We had even brought our bags to the Yee family Christmas party and parked our car facing the hospital in the event we had to leave suddenly. However, the baby didn't come that night.

My water began to leak at home and continued at the hospital, both in the elevator and admissions office. I couldn't quite believe that the registrar insisted that I complete all the paperwork while I was dripping water onto the floor of her office.

I knew that I wanted sodium pentathol to take away the pain. I had a good experience with it before with no side effects or aftereffects, and I had discussed this with Tom. But when I got to the delivery room, a nurse asked Tom to leave, as was the custom at that time, and I was in so much pain that I couldn't remember the name of the drug I wanted.

"I don't want to feel anything," I managed to say to the doctor.

"You don't want to take anything?" the doctor replied, a little surprised.

"No . . . I don't want to feel anything," I repeated faintly.

So the doctor administered a saddle block, which was the one drug that I didn't want. A saddle block would leave the back of my hips painful for months after the birth and left me nauseous and without an appetite for days. Afterward, the doctor recommended swimming to alleviate hip pain.

On December 27, 1964, at 11:05 a.m., a six-pound, six-ounce baby girl was born to me, whom I named Karin Kim. She was of average length at nineteen and a half inches, but she was so skinny and frail that I wondered if her little neck would ever be able to hold up her head. I am lactose intolerant and could not drink milk during the pregnancy, nor did I have calcium supplements. What calcium she could get to build her tiny bones was depleted from me. She would always be small-boned.

After the birth, the nurses whisked her away to be cleaned and wrapped. I held her briefly, and then she was taken to the maternity ward to sleep and be fed in a bassinet so I could rest. When Tom came to the window, a nurse held her up for viewing. I hardly saw her during my hospital stay. I held her once, but, generally, nurses picked her up when she cried and fed her formula from a bottle.

There were few births when I gave birth to Stephanie during

World War II, so I stayed in the hospital for over a week, and the hospital staff pampered me. A nurse even came in every day to comb and arrange my hair. But as Karin Kim was born at the end of the Baby Boom, the maternity ward was so packed that I had to leave the hospital after a stay of only one night.

People stared when Tom and I took her out in the baby carriage. The Civil Rights Act had only just passed, outlawing segregation between the races in schools and public places. Although interracial marriage had been legal in California since 1948, it was rare. In many parts of the country, interracial marriage between whites and other races was still outlawed. After interracial marriage was legalized nationwide in 1967, it became a little more common to see couples of different races together, but not so much in 1964.

People on the street would look at me and then at Tom and then discreetly or not so discreetly try to look down into the carriage to see the child. Educated people were typically more accepting. Less-educated people were often more judgmental. For instance, when I met Tom's teacher friends, they were all warm and welcoming. When we had an open house, they all came and were kind to me. But blue-collar people would often give us a mean look on the street. Still, I did not overly concern myself with this and only felt great pride as any new mother would.

It was funny how my relatives mostly thought that she looked like a little white baby, and Tom's relatives mostly felt that she looked Asian. Tom's Grandmother Hart always referred to her as her "little China doll."

Although I had named her Karin Kim, Tom never liked to call her Karin. He said that she looked like a Kim, which is what both sides of the family called her. Stephanie called her Kimmie because of a popular song called "Shimmy Shimmy Ko-Ko Bop!" by Little Anthony and the Imperials. Stephanie would dance the Monkey around Kim, singing, "Kimmie Kimmie ko-ko bop, Kimmie Kimmie bop!" Soon, we all called her Kimmie.

In the summer of 1965, we traveled to Oklahoma so that Tom's parents could meet their new granddaughter. Sentinel, the town closest to their farm, is in the southwestern part of the state. It was then a small town of about a thousand people set amid vast plains of wheat and cotton farms and beef cattle ranches. Primarily farmers and cowboys made their home in that region. It was the kind of place that was family and church-oriented. Everyone knew all their neighbors and looked after each other's kids. No one locked their house or car doors, and everyone left their car keys in the ignition. Tom's father once explained that he never wanted to bring the car key into the house as he would probably just lose it. Anyway, a friend or neighbor might need to borrow the car now and then, so keeping the key in the ignition was the handiest.

The people of the region worked hard. When the men took their hats off in the evening, their foreheads were white, and their faces ruddy brown below the hat line from working all day in the sun. Free time was often spent in church activities, watching high school sports events, or visiting friends and family. As no one locked their doors, neighbors freely dropped in on each other for chats. The men in their work hats might sit on the curbs in front of stores talking together, or else they might meet somewhere to play dominoes or cards.

Tom's parents warmly welcomed me upon my arrival. Moms said, "I've told all my lady friends about you, and they are going to give you a coffee," meaning a ladies' party where the hostess serves coffee and dessert. Moms had seen a photo of me in a green Chinese dress that I wore as a cocktail waitress at the Marco Polo restaurant. Before we made the trip, she asked me to bring that dress, and now she wanted me to wear it to the coffee. It would be the first time that many of the women had met a Chinese person, and Moms thought it would be charming for me to look the part.

The women in their tea dresses were gushingly friendly and complimentary. They all said how pleased they were to meet me, and I tried to be charming in return. In all, I had a pleasant time, and afterward, Moms and I went to the grocery store to pick up some items that she wanted for dinner. I was following her around the store when we came upon a man getting an ice cream bar from the freezer. He had just opened the wrapper and was about to take a bite when he caught sight of me and froze with his mouth open. I suppose that in my form-fitting, poison-green, satin Chinese dress, I was a singular sight in Sentinel, Oklahoma, in 1965.

When we later visited Tom's grandparents, they were also excited to see us and warmly welcoming. While Grandma retreated to the kitchen to prepare some refreshments, Grandpa invited us in and asked how we were getting on.

"Oh, I'm fine, but Helen can't tolerate this kind of heat. She's not holding up too well," Tom replied. "She's used to the cooler climate in California."

So Grandpa tried to turn on the old ventilation system, but it didn't work. Then he opened some dining room windows in the front of the house and pulled aside some curtains to open the shades. The windows, curtains, and shades looked like they hadn't been opened in years, and upon being disturbed, a good deal of dust went into the air. When Grandma came out and saw the mess, she scolded Grandpa.

"Good land! What do you want to open the windows for?" she said. I think she was embarrassed, and I felt bad about causing a commotion. Soon enough, however, Grandma only had eyes for Kimmie, and she gushed and fussed over her to her heart's content, much to Kim's delight.

Afterward, she would write a series of letters to Baby Kim to let her and us know what was going on in her life. The first began: "My dear little China Doll, you will never remember seeing me, but I held you in my arms when you was only 7 months old, and you was so precious and sweet and such a pretty baby and how I wish you was here with me this evening . . . "

After we had visited for a while, Grandma said, "Now, Helen, while you're here, I want you to cook us an authentic Chinese meal, so we'll know what that's like."

So I went to the store to buy some ingredients, and when I returned, I prepared sweet and sour pork ribs, sautéed vegetables, and steamed rice for dinner—or supper, as they called it. Tom's brother Bob and his wife, Pat, were invited to join us as they lived nearby.

It was customary in that part of the country to eat meat exceptionally well done. Steak, for instance, was typically rolled in flour and then fried in grease to an almost jerky-like consistency. Typical side dishes were mashed potatoes, canned corn or peas, biscuits, and gravy made from the steak grease and giblets mixed with flour, milk, and water. Alternately, steak might be deep-fried in fried chicken batter, again to the point of being well done, and this was called a chicken-fried steak. This food fueled the long days of physical labor.

This food also caused indigestion and acid reflux in older folks. Tom's Dad, for instance, almost always had a roll or jar of Tums on hand, and he was locally famous for the loudness of his burps. Much to Moms's embarrassment, neighborhood children visiting the house took great delight in getting to hear one of Pops's burps and would exclaim over it.

In any case, my lightly sautéed pork ribs, prepared with vinegar and sugar for the sweet and sour flavoring and cooked medium to medium-rare, were not so well received. I observed the party picking at them and fishing out the tomatoes. At the end of the meal, Grandpa Hart declared, "Well, Helen, everything was real good, but I believe that I prefer my rice in a pudding."

Grandma Hart genially added, "Yes, I like to eat rice as a cereal with milk and sugar."

After dinner, we chatted in the living room for the remainder of the evening. "Now, Tom," Grandma Hart asked, "if America goes to war with China, whose side will you be on?"

Tom laughed. "On the American side, of course, Grandma. Helen and I are both Americans. We'd both be for America." I nodded my agreement, and Grandma appeared relieved to hear it.

So this was our cultural exchange.

The heat and humidity were unlike anything I had ever experienced. I showered frequently and bathed Kimmie three times a day, and she still felt sticky to me. I learned afterward that Pops was upset about all the bathing that I did. I didn't realize that the house was using well water from the front yard, so the supply was limited. I might have guessed that the water was from a well as I had observed a crystalline layer of mineral deposits in the bottom of Moms's coffee pot. The hard, unfiltered water contributed to the stickiness.

Tom took me for a walking tour of his father's farm. Grasshoppers parted before us in sprays that were higher than my head. And while the grasshoppers were flying away from us, chiggers were descending upon us. Where they landed, they raised small, intensely itchy bite marks on Tom and egg-sized welts on Kim and me. After that, I decided that I didn't want to go into the fields again.

However, at noon, Moms asked us to deliver a jug of cold water to Tom's brother Bob, who was plowing his fields. Tom drove the car as close as possible and then walked out to Bob's tractor to give him the water. However, it so happened that a plow part had gotten clogged, and Tom needed to help Bob unclog it, which took some time. The heat in the car was intense. When I couldn't stand it anymore, I began honking the horn, and Tom came running back. He could not believe that I had stayed in the car with the windows closed when it was a hundred degrees in the shade. However, I was afraid to get out of the vehicle or open a window for fear of getting more egg-sized chigger welts. Tom drove us home, dropped Kim and me off, and then returned to help Bob with his plow.

Suffice it to say that I have never returned to Oklahoma in the summer again. After this trip, we visited only in the winter. It was a magical place for Kimmie, so different from her city life. In second grade, she won first prize in a school contest for her essay about visiting her grandparents' farm. She talked about going out to the hen coops with her grandpa and collecting the fresh, warm eggs, helping him feed the cattle hay and cottonseed, and getting to see how cotton grows on plants.

She liked to climb the bales of hay in the hayloft, to rest her eyes on the vast open space, and to see the Milky Way glowing in the night sky. She liked as much to explore the nearby creek bed with its high walls of red clay as to walk into the little town of Sentinel and drink a milkshake at the drug store soda fountain. Now and then, a rugged cowboy would pass through town in his chaps and cowboy hat, and we would feel as though we had stepped into a Marlboro commercial.

"How y'all doin'?" the friendly shop owners would ask as soon as we walked in. They were always ready for a good chat and gossip. Most of them still knew Tom and were glad to catch up on his news. When we were leaving, the owners would call out with a friendly smile, "Y'all come back real soon, ya hear?" Her grandparents' farm and the little town of Sentinel would be a place of happy memories for Kim.

I stayed home during Kim's newborn months. But after six months, I began to work on Saturday and Sunday evenings as a cocktail waitress at Marco Polo restaurant. Around the time she entered preschool, I worked some other evenings each week at Father Earl Hines's nightclub again.

Father Hines had been a well-known jazz musician of the Louis Armstrong era. He still played a mean piano and trumpet, and he liked to dress the part, swaggering around the nightclub in his zoot suit pants with chains hanging from his pocket, looking like a cool old hip cat. After I had worked there for a few weeks, he asked if I would bring in a photograph of myself. I didn't know what he wanted it for, but when I gave it to him, he put it in the display case in front of the restaurant with the photos of the performers as though I were one of the attractions. I suppose I ought to have been flattered, but it made me uncomfortable. I considered it unladylike to be on display.

When Kim was about one year old, Tom and I bought a house in the Oakland Hills at 6900 Sherwick Drive. The house was on stilts and had a sloping terraced yard, where we fought aggressive poison oak. Calamine lotion became a staple of our medicine cabinet. We broke out in a rash so frequently that Kim drew a rash on her teddy bear with a yellow marking pen.

Still, the house was out of the downtown area, so we felt safer. Kim could play in the yard without my worrying about her, and she and Tom liked to sit on the patio on summer nights and count the stars. On weekends, they would hike along nearby trails to overlooks, where they took turns throwing pebbles down the hill and enjoying the view of the East Bay. We didn't have money for extras. Still, I sewed beautiful clothes for her Barbie dolls from fabric scraps, made a stove and refrigerator from cardboard boxes, and gave her some of my old clothes and shoes for dress-up play. "Where there's a way, there's a will," I always said. Tom would laugh when I said that. He said that I had it backward. But I always thought that if there was a way to do something, I had the will.

When Kim entered the first grade at Kaiser Elementary, I started working full-time at Francesco's restaurant in Oakland. I worked a split shift from 11:00 a.m. to 2:00 p.m. and then from 5:00 to 10:00 p.m. I could drop Kim off at school in the morning and pick her up in the afternoon. I was then home with her until Tom came back from school. Or during track season, when he was coaching after school, I dropped her off at the track field. She would tag along after him as he paced back and forth, yelling encouragement and corrections to his runners. I will forever be grateful that my career as a waitress and Tom's career as a schoolteacher made it possible for one of us to always be with Kim.

There was one drawback to the new house. It did not have a quality elementary school. We hadn't cared when Kim was a toddler and a preschooler. However, at Kaiser Elementary, many of the kids were aggressive, and even in first and second grades, Kim was afraid of some of them. She was a good student who often won prizes of gum or candy from her teachers for her high marks. Then a gang of little girls might gather around her at recess with their arms crossed, saying, "You gonna give us some of your gum?"

Tom read to her each evening, and we both helped with her homework. By second grade, she was the best reader in class. Her classmates, emerging from school with a note pinned to their jackets, would flock around her, asking her to read it so they would know what their teacher said to their parents. They could not read it themselves.

The junior high and high school were not going to be any better. So, during Kim's second-grade year, we began looking for a new home where she could attend a high-ranking school. However, we weren't sure how a schoolteacher and a waitress were going to afford a quality neighborhood and schools.

Still, I promised Kim this: "If I have to scrub floors on my hands and knees so you can go to college, I will do it." She was young when I said that to her, but I could see that it touched her heart. She worked hard in school, and I was glad. I didn't want either of my daughters to live the kind of life I had lived.

34

LOSING STEPHANIE, FINDING STEPHANIE

As part of my divorce with Oliver, I received full custody of Stephanie, who was fourteen at the time in 1961. Oliver had visitation rights on Saturdays. Sometimes he called, and sometimes he didn't. When he did, he brought her to his new girlfriend's home. This girlfriend had a daughter who attended the Presbyterian Church in San Francisco's Chinatown. This church was connected to the Cameron House, a Christian organization aiming to provide wholesome social activities and counseling for Chinese Americans. Donaldina Cameron, the Presbyterian advocate for social justice, founded Cameron House. She had also established the Ming Quong Home for orphaned girls, where my sisters had lived when they first came to America.

At this church, Stephanie met a young man named Jim, who also participated in activities at the Cameron House. Stephanie was then a Hayward State University (HSU) student, working on her bachelor's degree. Tom took classes with Stephanie at HSU as part of his continuing education. This helped them bond. When Tom had first moved in with us, she was frequently defensive when he tried to tell her what to do as a father would. They had to adjust to each other. However, as fellow students in college, they enjoyed chatting about their teachers and classes.

Tom observed several young men approach her at the university. She had grown into an attractive young woman. One even sent flowers to our house for her, but she rejected them all—until she met Jim, with whom she felt an immediate connection.

Jim was not exactly orphaned, but his parents were divorced.

His father, who had custody of him and his two brothers, had remarried a woman from China with whom he had a baby son. As a merchant marine, Jim's father was gone many months at a time to sea and so was not present in his sons' lives. Their stepmother did not speak English, and Jim and his brothers spoke little Chinese.

In the meantime, Jim's mother, Mona, a flamboyant woman who had worked as a Chinese opera performer, had moved to New York. She got remarried to the gangster Dominick Dickie Pallatto, a member of the Mob. Together, they owned and operated King Wah Chinese Restaurant, which served as a meeting place for the mafia during off-hours. Under these circumstances, Jim found solace and guidance at the church and Cameron House.

Perhaps this background created a connection and understanding between Jim and Stephanie. They fell deeply in love and married when Stephanie was twenty years old. I gave her a beautiful wedding at the Chinese Presbyterian Church in Oakland with a reception at a restaurant in San Francisco's Chinatown. I made her wedding gown myself, and she asked Tom to walk her down the aisle and give her away since her relationship with her father was stormy.

Jim had gotten a job with a San Francisco post office. Stephanie intended to continue her studies at Hayward State. However, she took a part-time clerical job at Pacific Bell telephone company so they could get an apartment together. They furnished their rental with my old bedroom set and a couple of chairs, and a small table that I gave them.

Fate, however, did not deal kindly with this young couple, who had already endured so much. One week after their wedding, Jim became severely ill. Stephanie assumed at first that it was the flu. However, when he didn't improve, they went to the hospital. They found that he suffered from kidney failure because of a genetic disorder. The hospital administered dialysis, which was then a new type of treatment.

As Stephanie and Jim were without means sufficient for further treatment, Jim's physician submitted his case for research at the University of California San Francisco (UCSF) hospital. Jim was one of the first people ever to get a kidney transplant, a new type of procedure. Stephanie now commuted to UCSF every day after school and work. Also, she soon inherited Jim's younger brothers, Phillip and Harris. They had grown unhappy living with their stepmother due to communication issues and cultural differences. Though they were Chinese American, they were Westernized in behavior, which conflicted with their stepmother's old-world views. Phillip was still in high school, and Harris was just out of high school and without work when they came to live in her apartment.

And so, at twenty-one, Stephanie was now caretaker for a sick husband and mother to his younger brothers. Phillip rebelliously said he didn't see the point of staying in high school and wanted to quit, and Stephanie didn't try to fight him. She said simply and quietly, "That's fine. You can drop out of high school, but then you will need to find a job and move out of my apartment." That changed Phillip's mind, and he decided to stay in school until he graduated. She found Harris a job as a line worker at Pacific Bell, her place of employment.

The toll of these responsibilities caused Stephanie's grades to plummet, and, sadly, she decided that she would have to break from school. Jim remained at death's door for over a year. He received a kidney transplant, and it worked for a short time. Then it ceased functioning. His doctor had to remove it, and Jim returned to dialysis and waited for another transplant. He was in and out of the hospital, always just well enough to stay alive but not well enough to be healthy. Stephanie's soul and happiness were continuously in the balance as she never knew when or if there might be hope.

On the radio, I heard an advertisement for a type of government assistance for which I thought they would qualify. I directed Stephanie to apply so they would have some income besides her small wages from working at Pacific Bell. I also bought her little necessities like underwear here and there. This situation went on for over a year.

The doctor found a second kidney donor, and there was hope. Unfortunately, Jim's experience with the first kidney was repeated. The new kidney worked for a while, and then it, too, failed, and dialysis resumed. Stephanie then saw hope evaporate from Jim's spirit. He didn't want to fight anymore. One day, he told Stephanie that he loved her very, very much. He died a little while later when she was at work. She was thankful that he wasn't suffering anymore, but grief tore her apart.

In the weeks that followed, I had to take over her life as she was so devastated that she could hardly function. I brought her home to live with me so that she wouldn't have to cook or be alone. After he died, Jim's younger brothers had gone to New York to spend time with their mother, but when they returned, they stayed at Stephanie's apartment. I stood up for her and told them that they needed to find their own place now, and they agreed to move out so she would feel comfortable moving back in.

Stephanie was now at loose ends. She had no spirit or mind to return to school. San Francisco and her apartment were full of sad memories. What doubly hurt her was the reaction of their friends' wives, who had previously been cordial. They were now aloof and possessive, as though Stephanie was potentially a threat to their marriages because she was newly single. She was stunned.

Her friend Shirley invited her to apply for work as a flight attendant with Overseas National Airways, where Shirley was already working. Stephanie grasped at the opportunity. She was young and lovely with a good work ethic, was quickly hired on, and was asked to relocate to New York, where ONA was based. Just like that, Stephanie left, leaving most of her possessions and furniture behind so that Tom and I had to collect them from the apartment. I sold many of her things and sent her the money. She would never again return to the Bay Area except as a visitor.

In the first few months of her employment, she worked on a DC-10 airplane, preparing to fly from Kennedy International Airport in New York to Saudi Arabia. Birds somehow got sucked into the plane's right engine during takeoff. Fuel and friction caused a fire, and the pilot chose to abort the takeoff while he still could, using the entire distance of the runway to stop and almost skidding into Jamaica Bay. Working with her fellow crew, Stephanie helped evacuate the burning plane in forty-two seconds flat from the moment the doors opened. No one died, and everyone got off with only minor injuries. Shortly after the evacuation, the entire plane except the tail burned completely.

The media initially reported fatalities. When Stephanie heard this, she called to tell me she was all right. I was so emotional that I only said, "Thanks for telling me," and hung up to burst into tears, leaving Stephanie dumbfounded. It was not until I was sufficiently calm that I could call her back.

Stephanie continued to fly, especially to the Middle East and Europe, and around the United States. She made new friends in New York and focused her life around them. In the meantime, I became ever more involved with my new marriage, my new life, and Kimmie. Stephanie and I drifted apart. Though she was now a grown woman, I had trouble treating her that way. I didn't always feel that she made wise decisions about her life and told her so when we spoke. She resented that. One day, she moved and didn't tell me where she had gone. She disconnected her phone and left no forwarding number. My heart broke.

I thought for a long time about our life together and how life had been so unkind to her. Her father had been absent, and I had often taken out my anger on her, both in snappishness and by hitting her when she was a child. Trying so extremely hard to pull us up out of poverty, I had often come home between my lunch and dinner shifts and spent the time on home repairs and improvement. I painted the interior of our home and my rental property. I sanded and refinished the hardwood floors at our Hoover Avenue home and even repaired the roof when it was leaking. I sewed clothes for myself and Stephanie. I was scrupulously frugal, and I worked and worked and worked. I loved her by making sure she had a roof over her head and food to eat and a quality school, that she did her homework, and that she had lessons so that she would be an accomplished young lady.

But what Stephanie wanted was my company. Often, she had asked, "Mom, why don't you hug me?" I didn't know how to answer that. My parents had not hugged me. I felt like I didn't know how. My father had disciplined me without imparting warmth. But she saw other mothers hugging their daughters. She had wanted that so much, and she had not gotten that from me.

I called up her friend Shirley and asked for Stephanie's new number, but she wouldn't give it to me. She thought that if Stephanie had not given it to me, then it wasn't her place to tell me.

My voice breaking, I said, "Shirley, listen, Stephanie was my whole life and my pride and joy for eighteen years. I can't lose her now. Please tell me how I can find her." There was a long pause, and then Shirley told me that Stephanie would be flying into Oakland Airport on a particular day and time and that I could find her there.

On the appointed day, I went to the airport gate. I watched as every one of the plane's passengers debarked. I knew the crew would be last. I watched as the pilot came out, the copilot, and the other flight attendants. Finally, Stephanie came out. I stood and held open my arms.

Seeing me, she stopped cold in her tracks. Then she burst into tears—aching, wrenching tears. I came to her, and we hugged for a long, long time.

Over the next few years, we repaired our relationship. We called each other more and sent cards. We spent the holidays together. In short, we made an effort. Mostly, we learned to accept each other. Family is precious. I am grateful that I didn't lose my daughter.

35

HOME AT LAST

In the late 1960s, Tom and I saw advertisements for a new community of outstanding natural beauty along the Sonoma County coastline. This community was being developed for private homes and as a unique vacation destination. It was called The Sea Ranch. This place was remarkable for several reasons. First, it was accessible from the Bay Area only by the narrow and winding Highway One. Furthermore, being only about a mile in width along a ten-mile stretch of coastline, it was unlikely to become an overcrowded resort-style destination.

As described in The Sea Ranch Association's report, *The Sea Ranch, Concept and Covenant,* "The terrain is rugged, the surf treacherous, the ocean cold. Winds have sculpted cypress and pines into rhythmic shapes. The climate ranges from bright sunshine to dense fog, howling winds, and pelting rain—sometimes all in a single day. The weather, the season, and the time of day all contribute to The Sea Ranch's dramatic beauty."

At the time, "hippie" values of sustainability, organic living, and consciousness were just starting to be topics in broader society. The Sea Ranch community intended to respect and work to protect the natural environment by living lightly on the land. This vision and these values became known as The Sea Ranch Concept. It was a grand experiment, and it attracted worldwide attention. We were intrigued.

We drove up on a day trip and fell in love with this slice of the California dream. We found that homes in The Sea Ranch would have to meet specific design review requirements so that the buildings became part of the landscape and didn't dominate it. Building design details included exteriors of unpainted wood or muted stains, a lack of overhanging eaves, and baffles on exterior lighting to subdue the appearance of the buildings in the landscape and minimize nighttime light pollution. There would be no streetlights so that the nighttime sky could remain forever dazzling. The lack of roof overhangs allowed the near-constant strong breezes to pass over the buildings without the turbulence the overhangs would create. There would be community swimming pools and playgrounds. However, the place's appeal was mostly in its natural beauty of ruggedly beautiful beaches, sea-carved cliffs, and pine and redwood forests, preserved by strict building codes.

We stopped into The Sea Ranch Lodge, where there was a realtor's office, took a card, and said we were interested. Soon, the realtor invited us to come and stay at a cabin for a free night's lodging so that he could spend a weekend showing us properties for sale. Lots on the coast were pricey, but we found in our price range a wooded half acre up the hill on Moonraker Road. There were soaring redwood trees, a filtered view of the coast, and an abutting wooded ravine that felt sacred and primal in its deep quietness. We agreed to buy it that day. We would not develop it for many years, but we liked knowing that we owned this piece of paradise. We would come up on weekends throughout the year, stay at the Surf Motel just north of Sea Ranch, and enjoy the coast and forests. We had leisurely picnics on our lot while Kim explored the woods and ravine.

I was also interested in The Sea Ranch as an investment. As is common in my culture, I value real estate above all other types of investment. Real estate is something that I can understand and see and touch, and its value is self-evident. Even if its value falls, it still exists and can serve a function. I didn't care about having a fancy car or expensive clothes, which lose value as soon as you buy them. However, I always wanted to own land, which is of enduring value.

When we bought our home on Sherwick Drive in the Oakland

Hills, I kept the houses on Hoover Avenue and Frisbie Street in Oakland. I rented them to cover their mortgages and build equity. Soon, I would sell the house on Hoover Avenue as the renters there had such difficulty making payments that it became a headache. However, I continued to rent the Frisbie Street house to a gay couple. Gay couples sometimes had trouble finding places to rent, but I was content to rent to them as they paid on time and kept the house beautifully. They were excellent tenants, though they were particular about the colors I chose when it was time to paint the exterior.

Now I had my eye on the future. There was the problem of affording a neighborhood with excellent schools for Kimmie. I had some savings from the sale of the Hoover Avenue home. We could sell the Frisbie Street home at some point, but after paying off the mortgage and some other debts that Tom had when we started our marriage, I wasn't sure that would be enough. The Frisbie Street home was in a poor neighborhood and not of high value.

I thought that if we had fallen in love with Sea Ranch, others would too. It was still a new development with a good deal of property for sale. However, it was garnering global attention for its concept and style of architecture. *Sunset Magazine* featured beautiful glossy photos and a story about the community in its pages. Sea Ranch and its surrounding communities appeared poised to rise in value.

I convinced Tom to let us invest in two other lots. One was a lot along the coast, which would be in high demand. The other was a lot in Gualala, just north of Sea Ranch. With my own money, I bought a third lot also near Gualala. Tom was reticent about this type of investing, being unused to it, but I felt strongly that this would be worthwhile and convinced him. By 1973, we were able to sell the three lots at a profit. I also sold the Frisbie Street house, and now we had money in hand to look for a good neighborhood.

Tom had got a job teaching math at Piedmont High School. Piedmont is a small, primarily residential city surrounded by Oakland. During the 1920s, locals dubbed it the "city of millionaires" because there were more millionaires per square mile than in any other city in the United States. Many of these millionaires built mansions that still stand. While no longer at such a peak of wealth, Piedmont was still an upper-middle-class enclave with highly rated schools.

I had tried to buy property there before when I was looking for a house with Stephanie. However, though I had a down payment and steady income, I had been denied service by the realtor I met. At the time when I was looking with Stephanie, people in better neighborhoods wouldn't sell to Chinese, and he had declined even to show me any homes.

Now there was a realtor who invited the teachers of Piedmont High to meet with him and discuss the possibility of their buying homes in the city where they worked. Knowing my history, Tom brought up the issue of race.

"I'm interested, but my wife is Chinese. What would you have to say to that?" he asked.

The realtor replied, "Sure, I'll take that question," but then he didn't answer it. He talked in circles about his company's reputation for customer service without addressing whether he was willing to represent a person of Chinese descent.

When Tom shared this with me and described the appearance of the realtor, I recognized him as the one who had turned me away before, so I knew we wouldn't be able to work with him. Nonetheless, we obtained listings of properties for sale and drove by homes. In addition to the excellent schools, it would be wonderful if Tom could walk to work.

When we stopped by the house at 330 Pala Avenue, a realtor was showing the home to another couple, who sounded undecided. When they left, we asked if we could also see the house, and the realtor accommodated us. For Piedmont, it was an unusually modest home of two bedrooms and one and a half baths.

It sat wedged between a large house and a mansion so big that its lot extended from Pala Avenue to Scenic Avenue on the hill above. However, with its hillside location, the house had panoramic views of the East Bay and San Francisco from the living and dining rooms and kitchen. There was an office in the lower level where Tom could grade student papers. With our limited means, the modest size was appealing.

Tom again brought up the issue of race, describing how another realtor had rebuffed me from buying in Piedmont in the past. The realtor said she would discuss this with her boss. However, when her boss heard this concern, he contacted us immediately. He assured us in no uncertain terms that his office welcomed our business and that he had instructed his realtor to be of every assistance to us. I think, in part, times were changing, but I believe that it also helped that I was married to Tom.

An estate attorney was selling the house in a probate sale, meaning that the owner had died without bequeathing the property to an heir. As a result, the attorney had to sell it under court supervision to liquidate the asset and distribute the money to family members. Like a foreclosure sale, where banks typically sell properties as is and as quickly as possible, probate sales are an opportunity to buy property below market value.

We would have to submit a bid in court on a specific day and time. Tom took the day off work, and our realtor accompanied him to ensure that he followed the correct procedures. They arrived early in hopes that he would be the first to bid. Anyone bidding after the opening bid would have to offer at least several percent more. This rule ensured that someone wouldn't propose just one dollar more or one hundred dollars more, creating a lengthy bidding war. At the appointed time, Tom submitted our bid of forty-nine thousand dollars.

I was at work on my lunch shift and could hardly focus because of being so nervous about whether our offer would be accepted. When I arrived home in the afternoon, Tom was there. I looked at him expectantly. He smiled and said, "We got it."

36

MY SLICE OF HAPPINESS

The year we moved into the house in Piedmont was when I turned fifty years old, and Kimmie entered the third grade. The next few decades were the happiest of my life. Finally, there was stability and a sense of getting ahead. Two years after buying our home in Piedmont, Tom and I built a vacation cottage on our lot in Sea Ranch, the one we had been visiting for picnics for many years. With its deck looking out on a distant coastal view and blue jays chirping at us from trees all around, this cabin in the woods became a place of refuge, restoration, and happy memories. For Kim, it was a magical place to commune with nature and nurture creativity away from the bustle of urban life.

In 1981, when I was fifty-eight, I won a makeover contest sponsored by Woman's Day Magazine. The competition solicited before and after photos to demonstrate how everyday women transformed themselves with makeup. I was one of three grand-prize winners flown to New York for an interview and photoshoot with famed photographer Barry O'Rourke. Woman's Day featured the three of us in its January 12, 1982, edition.

A professional makeup artist interviewed me. When she saw how I did my makeup, she was surprised to see my worn brushes and how I used only drug-store brands, and she was so amazed by the worn stubbiness of my eyeliner brush that I was embarrassed.

"Can you draw a straight line with that?" she asked, incredulous. I demonstrated that I could.

However, I stayed in a beautiful suite at the Berkshire Hotel for three days, where flowers and a silver platter of fruit welcomed me on my arrival. I received limousine service, a one-thousand-dollar prize, and tickets to see *42nd Street* on Broadway. I was an honored guest at a dinner for New York cosmetics professionals. In the autumn of one's life, a Cinderella experience is especially sweet.

I also had the pleasure of seeing Stephanie return to college, earning a degree in computer science. She went on to a distinguished career at the National Aeronautics and Space Administration (NASA) Jet Propulsion Laboratory, where she received numerous employee awards. In the same year that Stephanie graduated from California State University at Northridge, Kimmie also graduated from the University of California at Berkeley. They both gave me their graduation tassels as a way of saying that I had earned those tassels as much as they had. I hung them on either side of the makeup mirror at my vanity table, where I enjoyed seeing them every day.

In my sixties, I suffered a heart attack, so I quit full-time work. Oh, how I hated to stop work entirely. I took so much pride in being of service and earning money, and I valued the friendships with my coworkers and long-term customers. I was fortunate that my employer allowed me to work part-time—just the lunch shift behind the counter, where I didn't have to carry dishes far. I continued working part-time until I was seventy.

Also, in my sixties, Tom and I began to travel. We set a goal to visit every continent, and we did. One of the trips that I enjoyed most was seeing Antarctica. There were classes onboard the ship to learn about the region's natural history and wildlife and climate science. Some five decades since my last time in class, it was a chance for me to remember how much I had once enjoyed being in school and learning.

The year that I turned eighty was the year I got my first grandchild—Kim's daughter, Avril. Finally! How long had I been knitting only for myself and Stephanie and Kim? Avril was born prematurely and was so tiny that even newborn clothes made her look like Dopey from Snow White. That bugged me. I took her measurements while she was on the changing table and, from a remnant of soft flannel, fashioned for her a perfectly fitted set of clothes with pants, top, and bonnet. I enjoyed seeing her look fashionable, even as a newborn.

I told Kim that I wanted to babysit. Two years later, Avril's sister, Anika, was born. The greatest pleasure of my winter years was getting to look after those two. We took them to parks, bought them donuts and milkshakes, watched movies with them, laughed at their antics, and just spent time with them.

Every so often, we would be out somewhere, and I would look around at all the impossible luxury that we enjoyed. There was clean running water, electric lights, a closet stuffed with clothes, and a van with built-in child seats that we bought to haul the grandchildren around. I would remember how far I had come. This way of life is all that my children and grandchildren have ever known. I am glad, but I never forgot what it was like to be King Ying living in a remote Chinese village and dreaming of bread and butter.

Ever since Kimmie was little, I have told her my stories. I wanted her to know where I came from, what life can be like for those born into less fortunate circumstances, and how life isn't always fair. I especially wanted her to know how hard some people have to fight for their slice of happiness. I am grateful and proud that I was able to enjoy some of the blessings of this world before I passed on and that I was able to help my family do the same.

EPILOGUE

KIM SPEAKS

John Quincy Adams, sixth president of the United State, is supposed to have said, "I am a warrior, so my son may be a merchant, so his son may be a poet." I understand the sentiment. I have often thought, "My mother was a waitress, so I could be a professional, so my daughters can be anything they want."

My mother was my best friend, hero, and good luck charm. Yet when I was young, I was often intimidated by her. She set such high and specific expectations for me that I sometimes lost my dreams trying to achieve hers. Mother wanted me to follow a sure path to middle-class comfort so I would not suffer the degradation of poverty and ignorance that she had. And so, I didn't often feel room to strike my own path in the world. I was aware every moment how hard she worked for our home, for our comfort, for my education and that she had no such luxuries in her youth. How could I not feel an obligation to follow the path she set for me?

By twenty-six, I had been valedictorian of my high school, won local beauty pageants, earned my master's degree, was married, and owned a home. Yet not my career nor my husband, nor the house suited me. And so, I bumped around for many years before settling on the proper husband, home, and work. I was well into adulthood before I knew what I wanted for myself apart from what I wanted to achieve for my mother.

What more than made up for this overachieving immigrant's child syndrome, as I'll call it, was knowing at every instant how intensely Mom loved and valued me. I remember her attending a beauty pageant in which I competed. Afterward, when I came into the audience to see her, she said with a broken voice and tears in her eyes, "I'm sorry. I was so busy being proud that I forgot to take any pictures." All I could do was give her a big hug and know that her being there and loving me so much were way more important than any pictures she could have taken.

She taught me how wise money management is a powerful tool of feminine strength. She knew how to be frugal and imparted its value in getting ahead to me. She also taught me how to invest in mutual funds and real estate. She encouraged me to drive a cheap car and use secondhand furniture until I had saved enough to buy my own house. Feeling confident in my ability to manage money has given me self-confidence and the ability to shrug off small slights. There is peace of mind in knowing that a sudden unexpected expense isn't going to derail me from my dreams.

She valued family, integrity, courage, and hard work. She showed me how to play the hand you are dealt no matter how poor the cards. She demonstrated that when the going gets tough, it is possible to find reserves of strength that I didn't know I had. And she taught me that when the going is good, to laugh with your whole body and heart. She taught me to take nothing for granted and to be grateful for the gift of life. She taught me how to approach life with zest, knowing there is always something worth working for and some new place worth exploring.

I am sorry to say that in her very final years, as her health declined and dementia encroached, she suffered depression. In the quiet stillness, old memories of past hurts resurfaced and haunted her, and it was my great sadness that I couldn't always help her lift the cloud that descended upon her soul. She slowly lost her physical and mental abilities. After a stroke, for instance, she lost the ability to speak in complete sentences.

Now and then, the clouds would part for an hour or so, and we cherished those moments. One afternoon stands out in memory. As a way of spending time with her, I offered to help her purge an overstuffed closet. Boxes of old curlers, cosmetics, and clothes brought back happy memories of past times. When we came upon a box of hair supplies from the 1960s, she was able to demonstrate how she had styled a bouffant back in the day. That made me so happy.

This book is my way of not letting those final days be the last word. Most importantly, I have set down these stories for my daughters to understand where we came from and what a debt of gratitude we owe to those who came before us. Mom was a blessing and a miracle.

PHOTOS

San Francisco Chinatown, between 1920 and 1930
(Arnold Genthe, Public domain, via Wikimedia Commons)
(Chapter 1)

Ho Sin (Ba) and Bo-Leng (Ma) with King Ying (standing) and
King Shu, about 1926
(Chapter 3)

Ho Sin (Ba), Yuk Moy (Seam), and Shew Min (James), 1936
(Chapter 11)

From left to right: Ding Ping (May), King Shu (Katie),
Tuey Jean (Jean), Fay Thleem (Wanna), Shew Min (James),
King Ying (Helen), Tuey Ngaw (Margaret), 1930s
(Chapter 14)

King Ying, 1942
(Chapter 22)

King Ying (Helen) and Oliver
at the Andy Wong Sky Room nightclub, San Francisco,1940s
(Chapter 25)

Asian American lounge waitresses of Pland's Restaurant with manager Mike Lynn, late 1940s. King Ying (Helen) is in the top row, 4th from the right. The restaurant's brochure advertised, "Lounge waitresses and assistants to assure you of good service with that Oriental atmosphere."(Chapter 29)

King Ying (Helen) and Stephanie on vacation in Hawaii, 1950s
(Chapter 30)

Tom and King Ying (Helen)'s engagement photo,
Tonga Room restaurant, Fairmont Hotel, San Francisco,
February 14, 1963
(Chapter 32)

Stephanie on her wedding day with Kim and King Ying (Helen), late 1960s (Chapter 34)

King Ying (Helen) in front of her home in Piedmont, California, 1970s (Chapter 35)

ACKNOWLEDGMENTS

This book results from extensive interviews with my mother, aunts, uncle, father, and sister and historical research. Although I began interviewing my mother in 2002, she shared stories informally through my childhood. When I decided to set them down, I could hear her voice so clearly that I wrote from the first-person point of view.

My progress slowed when my children were born until I set the manuscript aside for years when it was 90% complete. With my mother's health deteriorating in the late 2000s, I couldn't bring myself to finish her story.

Years after she passed in 2013, I completed the draft in 2018 to share with friends and family. When the Covid pandemic took away my employment for a year, I edited the manuscript and began the long querying process for publication.

I sincerely thank my family for their generosity in sharing stories. I am so grateful for my Aunties Katie, Jeannie, Margaret, May, and Wanna, Uncle James, my Dad, Tom, and sister, Stephanie. I thank my cousins, Julie, Jackie, Janis, Mellissa, and Sebastian for facilitating interviews and helping me pin down details. Thanks to my cousin, Renee, who sparked me to start the publishing process. Thanks to my husband, Sven, for his unwavering support.

Thank you to Nicole Zamudio-Roman for her belief and for recommending Balestier Press. Thanks to Helen Harris for sharing knowledge and the lovely folks at We Love Memoirs for their enthusiastic support of memoir writers. Thanks to Marketa Glanzova and Roh-Suan Tung of Balestier Press for making this book possible.

Thanks most of all to my mother for her remarkable life and spirit.

FROM THE AUTHOR

Thank you so much for reading my book. I am honored and grateful to share my mother's extraordinary story with you. If you've liked this book, won't you take a moment to leave me a rating or a review? It really does make a difference, and I am truly interested to hear what you think. Thanks again.

BIBLIOGRAPHY

Asbury, Herbert. *The Barbary Coast: An Informal History of the San Francisco Underworld.* New York: Basic Books, A Member of the Perseus Books Group, 1933.

Boissoneault, Lorraine. *The True Story of Brainwashing and How It Shaped America,* The Smithsoniam magazine, May 22, 2017

Brownstone, David M. *The Chinese American Heritage. United States: Facts on File,* An Infobase Holdings Company, 1988.

Chang, Iris. *The Chinese in America.* New York: Penguin Group, 2003.

"China Mike." *The Cult of Face in China.* 2020 (Internet Blog).

Donovan, Frank. *Wheels for a Nation.* United States: Thomas Y. Crowell Company, 1965.

Dong, Arthur. *Forbidden City USA.* A Deep Focus Production, 2016 (DVD).

Siu, Paul C.P. *The Chinese Laundryman: A Study of Social Isolation.* New York: New York University Press, 1987.

Tow, J.S. *The Real Chinese in America.* New York: The Academy Press, 1923.

9 781913 891299

Ingram Content
Milton Keynes
UKHW042024
421241UK00

BIBLIOGRAPHY

Asbury, Herbert. *The Barbary Coast: An Informal History of the San Francisco Underworld*. New York: Basic Books, A Member of the Perseus Books Group, 1933.

Boissoneault, Lorraine. *The True Story of Brainwashing and How It Shaped America*, The Smithsoniam magazine, May 22, 2017

Brownstone, David M. *The Chinese American Heritage. United States: Facts on File*, An Infobase Holdings Company, 1988.

Chang, Iris. *The Chinese in America*. New York: Penguin Group, 2003.

"China Mike." *The Cult of Face in China*. 2020 (Internet Blog).

Donovan, Frank. *Wheels for a Nation*. United States: Thomas Y. Crowell Company, 1965.

Dong, Arthur. *Forbidden City USA*. A Deep Focus Production, 2016 (DVD).

Siu, Paul C.P. *The Chinese Laundryman: A Study of Social Isolation*. New York: New York University Press, 1987.

Tow, J.S. *The Real Chinese in America*. New York: The Academy Press, 1923.

Ingram Content Group UK Ltd.
Milton Keynes UK
UKHW042024040523
421241UK00003B/3